Ysenda Maxtone Graham writes features, book reviews and columns for many newspapers and magazines. She is the author of six books, including *The Real Mrs Miniver*, which was shortlisted for the Whitbread Biography of the Year Award, *Terms & Conditions: Life in Girls' Boarding Schools, 1939–1979* and *British Summer Time Begins: The School Summer Holidays, 1930–1980*, which was a *Sunday Times* bestseller.

'Maxtone Graham [has a] unique blend of high comedy and shrewd social observation ... The book thrums with life and noise ... With freshness and immediacy, *Jobs for the Girls* illuminates a period of our very recent history' *Spectator*

'A riotous new history of women's decades-long struggle to be taken seriously at work' *Mail on Sunday*

'There are many beguiling stories in *Jobs for the Girls*, receding echoes of another century, bound together by the author's equally beguiling voice and the crisp intelligence of her observations' Lucy Lethbridge, *Tablet*

'Maxtone Graham, who mined the memories of more than 200 women for their personal job stories, excels in the quirky, comic and often poignant details that resonate with her readers' Melanie Reid, *The Times*

'Ysenda Maxtone Graham has a talent for conjuring the atmosphere of times past, both comical and tragic' *Country Life*

Ysenda Maxtone Graham

FOR THE

How we set out to work
in the typewriter age

abacus
books

ABACUS

First published in Great Britain in 2023 by Abacus
This paperback edition published in 2024 by Abacus

1 3 5 7 9 10 8 6 4 2

A CIP catalogue record for this book
is available from the British Library.

ISBN 978-0-349-14441-2

Typeset in Garamond by M Rules
Printed and bound in Great Britain by Clays Ltd, Elcograf S.p.A.

Papers used by Abacus are from well-managed forests
and other responsible sources.

Abacus
An imprint of
Little, Brown Book Group
Carmelite House
50 Victoria Embankment
London EC4Y 0DZ

An Hachette UK Company
www.hachette.co.uk

www.littlebrown.co.uk

For Michael

Contents

Introduction

Flashbacks

This is the third in my trilogy on 'lost worlds of Britain' – recent lost worlds, still in living memory, as recalled all too vividly by people who were there. In this book, I proceed from the trials of childhood to those of early adulthood.

It was a quotation in my introduction to the first of the trilogy, *Terms & Conditions: Life in Girls' Boarding Schools 1939–1979*, that inspired me to write this one. Leafing through *I Was There*, a history of one of the girls' schools, St James's, West Malvern, I'd come across the Victorian founding headmistress, Miss Baird, still going strong in 1937, describing her dazzlement when her Old Girls came back to the school to visit her:

I do not know at what stage Old Girls interest me most. For instance, whether it is when they have just left the chrysalis stage after a time in Paris or Munich or Florence, and they come down here to dazzle us with their transformation. Or whether it's when they come and tell us about the varied and interesting courses of training or 'jobs' which they are doing so efficiently. Or, at another stage, when they come down as mothers of Present Girls.

The inverted commas around the word 'jobs' suggested that Miss Baird considered jobs for young ladies as a new-fangled concept, a slightly comic idea, and very much 'so-called'. 'Jobs', indeed! The transformation of her girls from cygnets to swans in the finishing schools of Paris, Florence and Munich (Munich in 1937 – that's what they were up to) was supposed to prepare them for a lifetime of marriage and opening fetes: for cutting ribbons, not for changing typewriter ribbons.

From that moment on, my 'jobs' antennae were out. I longed to find out what 'jobs' young women did on leaving school, if indeed they did; what happened when they emerged into the world of adulthood, or pre-adulthood aged just fifteen or sixteen, perhaps not having the faintest idea what to do next, having had little or no aspirational encouragement (beyond marrying a suitable man) from their teachers or their parents, who were more interested in the sons. I started asking women born from the late 1920s onwards – in other words, anyone still alive – how equipped they were when they left school to go into any kind of work, and what happened next.

Further 'jobs' curiosity was sparked while writing the second of the trilogy, *British Summer Time Begins: The School Summer Holidays, 1930–1980*, in which I widened the net, asking men and women from across the social spectrum how they spent the long unsupervised weeks of their childhood summers. I discovered that the habit of work was something that some developed early and others never did. The unspoilt ones, desperate for cash, washed up in restaurants from the age of fourteen, walked home in the dark and spent the proceeds at the local coffee bar, or saved up for a bike, often giving up half of their earnings to their mother to pay for their upkeep at home. They learned from an early age the truth about jobs – that they go on, unglamorously and exhaustingly, for hour after hour, day after day – but that being useful and earning money, even if not much, is an effective morale-booster and has an empowering effect. Farmers' children told me how they'd worked all summer, their annual treat being a week on their grandparents' farm, and they had to work there too. Daughters from rigorous middle-class households were paid by their mothers to do the vacuuming and empty the waste-paper baskets, or were sometimes not paid to do that, just expected to. Meanwhile, others just played tennis. I wanted to trace the trajectories and attitudes to work that followed those very different starts, and to investigate how, through the different trajectories, women were formed into the people they became. I hope this book explains our mothers, and explains us.

A few flashbacks from my own experience, which have kept me awake since 1984, made me curious to find out what starting out in the world of work was like for other people. I left Girton College, Cambridge, hoping to 'get into publishing' as a secretary, in 1984, so at the tail-end of the period of this book, its cut-off date being 'the end of the Typewriter Age', which I reckon to be 1992, when the Email Age began, reducing to an eerie silence the clattering noise of offices and the rushing about of post boys with internal memos in string-sealed envelopes with a grid of previous recipients' names scratched out. Did some of the character and fun go out of office life at that moment?

The flashbacks are as follows:

First, Rosemary Goad, the director at Faber & Faber, saying to me in September 1984, 'Oh, I've got a million and one things to do,' when she interviewed me for the job of secretary to the marketing director, and I asked her what she did all day. She either wouldn't, or couldn't, name a single one of those million and one things, and I've wondered ever since what people did in offices to fill the hours. I didn't get the job.

But what was an English graduate even doing applying to be secretary to the marketing director at Faber & Faber in 1984? My male friends were going straight in as editorial assistants – on another plane and at a higher pay scale. Girls like me were being variously entreated by our mothers, 'Learn to type! It'll get you a job anywhere' or 'Whatever you do, don't learn to type. You'll just get stuck being a typist.'

Then, the man in a holey jersey at the dusty desk of Zwemmer's bookshop in Charing Cross Road apologising for not giving me the job there either, as a sales assistant, explaining they'd had 1,200 applicants. Twelve hundred applications for a bookshop assistant! But my mother told me that when she started out in 1954 it had been 'easy to get a job' at the advertising agency J. Walter Thompson. Was it true that jobs used to be easy to get?

Then, climbing a narrow staircase in Old Bond Street in my gathered skirt, frilly-collared blouse and Rayne pumps, to be interviewed by a steel-haired woman behind the desk at an agency that specialised in placing young women like me (nicely spoken with free accommodation provided by their parents) in jobs as secretaries 'in the art world'. Who were these ladies in charge of young women's job chances, and did they always lurk at the top of staircases?

Then, Jackie Laing, another brusque woman, who was in charge of the girls at Christie's, where I did get a longed-for first job through that Bond Street agency, saying to me at my interview, 'I'm afraid we don't pay you very much, but we do give you a turkey at Christmas.' The salary was £3,500. I didn't last till Christmas, and have wondered ever since, did young men applying to Christie's also get interviewed by Jackie Laing? (No, I discovered. They were on a different pathway from day one.) Would a turkey at Christmas compensate for the tiny salary? (No.) And why a turkey? It turned out that a certain Mr Leadbetter, who'd run the front counter at Christie's in the 1960s, went off to run a turkey farm in Hertfordshire. He provided the turkeys – four hundred of them, freshly dead and driven up to London in a van – as Christmas gifts for the staff. Each member of staff got one, with giblets, in a Christie's bag, along with a copy of the *Christie's Review of the Season*. This was a perk, leading me to wonder what perks people at other offices were treated to.

Then, the unbelievable dullness of what I had to do: the paperwork that enabled pictures deemed not good enough to be sold at Christie's King Street to be transferred to the inferior Christie's South Kensington. I never saw any of the actual pictures – called things like *Forty Winks* – only the paperwork. Facing the expanse of time between the end of lunch and going-home time felt like stepping into the first mile of the Sahara Desert. You could feel profoundly homesick by three o'clock. Did time hang as heavily for others in their jobs? Did they too sometimes take refuge in the loo?

At my desk in the Old Masters Department at Christie's, 1985:
a long afternoon stretches ahead

Then, developing a crush on Brian, one of the porters. He gave me a reason to go up and down the staff staircase on errands, delivering memos or taking pieces of paper up to General Filing, an attic piled high with enormous quantities of paper being put into alphabetical order. I did eventually invite Brian to supper, but nothing came of it. He said that when people he worked with had crushes on him, it made him 'run a mile'. What better place to have a crush, though, than the office stairwell, whose bleakness needed relieving? What were other women's experiences of lust and love in the workplace? Did they get their bottoms pinched in the lift? I never did; was it just my bottom, or had that habit died out by 1984?

Then, hearing the sentence 'We have now had time to carefully examine your painting' being dictated to my friend Amanda Dickson each morning by her boss in the next-door room. I was pained by his split infinitive. He called Amanda 'child' when she misspelled the name Gervase. Out came her bottle of Tippex. What were people's misspelling memories, and what were their Tippex memories? 'My letters were mostly *straight* Tippex,' one former secretary would recall to me, bringing back the dandruffy weight of a heavily corrected sheet of foolscap. How clever, how eloquent, really, were the male bosses, and what else did they say to their underlings? Were the underlings just as clever as them, just less confident and less ambitiously educated?

I address these and other questions about the lot of the young women of the second half of the twentieth century in this book of first-hand recollections, for which I chatted to more than two hundred women from all walks of life, from all over the country – the backbone of British Janets,

Janes, Sues and Angelas, who were only too happy to have someone to talk to about how they'd made their way in the world of work. In this book we will hear their voices. The vast majority of them were happy to be quoted by name. Very occasionally they asked for anonymity and I changed their name.

Alongside those bad flashbacks, I have good ones from my four years as a subeditor at *Harpers & Queen*, which started in June 1985 under the enlightened editorship first of Willie Landels and then of Nicholas Coleridge. Almost forty years later, I'm still sustained by the fun of it all and the friendships that were made. I wanted to find out whether, at its best, work was like this for others.

The good flashbacks are these:

First, the extraordinary friendliness of a thriving, bustling open-plan 1980s office, where women were treated (so it could happen!) as equals to men. The endless chat and hilarity. All of us subeditors, in fact all the staff, have remained friends for life. Was it true that there was sometimes this family feeling in working environments? Or was being holed up in an office with colleagues all too often like 'being married to twenty-five strangers', as I've heard office life described? Novels about offices describe the ghastly, cliché-ridden false bonhomie of it all ('Welcome to the madhouse!'; 'Roll on, retirement!'), but in that office, the bonhomie and kindred-spiritedness were genuine and, thank God, there were no notices on the wall saying, YOU DON'T HAVE TO BE MAD TO WORK HERE, BUT IT HELPS. I think that kind of conviviality must have become rarer now, because during the working-from-home months of the pandemic in 2020, lots of people I asked said they didn't miss their office one bit, as it wasn't any fun there at all any more, just a lonely, silent slog in front of a screen all day.

Sub-editors larking about at *Harpers & Queen*, 1987.
Left to right: Jasper Rees, Anthony Gardner, YMG, Harry Ritchie

I remember fondly the comforting presence of the 'father' or 'mother' of the office – the older person who'd worked there seemingly for ever. In our case it was the production manager Bob Johnson, who cycled ten miles from south London each morning, arriving at 6.30 a.m. with his packed lunch of sandwiches, made by his wife, which he ate alongside an Oxo cube dissolved in a cup of kettle water. (I was fascinated by other people's lunch arrangements; people skulked off to goodness knows where; hence the chapter called 'Smoke; Drink; Lunch'.) Bob had a remarkable ability to see and treasure the uniqueness in each one of us. He also happened to be a polymath. Did other offices have such a person who held the whole place together?

One afternoon in 1988, Miles Kington came into the office and showed us how he could send off his freshly written column for the *Independent* by plugging in a machine that made a funny noise, and we all watched, dazzled, as his piece was sent across 'the internet'. Meanwhile at my open-plan workstation I was still typing out headlines and captions on a non-electric typewriter. I wanted to find out more about the evolution of mechanical typewriters into 'golf ball' ones, and then the challenges of word processors, fax machines and early computers, and the part these contraptions played in the working lives of young women.

So much of a girl's future depended on a turning point decreed by others when she was eleven. At that point it was largely determined, without her realising it, whether she would be 'working for' or 'working with' or even working at all. Let's start by sorting the young British females of the period into their various houses of aspiration or non-aspiration: the schools they were about to leave. To what extent were these any kind of springboard to a career, or even a 'job'?

PART I

THE DAUGHTERS
LEAVE SCHOOL

I

Girls Without a Maths O Level

'Sheila Cotton, after spending the summer
perfecting her French, is having a year at home'

'News of Old Girls', Lawnside school
magazine, 1969

One thing quickly became clear: that vital passport to
industrial mobility, the maths O level, was mysteriously
off the menu at both the very lowest-aspiring state schools
in the country and at the poshest private schools. At both
extremes of the social spectrum, girls were thwarted before
they started. They left school at fifteen (secondary modern
girls pre-1972, before the leaving age went up to sixteen) or
sixteen (privately educated girls) without that fundamental
paper qualification, a maths O level certificate, to wave at
any possible future employer. If in their mid-twenties they
suddenly decided they'd like to train as a lawyer, teacher,
physiotherapist or nurse, they couldn't unless they went
first to an adult education college and dredged up their
non-existent memory of how to calculate a radius. Their

schooling had failed them in the core aspect of what you might think schooling was for.

You might ask why anyone would need a maths O level in order to do a non-maths-based job, and it's a good question. The theory was that it proved that a person could think logically, even – and indeed especially – if the thinking was outside his or her comfort zone. Thus an ability to calculate the missing angle of a pentagon became a gateway to the professions. But girls were deprived of it.

There were different reasons and excuses for this omission, at the top and the bottom of the social scale.

At the top end, it was first of all the choice of the girls' parents to steer their daughters to schools at which the tap of career opportunity would be turned off. Fathers paid high fees for their daughters to emerge into adulthood prethwarted. For them, their daughters' schooling had never been about academic achievement or equipping them for a career. They saw themselves not as stiflers of potential careers, but as enablers of a good marriage and a secure adulthood under the protection of a man of means. They were confident they were opening that avenue, because their daughters were going to be making friends with similar girls, who had eligible brothers whom they would meet at parties.

Many parents were actively against their daughters leaving school with their brains stuffed with mathematical expertise, as they feared that if they were too brainy it would put potential husbands off. There was still an assumption among the upper- and middle-class pre-war generation of parents that the safest kind of marriage was between a pretty, good-humoured, domesticated girl, pliable thanks to her unambitious schooling, and a man who could mould her according to his tastes and needs. They didn't seem to question whether this was what the young men of the post-war generation really wanted.

Scottish St Mary's Wantage girl Cicely McCulloch's father was typical in his bluff comments on this matter. He said to her when she was seventeen, in the late 1950s, 'There's no point in your having a career, because you're perfectly bed-worthy and will get married.'

Cicely, who has been a relationship counsellor for thirty years, is the first in my large collection of pre-thwarted women who never got a maths O level, having been allowed to give up maths aged twelve. 'I've got through life without maths,' she told me, cheerfully. 'I *can* do my times-tables, though.'

One day in her mid-teens during the school holidays in Galloway, it dawned on her that two local schoolgirls were being better equipped for self-sustaining adulthood than she was. 'I used to ride past the house of two girls in my Brownie pack,' she said, 'who were daughters of a local farm worker. Their mother asked me one day as I rode past, "What are you planning to do when you leave school?" I didn't know what to say, as I didn't really want to do anything after school. I had no ambition whatsoever. Both of her daughters had passed the 11-plus to Dumfries Academy. One of them went on to become a civil servant and the other a teacher. I remember the feeling of shame and embarrassment of that conversation.'

When it came to ambition for Cicely, her mother was if anything even less aspirational than her father. Here are three of her morsels of advice:

'Darling, you don't need to get a job. You've got brothers and sisters with small children. You can go and help them.'

Then, 'Don't ever ask a young man what he does, because if he's a gentleman he doesn't do anything.'

Then, 'It's not fair to take a job out of the hands of another woman who might really need it.'

That last was an often-heard message delivered to the so-called privileged. Snaffling a job, if you came from a well-heeled family, was seen as selfish in the way that leaving the gristle on the side of your plate was, when there were 'starving children in Africa'.

To those pieces of advice, she added one more, on her daughter's expected future as a wife: 'You must never wash in the bath if your husband comes into the bathroom. You must just float like a lily.'

Cicely McCulloch at Queen Charlotte's Ball, May 1964:
'There's no point in your having a career,' said her father, 'because you're perfectly bedworthy and will get married'

So Cicely found herself with the projected future of a Jane Austen daughter, transferred to the 1950s. The fifties was a particularly backward-looking decade, she told me, having lived through them as a teenager in rural Scotland. A decade earlier, during the Second World War, young women like her and her elder sister (who was even more repressed by their parents than she was) would have been driving ambulances or working at Bletchley, and falling in love, knowing they might be killed the next day. Now their parents were clamping down, reacting against the louche behaviour of that reckless decade.

The desired trajectory for a girl from an expensive school was: leave aged sixteen, do the Season, attend a secretarial course in Central London, get a little job, meet an eligible man, marry, give up job, have children, run household, be a pillar of the community.

'My mother's approach,' said Rosie Wilson, born in the mid-1950s, who eventually managed to become a nurse after being a secretary, 'was that you were either (a) an attractive young woman, in which case you would not need any career, as you would get married and be supported by a husband, or (b) unattractive, in which case you would need to support yourself as a spinster.' In the latter case, you would need to become a secretary. Her father's belief was that his daughters should live at home until marriage, while her brother was sent to Winchester College and Cambridge.

Note those words 'attractive young woman', or 'unattractive'. 'Attractive' here was almost entirely synonymous with 'pretty'. At that moment in a girl's life, the more brusque mothers, such as Rosie's, divided the females of the world into 'pretty' and 'plain', and a seventeen-year-old daughter of the 1950s and '60s was made strongly aware of which category she was in. In some ways, the 'pretty' ones were in more danger, as they risked being snapped up and subsumed into marriage all too soon. The 'plain' girl would benefit from her parents' greater effort to prepare her for a working life, but she would then find it harder to get her first 'little job', as there was a marked prejudice in favour of prettiness among employers.

I noted in *Terms & Conditions* that 'sparky' was the favoured adjective used by fathers of their more attractive daughters, as it seemed more enticing than 'clever', suggesting sparks of brilliance rather than the dull honing of the brain in a classroom. The daughters would need to use that sparkiness to the full if they intended to buck the trend and make any headway in the world of work without a maths O level.

From day one they were fighting against the expectations of the previous generation. 'Turn off parental controls', the prompt we now see on streaming websites, would have been useful for mid-twentieth-century daughters at the moment when they stepped out of girlhood. Parental control was still extremely tight. For a stark example of parents in the driving seat of their cusp-of-adulthood daughter's life, take Jenny Boltwood, born in 1946, who went to Northwood College for Young Ladies, 'run entirely by spinsters', as she recounted to me. 'I left school aged fifteen without any qualifications at all, except for dancing medals. What my parents were most interested in was getting me safely married off to someone "important" or someone who would keep me. On our first family holiday abroad in Majorca in 1962, they spotted a handsome man sitting under an umbrella at the beach café, while I was bathing in the sea. My mother went up to chat with him. He turned out to be an ear, nose and throat surgeon from Stockholm, twenty-two years older than me, called Eric. My parents then invited him to stay with us in England, and he did, and he decided he wanted to marry me. I thought I was in love with him, and we got married – I was seventeen and he was thirty-nine. My parents thought they were doing me a favour, by encouraging me towards this "good marriage" to a successful doctor. And we did have a lovely life in the centre of Stockholm. His friends' children were the same age as I was. He was horrified that I didn't have any academic qualifications. Sweden was more advanced than Britain in the 1960s, when it came to women's education.'

Jenny Boltwood, aged sixteen, on the 1962 Majorca
holiday during which her parents found a husband for her
(twenty-two years older than she was) on the beach

The marriage was short-lived because Eric died a year and a half later. Jenny was widowed aged eighteen, 'and I came back to live with my parents in Harrow, and my father took control again. He wouldn't let me buy a flat. I went off to the Lucie Clayton School to do a modelling course.'

Thus the adult widowed daughter was a puppet of her parents. Her very lack of qualifications kept her near them.

Jenny and her father in their garden in Kenton, Middlesex, 1962

This low trajectory of intellectual aspiration for middle-class and upper-class daughters started as early as the nursery. Elizabeth Rolston, born in 1926, who went to Studley Horticultural & Agricultural College for Women in Warwickshire after leaving Harrogate Ladies' College aged sixteen, told me that when they were young children, 'Our father read the great classics of English literature aloud to our younger brother. He expected the nanny to read to us daughters.' From the very beginning, the brother's brain was being nourished in a superior way to the sisters' brains. 'My father started giving me Latin lessons on the deck of a ship back from Kenya when I was six,' Julia Wigan, born in 1960, said to me. 'He was keen on us three daughters learning, but he said it was "so we would have something to think about while doing the washing-up".'

Push against any of this and you were firmly pushed back

down. Agneta Hinkley, also born in 1926, was sent to school in Bruton when St Swithun's closed during the Second World War. 'I didn't do Higher Certificate and I got a very poor School Certificate [the equivalent of O levels] – I didn't even take maths.' After leaving school Agneta was kept at home because 'my brother had a heart murmur and my mother decided that because he couldn't go into the forces, it was very unfair if I did. I was allowed to do absolutely nothing. Not surprisingly, I had a breakdown – a quiet one at home. I spent three whole months in tears.' Thanks to an uncle who offered to pay, she was sent on a cookery course at the Gloucestershire School of Domestic Science, after which she went on to be a junior matron at a boys' prep school in Hampshire.

It seems extraordinary that, fifty years later, the very same social class of parents would be paying vast sums for tutors to help their daughters up the ladder of opportunity.

'In my entire growing-up life,' said Philippa Millar, born in 1953, 'what I might do in my adult life was never mentioned either by my parents or by the schools I went to.' As it happened, Philippa had started worrying from the age of eight about how she was going to support herself as an adult. 'I always had this feeling that I would need to support myself financially. Money was always a problem at home. My father moaned endlessly about the school fees. I couldn't think what I would do. I used to worry myself to sleep. Who on earth would ever pay *me* to do anything?'

The lack of self-belief that came from these enforced low aspirations, and the ensuing certainty that if one did get a job one was going to be an underling, seeped into girls' hearts. As Penny Eyles, born in 1938, put it, 'I never particularly got on with my father. He was demobbed from the Army at the end of the Second World War and finally came home when I was seven. He didn't know how to deal with little girls. We used to shake hands.' While her brother went to university to study for a profession, she and her sister were sent to domestic science and secretarial colleges – imbued with a sense of 'I'm a woman, so I'm going to be an assistant.'

So much for the parents. What about the schools? In their musty isolation and their emphasis on good manners over intellectual achievement, expensive girls' schools bumbled along well below the potential academic threshold of their 'sparky' girls. I've lost count of the women who said to me, vaguely, 'Our school didn't really do A levels.' 'Well, did it or didn't it?' I asked them. By 'didn't really do A levels', they meant there was a one-year sixth form that you could stay on for, doing a bit of French and history of art, just to keep you quiet and occupied till seventeen. No exams followed. You sailed out with lots of friends but all too often without a maths O level, and certainly no A levels. In the same period at private boys' schools, the only boys who didn't stay on for the whole sixth form were the complete 'thickos', considered almost 'backward'.

Marriage was the perceived destination for the daughters, and this wasn't even hidden; it was overt. On the final day of the summer term at the girls' school St Margaret's, Bushey, in Middlesex, it was the custom for the deputy headmistress, Miss Pullan in the 1950s, to walk each school-leaver in turn up the aisle of the school hall in the final assembly; this was their practice for being walked up the aisle of the church by their father, as it was expected they soon would be.

'Really, we want most of our girls to do something like marry into the Foreign Office' was what the headmistress of St Mary's Ascot, Mother Bridget, told prospective parents, as late as the mid-1970s. This was a selling point for the school. Parents went home enchanted by the vision of their daughter presiding over an embassy dinner party in Rome, at the opposite end of the long dining-room table from her ambassador husband.

Bee Bealey recalled a task that the girls in her class at St Mary's Wantage were set by their social studies teacher in the mid-1970s. Social studies! What a trendy new subject! But the syllabus appears to have been Victorian. The girls had to write down the most valued attributes they looked for in their future husband. 'We were expected to write things like "kindness", "tolerance", "good sense of humour", and so on,' said Bee. 'Mary Muir just wrote "grouse moor".'

It was hilarious, and no one ever forgot it, because it sort of hit the nail on the head. What more could a girl ask for in life than to marry a grouse moor?

Bee, who wrote respectable abstract nouns rather than 'grouse moor' in that task, was expelled aged sixteen for an accumulation of petty rule-breaking, having spent four years hiding in the library reading. She was, and continues to be, extremely well read. It was absolutely typical for girls like her to leave school aged sixteen without a maths O level. Those in her 'lower' maths set at St Mary's didn't even sit maths O levels; they sat the CSE (Certificate of Secondary Education), an inferior exam designed for secondary-modern students as part of a divisive two-tier system. CSEs only existed between 1965 and 1987, and they didn't count as a career-worthy qualification unless you got a top grade 1, which equated to an O level 'C'.

In her expelled state, Bee was permitted to return to the school just to sit her O levels, a mixture of GCEs for the subjects she'd liked and CSEs for the others. This was undertaken in a light and frivolous spirit. 'My father's company driver, the most adorable man, drove me back to school to sit the exams.

I hadn't even read the biology textbook, so I begged him not to take me as far as school. We just had a picnic by the river and shook hands on our secret. I got an A – at least, my father thought it was an A; he was very impressed and asked me, "Are you thinking of a career in medicine?" but actually it was a small "a" for "absent". I admitted that to him just before he died. I did take the CSE in maths, but didn't pass it.' This rendered her pretty well unemployable.

I heard countless chronicles of the under-qualification of daughters whose parents were paying for their expensive education. A few more voices of the educationally let down:

Penny Sheehan, who went to Downham School, Hertfordshire: 'I got five O levels. Five girls in my class got no O levels at all. We were given lots of elocution lessons, because we were going to be opening fetes.'

Hermione Waterfield, Burton's School, St Albans: 'It wasn't a very good school. The dining room collapsed two months after I left. No science. My father wrote to my mother, "I really think Hermione could do better than the sales counter at John Lewis."' (She would one day become the first female director at Christie's.)

Bumble Ogilvy-Wedderburn, at Summer Bank, near Dundee: 'The headmistress Miss White wanted me to do these tests aged nine. She said, "Honestly, I can see no help for you at all. I think you'll have to be a dustbin woman."' Bumble was dyslexic. Then she went to West Heath where she got three O levels, but maths wasn't one of them. 'Then I went to learn French in Switzerland, where the *dictée* was very difficult as it was read out by a German. I then failed my French O level.' She went the Cordon Bleu cookery school in Marylebone.

Alison Willatts (born in 1949), who went to Tudor Hall in the 1960s: 'I went for an interview to be a nurse at St Thomas's Hospital. You had to have two A levels to get in to those big London hospitals, whereas most nursing schools took you with five O levels, one of which had to be maths. I didn't have a maths O level, due to difficulty with the teachers at Tudor Hall. The lady who took over the maths syllabus wasn't qualified to teach O level. She'd been Froebel-trained and knew even less about logarithms than we did.' So how on earth did Alison get into St Thomas's? 'Well, I did have two A levels – I was the first girl from Tudor Hall ever to get two, even though they were Ds because we had to do them in one year as there wasn't an upper sixth at Tudor Hall.' But how did she get in to St Thomas's without the necessary maths O level? 'St Thomas's had its own maths exam for suitable candidates who didn't have an O level. Luckily I passed that.' Ah, so St Thomas's had had to come down to the level of its promising but under-educated candidates and hoik them out of their predicament.

It was a decidedly bumpy start.

Meanwhile, in the world of state schools, the fourteen year olds at Sidcup Girls' Secondary Modern in 1971 were all handed out a questionnaire to fill in one weekday morning, distributed across the local state schools by the Youth Employment Service of the London Borough of Bexley. Anna Maxwell kept hold of hers for the rest of her life and showed it to me.

'Here is a list of jobs,' it said. 'Think about each one in turn. If you think you would like to do it, put a RING round it. If you decide you would not like it, put a CROSS through it. If you are not sure, leave it blank.' Those capital letters in the instructions, for RING and CROSS, make one feel that the authors of this questionnaire expected their readers to be a bit sub-par in literacy and comprehension.

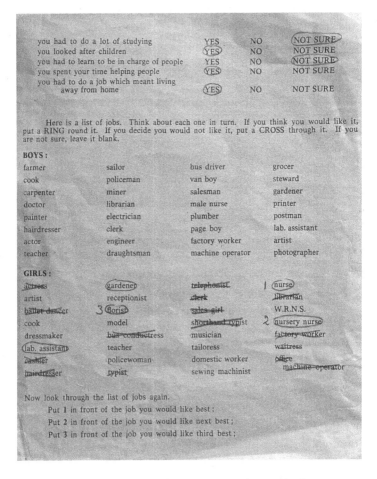

you had to do a lot of studying	YES	NO	NOT SURE
you looked after children	YES	NO	NOT SURE
you had to learn to be in charge of people	YES	NO	NOT SURE
you spent your time helping people	YES	NO	NOT SURE
you had to do a job which meant living away from home	YES	NO	NOT SURE

Here is a list of jobs. Think about each one in turn. If you think you would like it, put a RING round it. If you decide you would not like it, put a CROSS through it. If you are not sure, leave it blank.

BOYS:

farmer	sailor	bus driver	grocer
cook	policeman	van boy	steward
carpenter	miner	salesman	gardener
doctor	librarian	male nurse	printer
painter	electrician	plumber	postman
hairdresser	clerk	page boy	lab. assistant
actor	engineer	factory worker	artist
teacher	draughtsman	machine operator	photographer

GIRLS:

actress	gardener	telephonist	nurse
artist	receptionist	clerk	librarian
ballet dancer	florist	sales girl	W.R.N.S.
cook	model	shorthand typist	nursery nurse
dressmaker	bus conductress	musician	factory worker
lab. assistant	teacher	tailoress	waitress
cashier	policewoman	domestic worker	office
hairdresser	typist	sewing machinist	machine operator

Now look through the list of jobs again.
    Put 1 in front of the job you would like best;
    Put 2 in front of the job you would like next best;
    Put 3 in front of the job you would like third best;

The careers questionnaire handed out in class to the fourteen
year olds at Sidcup Girls' secondary modern, 1971

There was a different list for boys and girls: no 'doctor' or 'engineer' on the girls' list, nor anything as glamorous-sounding as 'photographer'. Even the boys were strongly not steered towards the professions, if you look at their options, but for the girls it was definitive.

The option you needed a maths O level for was Anna's first ringed choice: nurse. She did manage to become a nurse, thanks to staying on and sitting GCEs at the same secondary modern, which did have a GCE stream, after doing the worthless CSEs, so she never needed to resort to her second choice, 'nursery nurse', or her third choice, 'florist'. She remembers the filling in of that form as a moderately engaging and entertaining task, but nothing was ever heard of it again. 'There was no follow-up, and no careers advice.'

'The sense of failure clobbers one,' she said, feelingly, of not passing the 11-plus and being consigned to a secondary modern. It was the fate of so many: life chances determined at the moment before puberty when your parents opened the letter of acceptance or rejection. The subtext for those consigned to the secondary modern was 'Claw your way out of your assigned station in life if you dare or can be bothered to'. The general pull from then on, from both school and parents, tended to be downwards. 'Everything I ever wanted to do,' said Janet Garner, who left her secondary modern in Fulham aged fifteen in 1961, 'my mother said, "you're not clever enough".'

It was especially painful if you did pass the 11-plus to the local grammar school but still didn't go there as your parents couldn't afford the uniform, as happened to a great many, including Audrey Loper of Bradford, born in 1933. 'My parents couldn't afford for me to go. So I went to the secondary modern, where all my friends went. We didn't do O levels. I left at fifteen but didn't want to work in an office, so I sewed rugs at a works called Tankard's on the top floor of an old chapel from 7 a.m. to 5 p.m.' Thus were her life chances dictated by the price of a school blazer.

Until the school leaving age was raised to sixteen in 1972, most girls left their secondary modern at the end of the term (not year) in which they turned fifteen. Fifteenth birthday in October? You were out before Christmas, with no academic qualifications, and went straight to work after the weekend. Fifteen felt quite old and mature to be leaving, compared with these girls' mothers who'd left school and gone into domestic service or factories at twelve or fourteen, and had therefore only ever received a primary education.

'I left on Friday and started work on Monday,' lots I spoke to said. Qualificationless and suddenly cast into adulthood, the next thing they knew they were on a bus in the dark at 6.30 a.m. in their work clothes, with no school holidays to look forward to ever again. Diana Brooks, born in 1949, left her secondary modern in Huish Episcopi in Somerset on a Friday aged fifteen and a quarter, having been called stupid because she was dyslexic. 'Being made to stand up in class and read something out loud was my worst nightmare. It blew my confidence that I could do anything more interesting in life.' On the Monday three days later, she started at a factory where they made the stiff parts for the insides of bikinis. School had been work's waiting room.

The expression that rings in my ears to express this plunge into full-time work was spoken to me down the telephone by a woman in Sunderland who left school at fifteen and went straight to work in a department store: 'You just gorron with it.' The expected attitude was not to make a fuss, or have an existential crisis, but just to get on with it and do it.

Would it even have been worth these girls' staying on till the end of the school year to sit those CSEs? I'm not convinced it would, having asked women to sum up their CSE experiences. Those two three-letter abbreviations, 'GCE' and 'CSE', had a gulf between them. One denoted attainment and the other a lack of attainment. That second tier of the public exam system was not a springboard to anything much, except the possibility of becoming a nanny. Heather Hall, born in 1950, who went to the girls' secondary modern in Poole and did CSEs, said, 'They were not worth the paper they were written on. I did about six of them. The woman who was the deputy headmistress admitted to me in hindsight that they were worthless. The grade 1 was equivalent to a GCE grade C, and I only got one grade 1, in biology.' Glenda Herron, born in 1958, who went to the secondary modern in Sunderland, did CSEs at school and had to take maths and English GCEs at night school in order to have any hope of becoming a teacher. 'All the children I went to primary school with automatically transferred to the comprehensive school,' she explained to me. 'But I happened to live on the other side of the main road.' That was the cut-off point of the catchment area for the comprehensive. On Glenda's side of the road, the children had to sit the 11-plus, with no proper lead-up to it or preparation. 'So I didn't pass it, and went on to the secondary modern instead.'

There were gradations of 'not getting into the grammar school', some consigning you to an abject lack of qualifications, others giving you a chance. It was a matter of luck whether you went to the kind of secondary modern, such as a county secondary school, that aimed a notch higher, or that insisted that you did stay to sit some public exams, or that had a single good maths teacher, or that had a GCE stream for the girls who showed potential. 'County secondaries did have GCE streams,' Beryl Stoker explained to me. 'There were only two county secondaries in Leeds. I failed the 11-plus but got into the county secondary school when I was thirteen. I was in the GCE stream but was no good at exams so didn't actually get any.'

If you were at a secondary modern that suddenly went comprehensive, your life chances could be lifted by the sudden influx of ex-grammar-school girls with ambition. This happened to Christine Padgett, who did some actual O levels at Buttershaw Comprehensive, one of the first schools in the country to go comprehensive. 'I did a mixture of CSEs and O Levels – four of each. There were four streams and I was in the top one.' The dying strains of the newly discredited streaming system saved her, and she was able to train to be a nurse.

Christine Padgett, aged nineteen: able to become a nurse thanks to being allowed to do a mixture of CSEs and O levels (GCSEs) at her school that had just gone comprehensive

If, on the other hand, you were at a grammar school when it went comprehensive, you could be caught up in a swirl of chaos. This happened to Helen Shay, born in 1956 in Harrogate, who went to West Leeds Girls High in 1968 when it was still a grammar. It changed to a comprehensive in 1971 'and went dog-rough', as she described it. 'A lot of the older teachers had nervous breakdowns. I'd been in "the Latin stream". That went out of the window. The school was in chaos. Lots of the older teachers took early retirement. One old lady teacher was so terrified of the new influx that she couldn't look at the class any more – she was too nervy. I think I suffered from all that, as I was quite bright.'

As with the girls in the previous chapter, marriage was the perceived destination, but in this case it was marriage preceded by a full-time job from day one of leaving school. 'Working class' meant exactly that. Here's Helen Shay on Leeds in the mid-1970s: 'As a working-class girl, it's only with hindsight that I can see how bad it was. Your prospects were marriage. It was all about having a boyfriend and being attractive. The boyfriends I had were as thick as short planks, but if you had a boyfriend, you had kudos. There was huge pressure to go to the rugby club dance and prove yourself. All the girls who left school at fifteen went to work at a mill or a shop or to be a lowly secretary till they could meet their husband.'

To prepare their girls for the working life that would start three days after leaving, schools organised trips to visit factories. 'My older sister was taken on school trips to visit six factories, including the local chocolate one,' said Kathleen Hewitson, born in Leeds in 1947, who went to Calcott's Secondary Modern 'along with the whole neighbourhood'. 'I was really envious, and disappointed I didn't go on an outing like that. They stopped doing those factory trips in the year I was leaving, 1962. So I just worked in the factory nearest my home, Kauffmann Brothers in Harehills. I worked there full-time from the age of fifteen, and stayed for thirteen years.'

Those schools that provided some kind of bridge between themselves and the world of work were at least usefully plugged in to the real world – much more plugged in than the expensive schools whose headmistresses had no knowledge of the world of work, nor any interest in what their girls were going to do next, unless it was marriage to a man with a title.

The most usefully plugged-in state schools of all were the 'commercial classes', which really set their girls on a 'jobs' path for life.

'When I turned thirteen,' explained Jean Dace, born in 1935, 'there was a project at my secondary modern. Children were taken from various schools and interviewed, and if you passed, you became part of a class of forty children from all the different local schools, and that was "the commercial class" for the next three years. The one I went to was called Glastonbury Secondary School in Carshalton. It was an all-girls' school especially for learning shorthand and typing and bookkeeping. I thought it was very exciting. I fell in love with Pitman's shorthand. It was a new language, like hieroglyphics. Homework was never a problem from that moment on.'

Plugged in to the world of work, that school sent her straight off for an interview at a solicitor's firm in Central London, so aged fifteen she 'left school on a Friday and started on Monday', already supremely qualified as a capable junior secretary in a typing pool.

Childhood was over as suddenly as that.

2

Girls With a Maths O Level

**'I was a bookworm, so my father was convinced
I was going to be a librarian'**

Angela Hill, retired nurse

It was not 'you're going to grow up to be a famous novelist' if you were a bookworm, but 'you're going to grow up to be a librarian'. If you mended your dolls' legs with handkerchief bandages, it wasn't 'you're going to be a doctor' but 'you're going to be a nurse'. Parents meant it kindly; they really did. And both librarian and nurse are noble professions. To the daughter trained in self-effacement, it didn't seem insulting, just affectionate and realistic. But it wasn't exactly 'aiming high' as we would now think of it. Even parents who encouraged their daughters to work hard at school and 'cared about education for their daughters' seemed to go a bit weak and unambitious when it came to suggesting future jobs for them.

Swathes of girls who'd read the complete works of Dickens, and who did get a maths O level, and sometimes even some A levels, and sometimes even a university degree, were nonetheless directed towards helping, caring, supporting, tidying-up, making-institutions-run-smoothly-for-everyone-else careers. It made for a workforce of highly eloquent, well-read and knowledgeable librarians, nurses and secretaries. And the ones who did become librarians in Oxbridge colleges soon discovered that the Librarian with a capital 'L' was usually a male don who curated the whole priceless collection. The woman who did all the work, the actual librarian behind the desk, had a small 'l'.

'Don't let the girls get ideas above their station' was the underlying message from the advisors to teenaged girls wondering what on earth to do next. Schoolmistresses were so desperate not to allow their girls to become in any way arrogant that they went a long way in the other direction, ladling them with self-doubt and reminding them again and again that they must never boast or 'blow their own trumpet'. 'My girls' school, lovely though it was,' gardening writer Caroline Donald said to me, 'had no idea how to get the best out of its pupils or fill them with glorious self-confidence.' Thanks to one superb history teacher, Caroline did get in to Cambridge, but her mother sent her to the Oxford & County Secretarial College (known, with a hint of inbuilt misogyny, as the Ox & Cow) in her gap year to arm her for her future, and after a failed interview with Reuters, during which she got a nose bleed, she spent seven years after Cambridge working as a temporary secretary. 'It did at least lead on to a job on a newspaper eventually,' she told me.

Miss Burgess, headmistress of Malvern Girls' College in the early 1960s, said to Amanda Theunissen (who would later become a television producer) as she was about to leave, 'You're very intelligent but not an academic. You'll get into university but I don't think you'll get a degree.' So she didn't go. In hindsight one asks, 'How dare the headmistress presume that?' Malvern College was supposedly one of the higher-achieving girls' public schools, based on the boys' model, 'a good place for fat, happy girls who didn't have much of a social life,' as Amanda described it, 'and I'd been in the "A" stream all my life. But I don't think I had *any* dreams; no ambitions, no sense of what I could or couldn't do. My mother wanted me to be a secretary in the Foreign Office. She said I'd meet "interesting people". She thought I needed to get some kind of job – in the early 1960s there was no longer the social structure where you simply went back to live at home, played tennis, and waited till a man asked you to marry him. So I did go to secretarial college – Miss Judson's in Kensington.'

The tamping down of girls' aspirations was common practice. As Liz Jones, who went to Wycombe Abbey in the late 1950s, put it, 'Elderly spinsters are not the best role models for young girls. The word "university" was never mentioned in my hearing at Wycombe Abbey. Nor was the word "career".' Liz came from a particularly unhelpful family. She had been adopted by elderly parents, 'aged forty-one and fifty-one when they adopted me at six weeks. My adoptive mother was a complete nutcase. She tried to bring me up like a little Victorian girl, in a fantasy world, with a nanny in uniform, a day nursery and a night nursery. But she couldn't bear to touch me or be in the same room as me. She never gave me a word of praise. The two four-letter words I never heard, all through my childhood, were "Well done".' As for Liz's projected adulthood, 'My mother said, "I want you to marry a title." She thought I'd be invited to house parties at stately homes, but she was half a century out of date.'

One day she asked Liz, 'Would you like to go to university?' but she asked the question 'in such a fierce manner that it sounded as if she was condemning me to death'. Amazingly, after a spell at a boarding secretarial college in

Eastbourne, Liz did dare to apply to Trinity College, Dublin, 'a nice long way away', and got in, but she didn't complete her degree as she met a man and was soon a mother of two working as a secretary to a vet while her husband taught at Newmarket Grammar.

Quietly omit science O levels from your curriculum, as a headmistress, and you kept your girls safely in the 'nurse' rather than the 'doctor' camp. 'If I'd been allowed to stay on at my grammar school in Tavistock rather than going on to Tudor Hall,' said Alison Willatts, 'I would have done physics and chemistry O levels and might have had a chance of going into medicine. My father moved me to boarding school because he was in the Navy and being posted abroad. The only science at Tudor Hall was "human biology and hygiene", taught by a retired Army colonel. We got as far as the navel and started again at the knees but didn't do the bit in between. The colonel was good on sewage and drains, though, and he took us to visit an activated sludge plant.' Later, while training to be a nurse, Alison did sign up for adult evening classes to try to get those two missing science O levels. 'I took the exams, but I didn't quite make it.' It was too late.

'Did you have any careers advice at school?' I asked almost everyone I spoke to, trying to discover whether any adult, anywhere, really had a plan for these girls. The most common answer was 'there might have been a few leaflets put out on a table.' Or 'there was a little-used room with a few dusty pamphlets'. Pamphlets! I remember the much-vaunted 'Careers Library' at my co-educational senior school Dover College in the 1970s, a pamphlet-filled medieval gatehouse so little visited that it was the place where boys met girls for trysts after prep. After the snog, you could look up 'Hotel Management' under 'H' and be not helped by the enticing vagueness of what you found: black and white photographs of staff at a reception desk. At least my school was seen to be trying. That roomful of career-oriented brochures impressed the parents. Girls' schools of that period didn't have careers libraries, just a few leaflets lying around.

'Did you have people coming into the school to give careers talks?' I asked. Many told me that the only people who ever came to give careers talks at their all-girls' schools were, oddly enough, brigadiers and naval commanders – handsome middle-aged men in uniform, 'probably some distant relation of the headmistress'. These men's descriptions of their adventures on land and sea left the girls sitting cross-legged on the floor dazzled but none the wiser about how to proceed.

A 'fierce lady officer from the Women's Royal Army Corps' came to talk to the St Mary's Wantage girls in 1960, Cicely McCulloch recalled. 'She was bolstered in a hideous uniform: skirt, jacket, tie and brogues. We took one look at her and thought, "No, thanks."'

I never once heard anyone say that any careers advice they had received at school had been of any use whatsoever. The girls went in with the naive expectation that there must be some job that was particularly suited to their unique character, likes and abilities – one that they would love, but happened never to have thought of. But in truth there never was, and even if there had been, school careers advisors who'd usually spent most of their lives only in the teaching world, and were not plugged into the real jobs market, were never going to find it for them.

Of the girls who did take tests to see what career might be suitable, it was amazing how many of the tests came up with the answer 'florist'. Penrose Halson (born in 1940), highly intelligent and well read, was one of these. 'My parents sent me off to the National Institute of Industrial Psychology to assess and analyse me. They said, "We recommend either floristry or speech therapy."'

Penrose Halson in 1959: the careers advisor said
'we recommend either floristry or speech therapy'

There was an inward-looking tendency among the staff at girls' schools of the period that drove the girls who dared to dream crazy. Jo Fairley, born in 1956, who would go on to be the co-founder of Green & Black's chocolate, loathed Bromley High School for Girls for exactly that reason. 'The all-female teachers had gone from a similar educational environment straight to Girton and straight back again to teach, without really being in the world. They were not interested in anything beyond the walls of the school. My scripture teacher, Mrs Wootton, was also my careers teacher. In one class we were discussing what we might do and I said I'd quite like to start off as a secretary. She said, "Jo, if you manage to be so much as a Girl Friday to anyone, I'll eat my hat."' After Jo's appearance on *Desert Island Discs* in 2019, seven ex-Bromley High girls got in touch with her to say that Mrs Wootton had said something equally diminishing to them. 'Some of them told me it had been the spur to prove Mrs Wootton wrong; others said they'd "bought into" her naysaying, set their sights lower, and felt that she had really damaged their prospects in the world. In my case, it was a spur.'

On the day she left Bromley High, Jo walked to the bus stop and put her school boater under a bus tyre. 'I had a burning desire to grasp the world and be *in* the world.'

The only trouble was, if you didn't get good enough A levels, you couldn't grasp the world or be in it in the way you wanted to be, and some of those girls' schools had no idea how to get their sixth-formers to the required academic level. Rebecca Warren, who aged ten in 1959 was sent to a loveless boarding school in Shropshire at which she stayed for eight years, emerged at eighteen with inadequate A level grades thanks to the useless teaching of the desiccated ladies. They'd been fine with the O level syllabus, but simply couldn't cope with the next level. 'Of the fifty girls in my cohort,' Rebecca told me, 'one became a doctor, one a lawyer and one a teacher, but the other forty-seven of us came out not qualified to go to university.' Etched into her face, decades later, is her fury and sadness at the lack of help and advice given to her as a teenager, let alone the lack of pastoral care. 'Never, ever, during my whole time at the school, did I have a conversation with a member of staff who was interested in *me*.' When the disastrous A level results arrived, and Rebecca was upset, no one suggested she might retake them. 'My father didn't even write to the school to ask, "What on earth happened?"''

The whole subject was just dropped, and Rebecca started training as an occupational therapist, which she hated. Her older brother, meanwhile, who'd been sent off to boarding school aged seven, was on a totally different trajectory from the start: Winchester, then Cambridge, then a career at the Bar.

'None of us was stupid,' said Mary Burd, born in 1940, who left the (supposedly more academically high-achieving) Perse School in Cambridge in the late 1950s. 'We should all have gone to university.' But she and her two best friends all went straight on to secretarial colleges rather than to university, even though they did get good A levels. 'I didn't get in to Oxbridge,' explained Mary, 'and there was no question of being allowed to go to a red-brick university in those days.' (The reason being fear that at a red-brick university you might meet people with regional accents.) 'So I went to St James's Secretarial College.'

So, from almost-getting-into-Oxbridge, and armed with good exam results, girls found themselves in a classroom of young ladies typing in strict time to Sousa's marches.

'Only five girls out of our whole year at Queen Anne's, Caversham, went to university,' said Gillie Hanbury, born in 1943. 'They were the *real* eggheads. Careers advice was minimal. We were sent across to a separate building one morning, where we were asked whether we'd like to be nurses, physiotherapists, occupational therapists or secretaries. I fancied none of those. I said so to my parents. My mother said, "Well, you can always learn to cook". She herself had had to learn to cook when war broke out. So she sent me to the Atholl Crescent College of Domestic Science in Edinburgh.'

*

Surely, I thought, grammar schools aimed high for their girls? But I discovered it wasn't quite as simple as 'you were saved and enabled to do A levels and get into university and thus get a professional job if you got into the local grammar school.' At Wycombe Grammar in the 1950s, for example, as Glena Chadwick recalled, 'so many girls were going on to be nurses that there was a special sixth-form class for them, just one year long. It was the "Pre-Nursing Sixth". On sports day, all the girls in that class wore nurses' badges that they'd made out of cardboard.' So those girls had got their maths O levels, but then were encouraged to veer away from the more academic medicine stream into the world of nursing.

'The headmistress, Miss Dibb, at my grammar school, the Lilley and Stone Foundation High School for Girls in Newark,' said retired nurse Gill Robertson, born in 1936, 'was a real Oxford bluestocking – tweed suit, hair in a bun, lived with her lady friend – and she had real ambition for her "gels". The choice for us was: university, teacher training or nursing, but the nursing had to be at one of the top London hospitals – Guy's, St Thomas's or Bart's. Gill decided to be a nurse after a series of careers talks in 1952. A real nurse actually came to the school to talk about nursing. This was rare.

'In those days,' said Kathy Hay (born in 1948), explaining the 1960s state-sector norm to me, 'you only stayed at school after fifteen if you went to grammar school.' Ah, she did go to a Catholic grammar school, so did she stay on to do A levels? No, she didn't: 'My mother suffered from mental ill health so I had to take time off school and didn't even sit O levels. I left at fifteen with no qualifications and had to look after my younger siblings.' She was just one of many who, 'for family reasons', fell through the net of achievement even at a grammar school, while her friends who stayed on for the sixth form got themselves to a level where they could get a job at the National Insurance Office.

'Lots of girls at my grammar school left school at sixteen because of "family circumstances",' said Philomena O'Hare, 'even though they were clever. Their parents were poor and they needed the child to earn. So the girls went to work in Woolworths. Marriage was the only way out of that.'

'There are plenty of jobs. I don't know why you need to stay on at school,' Lynda Kitching's father said to his daughter (born in 1950), who had passed the 11-plus to Alwoodley Girls' High and passed her O levels. She was not allowed by her father to stay on, and 'as a dutiful daughter, I did what was expected. The headmistress was very disappointed that I left, but I explained to her, "My father said I should leave and get a job."' Not that the school had been much help when it came to career prospects. 'We had to fill in a form from cold, saying which jobs interested us. I ticked "air hostess", as I was quite good at French, but I'd never flown.'

Genuinely hard-up parents had an excuse for removing their daughters from school; they desperately needed the extra money earned by their fifteen-year-old daughter to support the household; but middle- and upper-class parents could be just as thrifty when it came to giving any kind of academic leg-up to their daughters. All the money was spent on the sons. 'Parents didn't want to spend any more money on one,' as Sal Rivière summed it up. She was one of only three girls at the joyless Beaufront School in the early 1950s who did stay on to do A levels, but she was then not encouraged to go to university. 'My mother thought that if we were intellectual no one would marry us. So I did the short course at Langham Secretarial College.' (The short course being cheaper than the long course.)

'You needed five O levels to be a nurse,' explained Gail

Nicolaidis, born in Leeds in 1946. She went to Steinbeck Secondary Modern, which did have a GCE stream as well as the lower CSE one, so she did get those five O levels. 'I could have sat the 13-plus to the grammar school where I could have got A levels – my sister did that, because she wanted to be a teacher. I didn't, because I knew I wanted to be a nurse.'

So, comfortable with her own aspirations, Gail self-sorted in her early teens. It wasn't only the parents and schools who did the sorting. If you knew what you wanted to do, and it was to be a nurse rather than a doctor or teacher, you positioned yourself accordingly and declined offers of academic promotion.

Certain 'brainboxes' (to use the unattractive term conferred on clever girls in the period of this book) were in fact the lucky ones when it came to having a dash of future opportunity thrown into the ingredients of their education. You come across seams of them in the higher-achieving grammar schools, and at the few top academic private girls' schools that did have ambition, such as Cheltenham Ladies' College, where Jennifer McGrandle, who was a new girl there in the early 1950s, was 'bowled over' to read in the prospectus that 'there will be a leaving scholarship for a girl who wants to study medicine with a view to surgery'.

It's in this narrow layer of British girlhood – not so upper-class that they were sent to a hopelessly unacademic, 'social' school, nor so low-aspiring that no one gave them a chance of preparing for the 11-plus to the county grammar – that we find the girls who, thanks to devoted headmistresses and rigorous teachers, got A levels and were encouraged to go to university. Barrister Barbara Rich (born in 1960) told me that the High Mistress (headmistress) of St Paul's Girls' School in the 1970s, who 'had a similar body shape and hairstyle to Princess Anne', had herself been a career civil servant. 'There was an Oxbridge expectation.'

Yet still, many of the girls, having got into Oxbridge, still went off to be secretaries afterwards. 'I'd taught myself to type aged fourteen, from the *Teach Yourself to Type* book,' Barbara Rich said, 'and the mother of one of the girls at St Paul's came in once a week to give us typing lessons in the sixth form.' So, even with her degree in English, off Barbara went to temping agencies, 'cubbyholes off Oxford Street' to sign on, turn up every Monday morning, and take whatever work was going in the typing pools of London W1.

'Watching the dissecting of one dead rabbit was the extent of my science education,' said Penrose Halson, who went to a succession of schools, ending at Millfield. She did get A levels, and was determined to get a university degree. Her parents thought they were sending her to a sort of university, but they had in fact been seduced by the brochure for St Clare's Hall in Oxford, which looked like an Oxford college but wasn't. The brochure said that its students could sit an external London degree. 'It had an attractive picture of Magdalen College Tower on its brochure,' said Penrose, 'but it was actually a semi-detached house on Banbury Road, and it turned out to be more of a finishing school. There was no library, just three Enid Blyton novels on a shelf. But I managed to get myself an external London degree by finding my own tutors, including a Spanish tutor in London.' She taught herself shorthand and typing at home and went to be a secretary to the friend of an uncle's friend in Damascus.

Alison Newton, who would marry the BBC presenter Peter Snow (an ITN newsreader when she first met him), also passed through St Clare's Hall in the late 1950s but had a better experience there. Her dream had been to get into one of the London teaching hospitals to study medicine. Astonishingly, considering the hopeless science teaching at Maltman's Green School in Gerrards Cross ('the lab was in an outbuilding with just one Bunsen burner', and 'nearly everyone left after O levels to go to secretarial college or be presented to the Queen'), Alison did stay on to do two A levels – botany and zoology. Those softer sciences were as near as the school would get to offering science A levels. 'I passed! My name was framed in the hall. I was considered *so* academic.'

So she now had the minimum requirement of two just-about-science A levels required for the London teaching hospitals. 'Without telling anyone, I applied.' This was 1957, and she got an interview at St Mary's, Paddington. 'The Dean had come from a boozy lunch, and there I was in my suit and sensible shoes and tights without ladders. "Now, Miss Carter," he said, "I see you were games captain at your school. We're very interested in games here. We have an unbeaten record at rugby." He offered me a place! Without a maths or a physics O level! I even got a scholarship, trading on my father's polio.'

But Alison's time at St Mary's, Paddington didn't last long. 'I failed at the first post, as I could not pass the physics exam at the end of the first year. I'd never been taught how to draw a graph. An elderly doctor taught us chemistry. He was very fond of me. As he taught me, he had his hand on my thigh. He tried hard to plead my cause with the Dean – couldn't there be a door left open for me? – but the Dean said no.'

Stymied, as so many medically minded women were, by the low standard of their school science teaching, Alison was out. But still she refused to take her parents' advice to train to be a secretary. She went to Dorset House in Headington to train as an occupational therapist but loathed it. 'The principal was a battleaxe, and I was no good at sewing, cord-knitting or basket weaving.' (In order to teach them you had to learn how to do them.) Then, at a wedding, she sat next to a girl who was at St Clare's Hall, Oxford, who said she should write to Miss Dreydel, the principal.

Miss Dreydel, who'd been paralysed from the waist down when her London house had been bombed, had been at St Anne's College, Oxford, Alison explained, 'and she felt sorry for all those girls going along to Oxford for an interview and not getting in, thanks to their poor schooling, and then having to go on to be secretaries. She wanted to help those girls get a degree.'

Alison's parents came to visit Miss Dreydel. 'My father, who was crippled with polio, got on like a house on fire with Miss Dreydel in her wheelchair.' At vast expense, they signed Alison up for an external London degree at St Clare's Hall, tutors were provided and she was welcomed with open arms by the real Oxford crowd (whom she never pretended to be part of), and she starred beside Esther Rantzen in the Balliol Players' production of *The Importance of Being Earnest*. 'And I got a 2:2 in history! 'The "bad" thing was, though, that I'd fallen in love with Peter [Snow]. That was a pity, because had I not fallen in love, I might have gone on to do higher things in my career.' In 1964, wedding preparations seemed far more compelling to her than a career ladder. 'I got a job as a medical secretary at King Edward VII's hospital in London, a snobby place, with fifty-two beds. "Miss Carter," said the House Governor, Vere, Lady Birdwood, "you can go and talk to the brigadiers and lords and ladies [the patients]." That was because I "spoke properly"; I was "one of us". I saw the job application forms. If anyone had an Indian name it was thrown into the bin.'

Alison newly married to Peter Snow, at home in London, 1964

Sporting prowess also helped Mary Piper (born in 1947) to get on to the first rung of her medical career. 'We hope you'll swim for the university,' said the chairman of the interviewers at the Royal Free Hospital when, after a series of enforced academic underachievements thanks to her schooling at Beckenham Grammar, she at last got in to medical school armed with three A level Bs. She'd been determined to be a doctor from the age of eleven, and had worked out at that young age that she would need physics, chemistry and biology A levels, as well as a Latin O level. She put her foot down when the school put her into the German rather than the Latin stream, and she refused to accept being made to do 'physics with chemistry' O level, which didn't count as either physics or chemistry, and thus would make it hard to do physics and chemistry for A level, essential for medical school. Her family's local vicar in Chislehurst was a friend of a doctor at Guy's Hospital and got Mary an interview with him. This was in 1964. 'So, why don't you want to be a nurse?' he asked her. To which Mary replied, 'If I was a boy sitting here, you wouldn't be asking him that question.' 'I didn't get in,' she told me, 'and what I'd said got back to the vicar. They all thought I was a Very Difficult Girl.' On she fought, so nervous about exams that the doctor prescribed barbiturates – 'the sedatives of the 1960s' – for her to take when she did her A levels, 'so I was like a zombie going into the exams, unable to think straight or draw a straight line. I got a B, D and E, and cried my eyes out.' The only thing to do was to go back to school to retake two of them. 'What other choice did I have?'

So even grammar schools were far from being an easy springboard into university or a profession.

Talking to women who did go to Oxbridge and then had to decide what to do next, I discovered that not only were there different rules for men and women found in bed together – the women were sent down, the men merely rusticated – and not only were women not allowed to be members of the Oxford or Cambridge Union until 1963, there was also a separate careers board for men and women. Celia Haddon gives us a glimpse. She got into Cambridge from Queen Anne's, Caversham, in the early 1960s. 'I went to the Women's Appointment Board, not *the* Appointment Board. The woman behind the desk offered me a job as assistant to Nikolaus Pevsner. She said, "You'll do the work. He'll get the credit."'

'No one's going to be very interested in your qualifications, my dear,' the woman at the Cambridge women's careers board said to Anne Oldroyd, who was about to graduate in modern languages from Girton in the early 1950s, already engaged to be married. 'You can go into teaching, or you can do a secretarial course, and if you do that, you might, if you're lucky, work your way up to being secretary to the managing director of Marks & Spencer.'

Sue (now the Revd Sue) Kipling read natural sciences at Girton in the late 1960s, having got in from her grammar school. 'In January 1970 I went to the women's careers board and told them I wanted to go into industry. "Well, we don't deal with that," said the woman behind the desk. "You'll need to go to the men's careers board for that." So I pedalled off down the Trumpington Road in my blue wool dress. I was interviewed by a colonel [the country seemed to be crawling with retired Army men impeding women's progress in their various ways], who strode up and down the office and said, "Women can't go into industry. We're not going to send you on the milk round." So I thought, "I'll just have to do this for myself." I saw a job at ICI advertised in *Nature* magazine, applied, and got it.' Off she went to the Billingham Plant in County Durham, where she was put up in a dormitory at the YWCA women's hostel, while the men were put up in hotels.

So young women needed supreme levels of drive to escape the confines of safe unambitiousness; of peeling out of university without the faintest, foggiest idea of what to do next. Sarah MacAulay, who read history at Cambridge in the early 1980s, recalled the moment when she woke up to this urgent need to do something. 'My boyfriend's best friend asked me one day, in the December before finals, "So, what are you going to apply for?" All the men were applying for jobs. Very few of my female friends were. Tim [the friend] said to me, "Well, if you don't apply, what are you going to do when you go back home to Scotland after finals, without a job?" I knew the deadlines were approaching, but until that moment I'd tried to avoid facing up to the application process.' That conversation was the spark that ignited her successful career in the City. She started by applying to every single one of the crème de la crème of merchant banks. She would have liked to apply to Swire and HSBC, but they still didn't interview women.

The banks enticed students by coming to Cambridge, setting themselves up in hotels – this was 'the milk round', so called because, in the way it delivered jobs to you at university, it was reminiscent of a milkman delivering the milk. The banks held drinks parties where 'the ratio of men to women was 50:1,' Sarah recalled. It was not that women couldn't apply; it was just not a familiar path for women leaving university.

You really did need guts – and ambition. For girls with only mild ambition, or vague dreams, or whose spark of ambition ignited only when they were in their late teens, it could be too late. If they hadn't made strenuous efforts throughout their schooling to keep themselves on the achievers' track – defying teachers, parents and retired colonels in order to do so – they could find themselves fatally under-equipped. They needed a burning ambition from the age of twelve to have a hope. It often came across as stroppiness. As for the millions of shy, self-effacing girls who kept their heads down and did what they were told, it was all too easy for their potential to be snuffed out early.

PART II

WHAT KATIE DID NEXT

3

The Two Extremes of Sewing

'Bridget Brocklebank has completed her
finishing course at the Château d'Oex and came
home by way of the Loire Valley, which she
found fully lived up to expectations'

'News of Old Girls', Lawnside school
magazine, 1969

Caught between two 1962 statistics – that menstruation started late, due to the worse nutrition, and that full-time work started early, due to the lower school-leaving age and the glut of available jobs – fifteen-year-old Kathleen Hewitson found herself having her first period in her first week at Kauffmann Brothers tailoring factory in Harehills, Leeds. It was embarrassing and she didn't know what to do. 'Mr James took me into the back office and gave me a little glass of Indian brandy – he said it warmed the tummy and would take the pain away. Then he let me go home early. The next day I came in wearing an enormous sanitary belt held on with hooks at the front and back.' No one could see this clunkily attached item, but Kathleen felt highly self-conscious.

Menstruation was a taboo subject and would carry on being so for some time. Eve Terry, who worked in a Tampax factory (*the* Tampax factory, supplying Tampax to the whole world) in Havant, Hampshire, in the 1970s, told me that as late as 1976, even though everyone used to pass their time juggling Tampax boxes three or four at a time when there was a lull on the conveyor belt, no one in the factory ever mentioned menstruation. 'The men would go home and tell their friends and families that they "made cotton wool".'

So hats off to Mr James, the foreman at Kauffmann's, who had clearly encountered this syndrome before in his New Girls, and kept a stash of medicinal Indian brandy (but no sanitary towels) in his back office in readiness for the required drill. The next morning Kathleen clocked back in at 8.30, 'pushing my card in and pressing the arm down the side', and got on with learning how to use a sewing machine. 'They gave us pieces of paper with lines and circles on them, to practise getting control. Molly was my teacher, twenty years older than me.' Molly was the 'mother' of this workplace, a woman of high standards and a kind heart, a trouser-machinist who looked after the new arrivals; five years later she would be the witness at Kathleen's wedding.

Kathleen's mother had come with her to Kauffmann's for the interview with Mr James, when Kathleen was still fourteen. It was normal for mothers to accompany their daughters to work interviews, and sit in on them, and Kauffmann's was reassuringly near home: 'I could run it in fifteen minutes and sometimes went home for lunch.'

This wasn't quite the dark satanic mill existence I'd expected to hear about. 'Family firm' could mean not only 'owned by a family' but also 'making the people who worked there feel like part of a family'. Kauffmann's was a small family firm, one of many such in Leeds, all in one large room, the men at the band-knife bantering at the far end, and you could tell when Bernard Kauffmann, one of the two brothers (the other being Cyril) was having his breakfast cooked in the kitchen because he liked his bacon burnt to a crisp. Kathleen was soon making four bundles of six pairs of trousers per day, all the way through except for the buttonholes and zips, and soon she too was training up new arrivals on the sewing machines. Esmeralda, a new West Indian trainee, was her first pupil. On Friday afternoons everyone bought sweets in, 'and they put the radio on and we all sang along with it, singing songs to Mr James.' (I pushed her for clarification on 'singing to Mr James', and she said they sang the love songs, as it were, *to* Mr James.) Only once during her thirteen years at Kauffmann's did a sewing-machine needle go through her finger, and Mr James got out his first aid kit.

Kathleen and Molly, her 'teacher' at Kauffmann's tailoring factory, on Kathleen's wedding day, Leeds, 1967

Susan Watson, also aged fifteen, wept on the bus every morning for the first six weeks of her full-time working life at Read's factory near Leeds Bus Station in 1963. She'd been determined to start work and her mother had telephoned Read's to secure an interview for her when she was fourteen: 'children don't use the telephone.' So Susan was a child when it came to not using the telephone and not going to an interview on her own, but an adult when it came to being expected to earn her keep. The habit of earning had been instilled in her since early childhood – her mother had brought her up with 'You can clean the bathroom and the hallway and then you'll have enough money to go ice-skating'.

These were the girls who were plunged straight in to the working world, no questions asked, and no gentle transition. 'It was such a long day, and you were shut indoors all day,' Susan told me. 'Bus at 7.30 and work till 5, and if you were one minute late they took fifteen minutes from you. That was called "being quartered". But I'd made my bed and had to lie on it.'

William Read Ltd in 1963, when Susan started working there aged fifteen (the woman in the foreground is not her)

This was tailoring again – piecework. The game was to take less time to do each piece of work than was allocated to it on the ticket, so that 'after a four-and-a-half-hour morning we'd aim to have eight hours in our wallet, and then in the afternoon we didn't work as hard. We'd aim to earn twelve hours' piecework in an eight-hour day.' Every now and then, the time and motion men would come round, 'these strange men in overalls watching over you. We worked slowly when they were there, otherwise they'd realise we were making too much money. So if the ticket said "20 minutes" we'd make sure it took at least eighteen.'

Workers' Playtime on the BBC's Light Programme played on the factory's radio all day, cheerfully broadcast from a different factory every day, interviewing workers, playing songs for them and singing 'Happy Birthday'. In Read's where Susan was, if one of the men was getting married the next day, the other men cut out 'male-body-part shapes' (would they now be called 'cock and balls'?) from left-over bits of tweed and threw them around the room. This was the sense of humour level and it was an eye-opener for Susan.

Saturdays were voluntary. 'There was no foreman or super-visor on a Saturday morning. We'd go in pretending we were going to work, but we'd bring our own material in and make something to wear to go out in the evening. The older ones would bring in material to make their curtains.' This cheeky stretching of the rules seems a far cry from the work ethic enforced in today's wish-fulfilment centres.

After work on each weekday, Susan took the bus home for the same cooked tea on a rota, versions of meat and three veg, and then changed into one of the frocks she'd made at work on a Saturday morning and got straight back onto the bus to meet her friends at the Conca d'Ora coffee bar. 'I gave my full three pounds a week wage to my parents and they gave me back some for spending.' By the age of twenty she'd had five years of full-time working experience, was married and had set up her own dress shop, called Gillian.

Meanwhile, girls from the upper echelons were being held back from the reality of actual work. Partly, they were being prepared for their future unpaid work – the hoped-for management of a large household; and partly they were just being given something to do while they waited for Mr Right – and being trained to be more eligible for him, in the process.

Often they, too, strangely enough, were doing sewing. Their parents, desperately needing to find something for them to do, sent them to various kinds of finishing schools as stopgaps. So, these daughters were learning exactly the same skills as the factory girls but with parents paying for them to do it, rather than being paid to do it and giving half their earnings to the parents. It shows how, when it came to the acquiring of accomplishments in early adulthood, an inadequate education could be a great leveller. Some earned; others merely learned; and the instant earners learned more about real life than the ongoing learners.

In a tall house in Pelham Crescent, South Kensington, girls were trained in the art of making clothes to a high standard, with sewing machines: this was a one-year couture course run by Mrs Bailey, described by her alumni as 'a beaky old bird' and 'a little old strict, cross lady' who taught them the skills to enable either the starting of their own couture business or (more likely) a wifehood of being able to run up a silk blouse, mend a husband's trouser pocket and make a daughter's smocked frock.

Far from 'clocking in' with their cards, as Kathleen had

done at Kauffmann's, the girls on this course 'had to fill in a registration card, entering our London address on the front and our country address on the back,' recalled Henrietta Lindsell, who would later start her own business, and who did attend Bristol university, but who left school 'lacking confidence in my own ability'. 'We made proper A-line skirts and fitted jackets. One morning each week was devoted to cooking lessons, and we were allowed to invite our boyfriend to lunch on that day.' That day of the week can't have been much fun for the girls who didn't have a boyfriend.

The word 'finishing school' has rather a final ring about it, suggesting that, just when you should be starting out in life, you were given a final polish-up before being cast into the happy ending of perfect wifehood. Switzerland was the usual setting for these establishments to which girls were sent to transition to adulthood. Non-earning sewing also went on in these places, such as Brillantmont, where sheltered daughters of the 1950s and '60s were taught to sew a perfect smocked dress by 'Madame de la Couture', as she was known, and an exquisite petticoat by 'Madame de Lingerie', who also taught them how to iron a shirt properly – 'a man's shirt, of course,' said Penny Eyles, who left Queen Anne's, Caversham, aged seventeen and spent a year in one of Brillantmont's three villas.

What were these girls doing suddenly holed up in Swiss villages? The motivation for their parents, again, was to pack their daughters off to somewhere, anywhere, where they would make suitable friends, be safely out of the way for another year, and acquire skills for a life of probably not having to make their own living, after a few years of doing 'little jobs'. It was all part of 'putting off the evil day', as it was called, the unspoken second half of the sentence being 'when, God forbid, they would actually need to earn some money'. So these 'sparky' and actually mostly clever, just badly educated, girls, found themselves in yet another world of dormitories, corridors and rules, this time run by Madame this and Mademoiselle that, but at least the Swiss ones were in a stunning place, geographically speaking. Most of them had their own chalets in the mountains where the girls could go skiing at weekends.

'My father did ask me if I wanted to go to university,' Mary Villiers (who would much later in life become editor of *Hansard*) said to me. 'But my friends were anti-bluestocking and I said no, and my father feebly gave way.' Ah, so sometimes it was not the parents who were anti-brainbox. Beaufront had instilled in its own girls, and the girls in one another, an anti-bluestocking bias. When Mary (a student there from 1948 to 1952) left, aged sixteen, she went straight to a finishing school called Mon Fertile (in 1953), 'and it was like being let out of jail'.

Mary Villiers, Mon Fertile finishing-school girl

There was an exoticism about the names of these establish-ments, enticing for sixteen year olds who'd been stuck at English institutions at the end of gravel drives for the first half of their teens. Parents sent them to finishing schools as 'compensation' for their hard time at dismal English boarding schools, as Camilla Trimble told me had happened to her after her horrible time at St Joseph's Convent in Taunton. How could they resist the tempting concept of Brillantmont, Le Château Mont Choisi, Le Manoir, Le Vieux Chalet or Mon Fertile? The last name stands out, seeming to sum up the fecundity of not only the Swiss setting but also the girls, many of whom had never yet kissed a young man and certainly weren't about to in this next closeted year of enforced French conversation with Madame at the lunch table, as they waited for grown-up life to start.

These places were aspirational: the message was 'if you come here and perfect your "finishing", you'll be accomplished enough to be the future wife of an ambassador. You'll know exactly how to get in and out of a car, speak fluent French and Italian, be at home in the international world, hold your end up in a dinner-party conversation about Renaissance art, make exquisite poached salmon and effortlessly manage the domestic running of the ambassadorial residence. You'll be the quintes-sence of faultless deportment, and your husband's shirts will be creaseless.' These establishments prepared a young woman for every aspect of her hoped-for future married life, apart from the wedding night.

'Mon Fertile was run by Mademoiselle Claire Panchaud and Miss Allen,' said Mary Villiers, 'definitely a lesbian couple. I was the Virgin Mary when we put on a piece based on Paul Claudel's sacred poem about the Nativity, in the dining room.' That was the improving level of entertainment. It was a lovely year of release from school, and Mary enjoyed studying Italian, history of art and literature, 'but my father then said, "you must now do a secretarial course".' Off she went to Miss Judson's in Kensington to be guided into a state of earning-potential, insurance against any disasters life might throw at her.

Some of the girls in transition between school and the world of work didn't get as far as Switzerland, as there were 'perfectly good' (according to the parents), and slightly cheaper, finishing schools in England, such as Hazelbury Manor in Wiltshire, the House of Citizenship in Hertfordshire, Eggleston Hall in Yorkshire, Cygnets in London and Tante Marie in Woking. The idea was that you learned a little bit of current affairs on top of the domestic accomplishments and bridge lessons. Penny Sheehan, who attended Hazelbury Manor, run by Mrs Crawford and Miss Bedds, told me she'd learned 'a little bit of this, a little bit of that, and a little bit of nothing', before being allowed to go to the glamorous Tah-Dorf in Switzerland, where she could ski at weekends. St Mary's Ascot had its own finishing school, Errolston, reached by walking through the woods from the school. A nun I spoke to told me she was sent to Errolston by her mother for one year of what would have been the sixth form if she'd stayed on at St Mary's. 'Twenty-four pupils, all boarders, and we learned dressmaking, laundry, cookery and housewifery, along with having religious lessons and outings. We dressed for dinner every evening, although most of us only owned one evening dress. We had to iron everything to perfection.'

All this while, the factory girls were already hard at work turning their skills into money, and the commercial-class girls were already on the secretarial ladder.

Some of the privately educated daughters, on leaving school and not wanted hanging around the home, were palmed off by their parents on to French families, or on to strange Parisian landladies who were supposed to teach them French and take them to see the sights. This was another example of 'shove them out, preferably abroad, hope for the best, facilitate them to acquire an accomplishment or two, and postpone the moment when they have to dip their toes into the cruel real world, if indeed they ever do.' Christabel Watson, born in 1939 – who was to become a racing driver for two years of her early twenties, thanks to being given a Mini by her family for her twenty-first birthday, into which her uncle then fitted a racing engine – was sent to the Comtesse de la Calle in Montmorency in 1955: 'a huge house in a square, with sixteen girls, and the Comtesse like a little owl. We learned French cooking with the cook and we did sightseeing with the Comtesse's daughter.' The Comtesse herself didn't lift a finger. The author and agony aunt Virginia Ironside, born in 1944, was sent to Mademoiselle Anita's in Paris, 'the crème de la crème of French finishing schools', but Virginia had to lodge in a box room with a 'very unpleasant family' and the son stole from her. Having been an only child at a London day school (Miss Ironside's, run by her two great-aunts), she didn't find it at all easy to be among girls fresh from boarding school 'whose crushes became obsessions. I found it weird.'

After being sent to a health farm in the summer of leaving St Mary's Wantage without a maths O level in 1978, Bee Bealey was sent to lodge in the Boulevard Jean Jaurès in Paris with Madame de Maille, her mother having vetted Madame first, interviewing her in Boodle's club in London, where 'Madame drank large quantities of wine and sat with her legs wide apart so everyone could see her black lacy knickers.' There were twelve girls lodging in the house in Paris, four of them best friends already, so none of them spoke any French. 'We were meant to do *Le Cahier* in the morning and *La Culture* in the afternoon, but Madame ran out of money so we never got to Fontainebleau.' Then it was back to London for a three-month cookery course at Mrs Russell's Cooking School in Wimbledon, where 'we just watched Mrs Russell cooking a three-star Michelin-style lunch all morning, and then ate it. After lunch we had to take dictation of all the recipes. We passed out from the heat and the food. We were perched on stools and there'd be a great crash when someone landed on the floor.'

Then it was time to start the Season, which Bee had no desire to do, not wanting to be married off to an eligible chinless wonder. 'I threw every invitation into the china umbrella stand in the hall. A dinner guest knocked it over and it smashed, and out came a dozen unopened invitations. My mother made me write a letter of apology to every single hostess.' Then she was allowed to 'crash' the St Clare's Hall history of art trip to Italy. 'That was heaven.' Only then did Bee's parents say, 'You've got to learn to type; if you do, you'll never be without a job.' And off she went to Mrs Thomsett's.

As with the sewing, unambitious schooling led to young women from very different social classes becoming experts at cleaning and cooking. For example, I spoke to Violet Downton, born in 1930, whose mother died aged twenty-seven. She loved maths and reading, but was never encouraged or helped to go in an academic direction. After being evacuated to a family in Wales during the war, where the mother of the house taught her to clean and polish, Violet was separated from her siblings and sent to a children's home in Chatham, Kent. 'When we were fourteen, four or five of us girls, still under the London County Council, were sent to a children's home in Herne Bay – we were told we were going to be trained to be nurses, but they just made us do the cleaning, from 7 a.m. to 8 p.m. every day. We used "the Polisher", a big, heavy non-electric thing. We had to go on our hands and knees first, putting polish on the floor and then the Polisher shone it. I enjoyed doing it – I liked seeing it all come up nice and clean. I earned 9s 4d a week. We slept in units up at the top of the building – just a bed and a bedside table. We grew up quickly doing that.'

One day, while she was polishing the hallway, her grandmother and aunt turned up and were appalled to find Violet cleaning all day rather than training to be a nurse. 'I went home with them to 68 Kimberley Road, Beckenham, and got a job in the general office of my Uncle John's works.' Marrying young, 'to a man who drank every day of the year except for Christmas Day when the pubs were shut', Violet then worked from day one of her married life, to pay the rent, and was a cleaner for thirty years.

Another straight-into-cleaning example: Alice Rourke, born in 1947, left school at sixteen, sent a letter to Mrs Swiny who lived at the nearby Dower House of Arbigland, and went straight into a job working as her cleaner, earning 'two shillings and ten-pence-halfpenny an hour' for the next seven years, before going on to work at the Big House, which was much nicer. Mrs Swiny was 'old school' – no vacuum cleaner, just a hard brush for the carpets, a special brush for the fringes and a soft brush for the wood. When it came to windows, Mrs Swiny's rule was 'Clean the edges and the middles will look after themselves.'

Meanwhile, as with the sewing, which some were paid to do and others paid to learn, when it came to cooking and cleaning, the non-earners were sent instead on fee-paying domestic science courses. These were another kind of finishing school: useful institutions, more practical than alluring, in which to park education-deprived daughters, some of whom intended to go on to earn money in domestic science jobs but most of whom didn't. The Glasgow and West Scotland College of Domestic Science was nicknamed, unceremoniously, 'the

Dough School'. At the more refined Atholl Crescent School of Domestic Science in Edinburgh, there was a year-long course specifically designed for girls aiming to be not employees, but wives. Its official name on the application form was 'Household Management', but it was nicknamed, again with great frankness, 'the Brides' Course'.

These girls, too, were being prepared for the world of work – unpaid work. They were expecting to run a domestic household, probably without much help from their husband (perhaps the 'grouse moor' they'd married), and would need the appropriate skills. In the earlier decades of this book, after the decline of domestic servants but before the rise of Magimixes, ready meals and Dysons, the work of a housewife was onerous and time-consuming. They might as well be prepared and equipped for their future existence.

'I was going to go on the Brides' Course,' said Gillie Hanbury, 'but my mother decided to put me on the Household Institutional Management course instead, which lasted for four terms rather than three. She wanted to get rid of me for longer.' This was in 1961, and the 'H.I.M.' course was a touch more vocational than the Brides' Course: 'we actually had to run the residential hostels, getting up at dawn to make the bread for the day and screw newspaper into knots to lay all the fires. The mistress in charge of us, with a moustache, put white gloves on and ran her finger along every ledge and shelf. She ticked us off if we hadn't cleaned the inside of a keyhole.'

That kind of perfectionism was instilled in domestic science college attendees, leading to half a century of polished light switches and well-dusted keyholes all over Scotland. The Atholl Crescent girls had to wear white overalls with 'bachelor buttons' pegged on that had to be taken out when the overalls went to the laundry and came back as stiff as a board. They improved their fine motor skills: in 'leather work', they were taught to make kid gloves with tiny diamond shapes between the fingers. The soft furnishings teacher taught them to do piping for cushions, and loose covers: again, sewing as wifely accomplishment rather than money-spinner.

When it came to recipes, this being 1960s Scotland, the first 'signature dish' the girls learned to make in their first cookery class, lined up in their starched white coats, paired up in alphabetical order, was sheep's head broth. The alumni I spoke to painted a picture of the scene. Behind the group of girls learning to cook, there were real workers who did the real work. 'The maids who worked in the kitchen had put everything out for us,' said Gillie Hanbury, 'and they did the washing-up.' She recalled Miss Rutherford coming in as the lesson began. 'On her desk was a tray full of sheep's heads, with their eyes still in. The first thing she instructed us to do was to take the grass out of their teeth. This was too much for some of the delicate flowers among us.'

'We were sensitive children,' said Elizabeth Ballantyne-Brown, 'and we had to make haggis from sheep's thorax. The thorax tube had to come out into a smaller pan to drain its contents. The smell! I've never eaten haggis since.' And behind each retching girl stood her long-suffering personal maid to take away her dirty pan. When it came to baking cakes, 'we had to beat everything by hand,' said Elizabeth, 'but we had a maid to do the washing-up.'

On laundry day each week, the girls were told to bring in a selection of men's dirty clothes to practise their laundry skills on, 'so we were very popular with the young men.' Edinburgh's young advocates could count on their washing being done for them in this way, by girls they were highly likely one day to marry. One young Edinburgh fiancé I heard about threatened to break off the engagement, on hearing that his fiancée had failed the hygiene exam.

The Atholl Crescent School of Domestic Science girls, 1961 –
Elizabeth Ballantyne-Brown front row second from left. They're
holding a chief tool of their domestic education: a knife sharpener

This kind of highly disciplined domestic training for girls who could have done better academically carried on late into the 1970s and '80s. Elspeth Allison, mother of the novelist Nina Stibbe – who longed to stay on at school, 'but my parents thought it was a joke' – was sent aged sixteen in the late 1950s to Cuckfield Park Domestic Science College, where 'a strict woman taught us to make trellis icing'. The girls were also trained in 'invalid cookery', the sad art of 'what to cook for an old person living in your house'. The answer was boiled fish. So, two antiquated theories were being kept alive here: what girls needed to be taught to do, and what invalids needed to be made to eat. Institutions such as this prolonged the age of appalling food in mid-twentieth-century Britain.

Winkfield Place in Berkshire, otherwise known as the Constance Spry School for Flower Arranging and Cordon Bleu Cookery, was heavily oversubscribed. Raine Capara, born in 1958, told me that her father, 'who was of the era that believed "little girls don't need to work; little girls just get married"', came across Winkfield Place in the *Daily Telegraph* magazine when Raine was sixteen, and suggested it would be suitable for her when she left school at the end of the year. 'My mother rang them and was told there were no spaces for the next four years.'

Winkfield turned out to be one of those places, like Eton, for which you needed to be 'put down at birth', 'put down' in this sense meaning not euthanised but registered. While her mother started ringing the college every Friday for eighteen months, asking whether a place had by any chance come up, Raine was sent to a modelling and grooming school in Manchester called Sheila Watson's, where she learned how to get in and out of a car and how to apply make-up. At last, a place came up at Winkfield for September 1975 and Raine started, under the headmistress Miss Holden 'in twinset and pearls, with a hairstyle like the Queen's. We cooked our three-course lunch in pairs every morning.' In the afternoon the girls did dressmaking, needlework and flower arranging, using the same tired flowers other girls had used in the morning, which made it harder as the stems had been cut down. Raine did become a florist – the head florist at Claridge's. 'Winkfield gave me my career.' First, she rang every hotel in London asking whether she could work as a patisserie chef, and each hotel wrote back saying 'We don't employ girls in the kitchen.'

Her cooking partner at Winkfield, Caroline Goss (they're still best friends), had a similar trajectory, although she'd been put down aged twelve, which was just young enough to guarantee her a place. She'd left St Felix, Southwold, with no qualifications except swimming for the school in the county finals. First, she went on a dressmaking and pattern design course at Lucie Clayton's modelling school, with deportment included. 'I wanted to be a fashion designer and to go to St Martin's, but couldn't because I had no O levels.' Then it was Winkfield and four to a dorm – 'really expensive: my father said, "I could have bought a Rolls-Royce instead."'

The girls, whose parents were paying for the privilege, had laundry lessons once a week in 'the sluices' (the laundry rooms), and learned how to wash silk and cashmere, rolling it in a towel to dry. They had driving lessons, taking their tests in Slough. 'Our Etonian friends said, "Soon you'll be ready to be a wife."' And indeed that did happen. 'Every Monday evening, we did Scottish dancing at Sandhurst. The idea was that one of the Sandhurst men would invite you to the ball at the end of the summer term and you'd marry him.'

For the working-class girls, the equation was simple: daughters were launched straight into the world of work, and the household had another instant source of income. The 'bank of mum and dad' now had the subsidiary 'bank of daughter'. The middle- and upper-class girls who went on those transitional courses got a whiff of enjoyment, freedom from school, and making lots of new friends similar to the experience of their counterparts nowadays in their first year at 'uni'. In a very few cases they learned skills that launched careers, or at least 'jobs', but in most cases, while picking up a few useful skills, they just had another year to grow up before having to face real adult life.

As for their parents, the 'cost of the Rolls-Royce' to send them on these courses was considered a worthy price for knowing that they'd done all they could to complete the upbringing of their daughters, so they would be an asset and a treasure to their future husband, their family and their social circle. Although the parents would never quite admit it, they probably secretly longed for a conversation with their highly satisfied future son-in-law: 'Thank you for preparing Jill for being the perfect wife. Never a crease in my shirt; never a blade of grass in my sheep's head broth.'

But, as insurance, just in case anything went disastrously wrong with that plan, these young women might need to learn how to type.

4

Secretarial Colleges

'Belinda North has been enjoying her time at
"The Marlborough" in Oxford where Rosemary
Gascoyne, Fiona Carlisle and Patricia Lewis are
also studying'

'News of Old Girls', Lawnside school
magazine, 1972

'The girl of today,' said the elegant 1973 brochure for the
Queen's Secretarial College in South Kensington, shown
to me by Vivien Ruddock who went there straight from
Benenden in 1974, 'has the satisfaction of knowing that, even
if she is not able to train for a chosen career, she can now enter
it through the secretarial side.'

'Not able to train for a chosen career', in other words,
because she had not been educated to the required standard.

The brochure continued: 'A secretarial course can be very
rewarding and, on its conclusion, every student has the satisfaction of knowing that she has equipped herself, not only
for the immediate future, but also for any emergency which
may arise later in life.'

Tactfully, on this brochure printed on top-quality Conqueror paper with a stiff card binding, looking remarkably like the Order of Service for a wedding at St Margaret's Westminster, the college didn't specify what kind of emergency 'later in life' this might be. But the 'D'-word hovered in the air: the unspeakable prospect of the break-up of a marriage. As Mary Villiers's father put it to her, on recommending that she should go for secretarial training, 'It'll be something for you to *fall back on*' – those last three words spoken with ominous intensity.

Whatever the reason, you would never be short of work if you could type and do shorthand. In those days when not a single business letter in the whole country could come into existence without being spoken aloud by a boss and 'taken down' by an underling, secretaries populated every corner of office buildings from basement to attic.

The 'commercial class' girls didn't need any of this post-school vocational training. They'd got a head start, having been trained as secretaries at school from the age of thirteen. They went straight off to be shorthand typists just after their fifteenth birthdays, catapulted by their schools straight into the world of office work. It could be a long commute from the outer suburbs for the fifteen-year-old beneficiaries of this system such as Jean Dace, who went straight into a typing pool in the City from her home in Croydon. She soon changed jobs, working in the typing pool at the local Cope's Pools in Hackbridge, a football pools firm. She started as one of the fifteen girls in the pool, taking dictation from any of the bosses who might suddenly call one of them in, but proved herself so capable that she was plucked from the pool and became the manager's secretary for the next three years, typing letters of congratulation to the big winners with a cheque enclosed.

'Jobs were ten a penny at the *Evening Post*,' agreed Carole Ellis, who'd also been trained in a commercial class in Leeds and also got her first secretarial job in an office above a shop at fifteen. 'Mum took me along for my first interview.'

She emphasised that she was a 'shorthand typist', not a secretary: just one of the girls in the office who could be called in at any time to take dictation. This office-above-the-shop existence was not the kind of job that the girls at the Queen's Secretarial College in London or its equivalents would be aspiring to. They wanted to go into a more rarefied world where their bosses would be eminent and, with luck, eligible. As Lawnside's 'News of Old Girls' of 1970 exemplified it, 'Francesca Peel has finished her secretarial course at Cambridge and is now working for eight doctors.'

How tough was it to learn the secretarial art? The 'News of Old Girls' at the back of school magazines frequently alluded to what hard work a secretarial course was: 'Paula Drysdale has been taking a strenuous secretarial course in Edinburgh'; 'Jane George is at the London College of Secretaries and is enjoying her course, although she says it can be very exhausting.'

They'd never had to work so hard in their lives, poor things. 'Nine whole hours of shorthand per week!' recalled Katie Thomas, who went to the 'Ox & Cow' after leaving More House School in the late 1980s, when word processors were starting to click into electronic action but email was not yet spoken of. 'So that was three full mornings of shorthand. We were drilled.' They had to wear a suit twice a week – to get into the office-going habit – and a skirt every day, and if they arrived with a ladder in their tights they had to sign a book to say they were going straight back to their digs to change. At break time, they would 'pile out on to the pavement and light up' (they lived entirely on toast and Marmite and cigarettes), and then it would be back for yet more strenuous work: nine hours of typing lessons per week, to match the nine hours of shorthand.

One dismal thing about starting on one of these secretarial courses was that, even though the girls had just left school and had therefore said goodbye to the world of *Crown and Parliament* by R. J. Unstead and *Understanding Geography Book 2*, they were presented on day one with ... yet another textbook. Katie kept hers and showed it to me: a heavy, laminated paperback called *Secretarial Duties* by John Harrison, in its eighth edition. The illustration on the jacket showed an up-to-date cuboid computer linked to a keyboard with a curly telephone-style cable, plus two house plants, and a clock displaying the unattractive time of five to nine in the morning.

Trendily, the male author noted in his preface that, 'In order to simplify the writing of this text, the feminine pronoun is used for the secretary, but I would like to make it clear that such references apply equally to men and a deliberate distinction between the sexes is not implied.' But the distinction was heavily implied in all the classes described to me by the women who attended them in the period of this book. They were told they would need to remember the dates of their bosses' children's ('his children's') birthdays; their whole working lives, whether long or short, would be devoted to the service of making life easy for their boss, always envisaged as a man. 'We were expected to grovel to the boss,' said Liz Jones who was trained at the Whitehall Secretarial College in Eastbourne, 'to humour him and cater to his foibles.'

The Oxford & County girls' hearts sank as they read in John Harrison's updated preface, 'I have extended the number and range of in-tray exercises which are given at the end of each chapter.' A typical in-tray exercise was to write a report on a 'sherry evening to demonstrate the new word processor in the Committee Room at 219 Barrington Avenue, Nottingham', to which the secretary had been sent to represent her boss. In the typically unfunny but trying-to-be-light way of textbooks, the third of the 'case studies' on which the book's exercises were based was 'Jane, private secretary to Mr Brian Dobson, the manager of a group of well-known singers known as the Secretairs'. The jaunty name of the pop group did not make the textbook exercises any more fun.

Towns were crawling with secretarial colleges, often in Victorian houses on the way to the station, but Oxford and Cambridge were particularly favoured by parents pushing their daughters towards them, as they hoped a bit of the varsity aura would rub off on them, just through their being in the vicinity, and also there was a chance they'd meet a nice eligible undergraduate at the imagined parties.

Katie Thomas and Carrie Donald, 1980s 'Ox & Cow' girls

The upper classes, as always, were adept at sorting themselves into separate strata from the rest of society. In the world of Oxford secretarial colleges, the girls at the 'Ox & Cow' in St Giles', though definitely 'above' the girls at Mrs Thomsett's, were aware that they were less exalted, socially speaking, than the girls at the Marlborough in the High Street. 'We were the ugly sister to the Marlborough College,' recalled Caroline Donald, who was sent to the 'Ox & Cow' after the Oxbridge term in 1981, 'the M&S to their Harvey Nicks. It was at the peak of Sloane Rangerdom, and they were so much better at it than us. Wearing their stripy pedal-pushers and upturned collars, pearls and velvet hairbands, with a cashmere sweater casually slung round their necks, they jumped into sports cars to go to lunch in Woodstock, while we biked off to the pub.' Meanwhile the no-frills local techs in every English city just taught girls to become secretaries with no added social graces attached.

Some secretarial colleges were even socially divided within themselves. Philomena O'Hare, who went to the Yorkshire Ladies' Secretarial College in 1979, recalled, 'the private pupils were upstairs. They had electric typewriters. We were on a government scheme, and had mechanical typewriters, downstairs. They paid us thirty pounds to do the course.' So as with the sewing, cleaning and cooking, the daughters from the lower echelons were being paid, and the upper-class parents were paying for their daughters, to do exactly the same thing, but in this case the paid ones had the more antiquated equipment. I spoke to Elizabeth Bennett (born in 1934), who was one of the private students at the college, having been educated at Westonbirt, and done A levels, but the only options offered to her after that were teaching, secretarial training, nursing, occupational therapy or librarianship.

She recalled the strict Yorkshire ladies who ran the college. 'The principal, Mrs Gould, was a fearsome chain-smoker. For one week in the year we had to be her secretary for a week. That was terrifying. You had to take dictation from her and work the telephone exchange.' All this in the uniform leaf-green long-sleeved overalls, worn because the typewriter ribbons were so inky.

In London, the St James's, the Queen's, Mrs Hoster's and Miss Judson's in Kensington and South Kensington seemed to be neck and neck when it came to high social status, while St Godric's kept up standards in Hampstead, with its four connecting houses in Arkwright Road and its boarding houses dotted about in the surrounding streets. At each of these establishments, there were the really keen girls who genuinely wanted to learn to be secretaries, and there were the ones whose hearts were not in it, who had been sent there by parents trying to make them be serious about something, and who left on the dot of 4.30 to get ready for the evening's parties, sometimes hemming their skirts up with a stapler before leaving.

'Good morning, ladies!' the mistress at the Queen's would say the next day. 'And which of you came back on the milk train this morning?' That was a euphemism for 'partied all night', and was as near as she came to attempting a witticism.

The syndrome of austere middle-aged ladies keeping blossoming young women under their thumbs rolled on, then, from the world of school into the world of secretarial colleges, along with some of the inbuilt snobbism. Amanda Theunissen described Miss Catherine Judson, who ran Miss Judson's, as 'clearly the daughter of several admirals'. 'The college was full of very nice young ladies,' recalled Amanda, 'queuing to go and be secretaries in the Foreign Office.'

At least it wasn't school any more. For Jo Fairley, going to the Langham Secretarial College in London in 1974 was a blissful release from the repression and dullness of Bromley High School for Girls. 'I completely loved it. They treated you like a grown-up. At last, I was doing something that had a practical application. I'd had stand-up fights with my maths teacher at school: "If you could tell me why I would ever need a logarithm ..."'

So, from her point of view, the maths O level she'd been made to take at Bromley High had been pointless. Why, indeed, would she ever need a logarithm? It wasn't as if she was going to be navigating a sailing boat at 3 a.m. in the mid-Atlantic. The agony of the slide rule had been just a painful rite of passage to prove she could stretch her brain. At last, at a secretarial college, she was learning something of real use, and, as she said, 'we knew we could choose which area we wanted to work in. And we didn't expect to be several rungs up when we started.' But, she added, 'It was a given that our boss was going to be a man. We had lessons in how to decipher bad handwriting – our boss's, or a doctor's illegible scrawl. You never imagined in a million years that you'd be working for a woman, or that you would one day become the boss.' By the age of twenty-three Jo would, in fact, be the boss. For Julia Wigan, likewise, secretarial college (hers was in South Molton Street) was 'the most tremendously exciting thing – my ticket into earning money, and meeting boys, and meeting girls who wore make-up.'

Each secretarial college had its unique selling point, be it geographical, social or practical. 'We have had girls from titled families,' boasted the 1962 prospectus for the Whitehall Secretarial College in Eastbourne. 'That was a real come-on for my mother,' said Liz Jones, the one who had been adopted and dressed in Victorian clothes. The Whitehall was run by Miss Chynoweth, described to me as 'a squat woman in a skirt and jacket' and 'stout with grey hair', who'd been at the 1919 Paris Peace Conference in Versailles as a junior secretary to Lloyd George. She was 'a tough nut' but a good teacher, training the girls in shorthand and typing to the highest standards. 'The great test,' said Liz, 'was whether you dreamed in shorthand.' Miss Chynoweth certainly did, and was quite one-track-minded about it. When Liz eventually admitted that she intended to go on to university, the ever-so-slightly disapproving Miss Chynoweth said, 'Well, at least you can take down your lectures in shorthand.' Alumni of her college, and indeed of all secretarial colleges, still find themselves scribbling their shopping lists down in shorthand, keeping up the skill drilled into them up to three-quarters of a century ago.

Miss Chynoweth's particular obsession was with paper clips. She couldn't stand it if her girls used an unnecessarily large one. 'Don't send a man to do a boy's work!' she would bark. Another of her rules was 'never write with the lid perched on top of your fountain pen'. It made the pen top-heavy and would slow the shorthand down. She was also strict about how to stick a stamp onto an envelope: not only did it need to be at an exact right angle, it also had to be equidistant from the top edge and the side edge. She aimed to instil in her students an extra level of general knowledge and initiative that would set them apart from the ones who had been trained merely at the local tech. 'She gave us a general knowledge test each week,' said Liz Jones. 'We were expected to keep up with the news, reading the papers every day, broadsheets only of course. We had to study the Court Circular in *The Times*.' 'If you're doing a letter for your boss,' she would tell the girls, 'and he says "send it to his London address", you will say, "Excuse me, I did happen to notice in the Court Circular that he was at the British Embassy in Paris this week."' This was the kind of initiative that would get you Brownie points, both at the Whitehall and in real life. 'Remember, you might be working for him one day!' Miss Chynoweth reminded her students.

It was freezing in that winter of 1962–63 when Liz was

at the Whitehall, and there was no central heating in the draughty Victorian Gothic building, just stoves in the two 'typewriter-infested teaching rooms', the girls clacking away with their red fingers. 'Perish the thought that our fingernails might be varnished. The length of our nails was inspected regularly. We had to dress conservatively, quietly and in good taste. No miniskirts allowed, and only the most discreet make-up. I was rebuked by Miss Chynoweth for appearing in a striped shirt that she said was "too masculine in style".'

When it came to typing, the rule was that either the students had to be blindfolded or the typewriter did, a metal cover coyly fixed high over its keyboard to make it invisible for teaching purposes. As the period of this book progresses, the music to which the students were made to type in strict rhythm evolved from military marches at Mrs Hoster's above the Cromwell Road in the 1950s, as recalled by Penny Eyles, where 'a wizened woman taught us typing', to Pat Boone tunes played by Victor Silvester's dance band, at the Queen's Secretarial College, also in the 1950s, as recalled by Penny Graham, who 'only lasted three months', to Abba's 'Waterloo' at the Ox & Cow in the early 1980s, as recalled by Caroline Donald, where the girls typed 'on manual typewriters, imagining we had tennis balls under our palms. Clack-clack-clack, it went, then you heard the whizz of the handle on the bar as you pushed it back to start the next line, and the zip of the wheel as you rolled out the letter and carbon paper.' The girls at South Molton Street, and the ones at Pitman's own-brand no-frills training college in Bloomsbury, just had to type in time to a metronome, with no music to jolly them along. That seemed harsh.

As with piano lessons, 'flat fingers' were not permitted. It was all about evenness of touch. 'If you clattered the keys down too hard,' Vivien Ruddock explained, 'their tops would get stuck up in the air together.' Slower music – pieces like the Slow March of the Grenadier Guards, or a very slow Pat Boone dance tune – would be played when the girls were focusing less on their speed and more on their evenness of touch. 'If there was a double letter,' said Liz Jones, 'the rule was that you must never try to shortcut with a quick double-click.'

Mechanical typewriters were used for teaching purposes deep into the electric era, rather in the way electric sewing machines were not allowed at many girls' schools long after they'd been invented. It was thought good for the soul to stick to the harder, more physically demanding, more antiquated method. 'We worked solely on mechanical typewriters,' Vivien said, 'just having one go on an electric one in the week before we left.' This was in the 'model office', a mocked-up office environment for leavers to get a feel for the real world. The danger of the lack of electric experience was that when you were first presented with an electric typewriter in your first real job, you tended to smash the keys down much too hard, damaging the keyboard.

As for shorthand, some fell instantly in love with it, think-ing of it as a thrilling new secret language that would unlock the door to adulthood. These girls went home every evening to practise, taking shorthand from the radio. Others found it unbelievably dull, for example Anne Oldroyd, for whom mastering the sound-based Pitman squiggles at Kilburn Polytechnic after Cambridge was an anticlimax. 'I'd never done anything so boring.' 'A dreary way of spending one's life,' said Penny Eyles. Virginia Ironside couldn't stand it either. On the first morning at her secretarial college in Oxford in 1962, the shorthand mistress arrived and announced, 'You must get up when I come in, and you must say, "Good morning, Miss Burnham," and I will say, "Good morning, people." I couldn't stand being with all those other girls,' Virginia said, '1950s relics, in their hairbands and pearls; I couldn't bear their camaraderie and giggling. I couldn't do the shorthand. I only lasted ten days. When I came home, even after those ten days, I had a stammer.'

'There were loads of "short forms" for things you had to scribble down most often,' Vivien Ruddock told me, explaining the Pitman's method, 'for example "Dear Sir", "thank you", and "company report".' The short-form Liz Jones remembered most clearly was 'L' for Lord. 'Why did we need to know this? Because lots of company directors and important people were Lords, so we'd be sure to encounter them.'

Shorthand was a tricky art to master, devised by Sir Isaac Pitman in 1837; oddly harder for people who were good spellers because they had to forget spelling and rely on sounds. 'I couldn't do the Pitman's,' Bee Bealey said, simply. To learn it properly, you needed those hours and hours per week of intensive drilling, and the problem about Mrs Thomsett's in Oxford was that, even though it had a whiteboard rather than a blackboard, which seemed very state-of-the-art, 'it wasn't a serious course – just two hours a day, a.m. or p.m. – and one prayed for p.m.' There was no way you were going to get on top of the system with this half-hearted approach. 'Eventually,' Alexandra Etherington, who went to the Queen's, said to me, 'I did learn to write shorthand. But I couldn't read it back.' And reading it back was literally half the point.

It might have been tedious, and all too like going back to school. Yet, as mothers said to their daughters to encourage them to keep at it, 'Darling, you'll always be able to earn some money.' (With that 'always', they couldn't help envisioning the horrid picture of their daughter being abandoned by some cad of a future husband.) The Morningside ladies in felt hats who taught at Dugdale's secretarial college in Edinburgh called their students 'Ladies', but apart from that they sounded just like Miss Jean Brodie. Lateness and truancy were not accepted at any of these establishments. You had to ring the doorbell and account for yourself if you were five minutes late. 'If we didn't turn up,' Annabel Charlesworth said, 'they rang our parents.' You can hardly blame them, but it was annoying for the 'milk train' types whose hearts weren't in it.

It wasn't always old ladies. The St James's Secretarial College in London had a sister college in Bridport, Dorset, run in the late 1970s by 'a terrifying, grizzly man called Fido May', as Amanda Graham told me. 'He allowed us to smoke inside the college, and we did.' The actual people who taught the classes were all women, though, just as at Newton Manor, the school Amanda had just left.

For those who couldn't stand or do shorthand, there was another option. Virginia Ironside spotted it on the tube, intrigued by an advertisement that said, 'gt a gd jb & mo pa'. This was a speedwriting course. So she went on it, in a little room up a flight of stairs in Oxford Street, and loved it. 'So much nicer; and it was my choice; and none of that "Good morning, Miss Burnham" nonsense.'

The only problem was that speedwriting, though easier to learn (it was mainly a matter of dropping vowels and silent letters from words) was simply not as efficient a method of taking down the spoken word as proper shorthand. Working as she soon did for Shirley Williams, who spoke very fast, Virginia found it hard to keep up, in the unheated office of the Fabian Society.

Depending on the typing and shorthand speeds you managed to achieve at these institutions, and the ambitions of their principals, you would proceed to anything from the Foreign Office at the top end to (if you were a low-achiever and never got the hang of Pitman's) having to go to the Kelly Girl agency and ask whether there were any vacancies for a receptionist.

5

'Little Jobs'

'Celia Hammond is looking after the animals' welfare in Harrods'

Stover School Magazine, 1959

'Little', as an adjective for 'jobs' seems to have meant not so much 'footling' as 'short-lived'.

'We wore our jobs lightly,' said Perina Braybrooke, born in 1932, among whose first jobs on leaving school was working in the watch department at Asprey's, where one of her duties was to take all the valuables out of the shop window before going home, 'and I took them out at 3 p.m. so I could get to my party'. Then she left and went to be an assistant vendeuse at the fashion house Worth. (That job title was always given its French name at the great fashion houses, elevating the working day far above the workaday.) 'I gazed enviously at Clarissa Churchill, who was having a dress fitting. I longed for a dress like that. I think we were all rather waiting to get married.'

It's confusing. We hear people saying nostalgically, of the

Olden Days (1950s to '70s), 'It was a job for life in those days, wasn't it?' We remember grey-haired fathers and grandfathers in suits who'd worked for the same firm for decades, doing the same commute every day, arriving home on the dot of six with the evening paper tucked under their arm, steadily working their way to a company car, an executive ashtray and a panelled office on the top floor.

That kind of job longevity could and did happen to women, for example the ladies who were 'the mother of the office' – the ones who'd worked in the same place for years, always looked after the new girls and had never risen up through the ranks. They were known as 'the salt of the earth'. The only thing was, young women starting out in the world of work took one look at them and vowed to do all they could to avoid becoming one of them.

Frances Pemberton told me about Miss Hargreaves, for example, who, in her 'cardigan with glass buttons', worked as a secretary – *the* secretary – to Douglas Bader, and had worked for him for decades: 'she was his gatekeeper, his right-hand woman. She was more like a mother to him; or like his nanny.' Barbara Rich described the two women who worked in the Chambers where she started as the first female barrister in the mid-1980s. They were the secretary and the cleaner, both of them middle-aged. They were both 'a fixture'. Anne, the typist, 'worked in a cubbyhole, and typed letters in strict order of seniority of the person they were dictated by. She wore terribly frumpy clothes. She was always reading – a life of the mind struggling inside her, that never got out. She downed tools on the dot of 5.' Bridget, the cleaner, was a doctor's widow. 'She didn't really approve of women lawyers in Chambers. She did the catering for the Christmas party: salmon mousse made from tins of John West salmon, and sausage rolls arranged on a plate in a Christmas-tree shape.'

Caroline Stacey described to me the 'fantastic old sub-editor' who worked with her at *Caterer and Hotelkeeper* magazine in the early 1980s and had been a fixture there for years: 'she kept a bottle of whisky in her desk drawer, but to mask the smell of whisky on her breath she chewed bits of raw garlic. She lived with a woman she told us was her cousin. She wore men's trousers and swore like a trooper; "bugger" in a plummy voice. She'd go to the loo and fart loudly. You knew it was her in the next-door cubicle. She always put a bit of lavatory paper on the seat before sitting down, and would then come out with a short tail of paper sticking out of her trousers. She was very strict about the split infinitive.'

An office treasure, in other words. In such women's cases, though, the longevity, one feels, was seen as more a sign of failure than of success. To be a Miss Hargreaves in a cardigan in her sixties, or an Anne in her cubbyhole, or a widowed Bridget mashing up the tinned salmon for a festive office occasion, or an old, farting subeditor, was not a desirable state. In his 1958 poem 'Business Girls', John Betjeman summed up the desolation of single working women soaking in their early-morning baths in their 'precarious bathrooms' jutting out from the backs of houses: 'Rest you there, poor unbelov'd ones,/Lap your loneliness in heat.' What did he know, as a man? That unbelov'dness was purely in his imagination. But Barbara Pym was writing from personal experience when she portrayed Marcia and Letty in her 1977 novel *Quartet in Autumn*: emotionally dried-up, ageing single women, for whom life had never quite taken off – there they still were, calcified in their obsolescent office clerking jobs, counting down the days to retirement.

It was precisely this kind of workplace stagnation that young women of the period of this book wanted to avoid. Far from aiming to prove their stamina by staying in a job for a long time – God forbid that they should ever become 'a fixture' – they aimed to prove their agility by dipping in and out. 'Wearing jobs lightly' was the aim. They drifted cheerfully, with no grand plan, into the world of work, plucking jobs as though they were apples in an orchard, and discarding them after two bites. What a casual attitude to employment, I thought, as I interviewed them! Nowadays, if by a miracle a young woman manages to snaffle a job, the chosen candidate from thousands of online applicants, she's obliged to wear it heavily, making herself indispensable in a climate of insecurity and job scarcity. It wasn't like that in the 1950s and '60s. You left the job voluntarily rather than the job leaving you. 'I temped one summer for fortnights at the BBC, *The Sunday Times* and the Harrods publicity department,' said Cicely McCulloch. 'Each of those employers said, "Please will you stay on?" but I said no. I didn't want any commitment. Jobs grew on trees.' She admits now that if she had stayed on in any of those offices, she would probably have worked her way up through them. But the urge to try something new was too strong. Some jobs were as short-lived as a mayfly. 'You could get one in the morning, leave it that day and get another in the afternoon,' said Sharon Scard, who told me that by the age of twenty-two she had already had twenty-five jobs.

Born in Hackney in 1956, Sharon was a grammar school girl whose sister was a secondary modern girl. Both left school at fifteen, Sharon's sister (who had been taught typing all the way through her secondary modern) to work in an office, and Sharon (who hadn't learned to type at her grammar, so was actually less qualified for employment) to work in a shoe shop, Trueform in Dalston, a job she got from the Reed employment agency. 'I was tiny,' she said, 'still growing, my skirt too long so I could grow into it. I worked five days a week plus alternate Saturdays. I earned seven pounds a week and gave half to my mum. She was a single mum and needed me and my sister to leave school and earn money.' Shoe shops like Trueform were kept going by these eager, hard-working, fifteen year olds who 'didn't get tired'.

'But I did get bored,' said Sharon. 'So I'd go back to the agency and get a job somewhere else, maybe in an office as a receptionist. Six months was a *very* long time for me to stay in any job.' There would be another fifteen-year-old available to fill the vacancy at the job she'd left, while she would walk into the space left by the voluntary leaver at the next job.

Sharon Scard, aged sixteen in 1972, with her uncle,
outside her aunt's bungalow in Jaywick, Essex. She'd had
twenty-five jobs by the age of twenty-two

A few years in to this existence, a girl's CV would be running on to its third side of foolscap. Did she even have a CV? I asked Sharon. Those documents were not much in evidence, she said. I wondered whether the extreme briefness of previous jobs might have raised eyebrows on the question of stamina, but she said, 'I don't recall any disapproval over length of previous employment.'

The song 'Find Yourself Something to Do', in Julian Slade's 1954 musical *Salad Days*, was sung by two fretting parents to the young man of the story, Timothy, just down from Cambridge, whose mother and father were desperate for him to find a job in a government ministry, and advised him to 'Go and see Uncle Sam'. Well-connected graduates like Timothy were expected to be swiftly absorbed into the network of old boys and old relatives who would lift them into the safety of a lifelong career. Off Timothy goes to have lunch with his uncle, while his friend Jane, who has just graduated from the very same university, sits in the sun and dreams of being 'in love by the end of the season'. This seemed the natural order of things to the original audience.

But even the girl needed to find herself *something* to do. Jane in *Salad Days* agreed to look after a magic piano for £7 from a passing tramp. In real life, girls like Jane just went and got their first brief job, often through knowing someone who knew someone, and then got another one, subsisting on a very small wage (£3 a week for Perina Braybrooke at Worth) and being taken out to dinner by men who earned more than they did. The usual way of describing this existence was 'I floated about'.

It's an evocative expression, exuding an image of wafting dreamily in a gauzy dress from one form of employment to another, lodging with other girls who were similarly floating about, waif-thin through not eating enough, living in draughty digs with penny-in-the-slot meters, meeting all kinds of fascinating men, one of whom would eventually whisk you off to a life of solid, grounded wifehood. 'It was quite usual to be rescued by a man,' as Josceline Dimbleby summed up the vaguely hoped-for goal of that existence.

They needed to be on standby, because at any moment in this floating-about period, daughters might be called away from their job to help with a family crisis. Elizabeth Rolston left Studley Horticultural & Agricultural College in Warwickshire and went to work with a dairy herd in County Durham in 1947 ('a freezing winter, and there was a German prisoner of war still working there, and two land girls'). She was suddenly called south to go and live with, cook and clean for her uncle, who'd just returned to Sussex after being a missionary in Burma. She did this, unpaid. Nor was this just a 1940s phenomenon. In the mid-1950s, Frances Pemberton, while working happily in a little office above Threadneedle Street, was suddenly called home because her father was ill. 'My mother expected me to stop having a nice time and go home. One had to give up having a life, and just go back and help.' 'I'd just started as a nursing probationer at St Thomas's Hospital in 1951,' said Agneta Hinkley, 'when my mother fell downstairs and fractured her skull. My parents sent for me. I had to go back home to Bruton to look after them. I was twenty-five, just coming up for preliminary nursing training. I tried going back to St Thomas's a year or so later, but it was useless: too late.' I spoke to women who, deep into the last decade of the twentieth century, had been 'called home' to run the household and fetch and carry when summoned by an ill mother or father who 'didn't want to pay for a carer' or 'didn't want a stranger in the house'. This kind of instant, dutiful self-sacrifice was not required of sons.

Parental control continued to reach its cold hand into the finding of paid employment – because the jobs needed to be 'suitable', for the sake of the Reputation. 'They sent me' is how Elspeth Allison described being pushed off into various jobs, after the detested domestic science college her parents had sent her to on leaving school aged sixteen in the late 1950s. 'They' referred to her parents. 'They sent me to work in a council day nursery.' 'They sent me to a boys' home – an orphanage.' 'Then they agreed I could go to typing college, Miss Harrison's in Leicester.' 'I got a really good job with a local solicitor in Leicester, but it didn't last as I started going out with a friend of my brother's, whom my parents disapproved of. They decided I should leave the job and leave home. They sent me away to work for the local vicar's daughter in Berkshire – I was to go and look after the vicar's grandchild.' You can sense the 'find yourself something to do, dear' urge here, so strong that it spilled over to the parents bossily finding their daughter something to do. Parent power was palpable; and Elspeth's parents' chief desire was that their daughter would, through her job, find a suitable man to marry, which indeed Elspeth did, at that job in Berkshire.

If a job wasn't considered suitable, parents put their foot down. 'I was offered a job on the local paper when I left school in 1952,' Josephine Boyle told me, 'but the idea was met with horror at home. My parents had an image of me meeting drunken journalists in dirty macs. They were *so* disapproving. So instead, I went to be a junior matron at a boys' prep school in East Sussex, changing their sheets and emptying their chamber pots: one communal chamber pot for each dorm and it was full in the morning.' The journalist job would have been far more educational for Josephine, but, she told me, 'it was just out of the question, socially speaking. Our parents didn't want us to meet people from different walks of life.'

The jobs you could find yourself doing, in the lottery of short-lived employment, were unpredictable. 'Find yourself doing' is the apposite expression here, because once they were in 'digs' of their own and had thus escaped the daily power of parental control, these women floating about were so curious about life, and so ignorant and innocent of the facts of life and of worldly behaviour, that they said yes to things, and could suddenly find themselves working in very weird, remote, unsupervised places, for quite strange men. While so doing, they did indeed find themselves, or at least discover what they didn't want to spend the rest of their lives doing.

This was long before the days when most jobs in the world involved the safe pastime of staring at a screen all day in a heated, open-plan environment. Georgina Harding, born in 1940, who spent her 'entire life up to the age of twenty-six aiming to get married', did a few jobs to pass the time till that marriage came to the rescue. One was to work for the publisher and Conservative MP David James, who had founded the Loch Ness Phenomena Investigation Bureau. For two long summers running, Georgina, an alumna of Riddlesworth Hall, who'd also been to boarding school in the wheat belt of Australia, where 'I had a nervous breakdown but they just called it "hopeless"', was sent up north by him to live in a caravan on the shores of Loch Ness and keep a lookout for the monster from the moment she woke up every morning till the moment she fell asleep. 'I shared the caravan with various other people, and we'd all been sent up there by him,' she recalled. 'We were told by the monks who lived at the end of the loch that they saw the monster often. The caravan was at Drumnadrochit, with a pub within walking distance.' The pub certainly helped, when it came to giving everyone the illusion that they definitely had seen something stir in the loch.

Penny Eyles, aged twenty-two in 1950, found herself working at a very strange laboratory a short bus ride away from the damp-walled high-ceilinged flat in Oxford where she was lodging with two friends who were doing secretarial jobs. She answered an advertisement and found work at a place called the De La Warr Laboratories. George de la Warr, who ran them, was 'Mr de la Warr' to Penny, who was there to type letters for him and Mrs de la Warr, addressed to their patients. 'There were lots of black boxes lined up along the wall,' said Penny, 'each labelled with the name of the patient it belonged to – Lady this, Lord that. Inside each box were samples of the patient's blood and hair, and various knobs and dials, and just inside the lid there was a strip of rubber. Every week, a medium, Mrs Boulder, would arrive and "treat" the patients by rubbing the piece of rubber, and the dial markings would move.' It all seemed quite far-fetched, to do with the power of radio waves, but Penny spent the whole working day writing letters acknowledging receipt of large payments of fees from the aristocrats who swore by the treatment. (De la Warr was later sued in the High Court by a disgruntled customer.)

'Then I got a letter from a school friend,' said Penny, 'who was a nurse and said she'd got a flat at 71 Wimpole Street and would I like to go and live there with three other nurses?' So it was goodbye to Oxford and hello to working for some 'ex-Army posh boys' in an advertising agency on Waterloo Bridge. This was a typical flit from job to job in the 'floating about' existence.

It was hard to keep up, as I scribbled the flits down. 'Hold on, hold on, you did what? Ah – Universal Aunts; you had to collect girls who needed to be ferried across London. Did you need any training or paperwork for that? No? OK. Then what? Ah, you worked for an antique dealer who was "very mean" and had trained himself to drink coffee with "off" milk, and sent you downstairs to be out of sight when famous people came into the shop. What was his name again? Ah, Henry Woods Wilson. Got it. And then you went to be a paid companion to ... who? ... where?' This last was the trajectory of future fashion editor of the *Evening News*, *Woman's Own* and *Cosmopolitan* Penny Graham (born in 1940), after her brief stints doing the Season and going to Queen's secretarial college. 'Captain Buckmaster's family were worried, as he wasn't eating,' she explained. 'So could I go and have lunch with him at Buck's Club in Clifford Street every day and be paid for it? I said yes, and had a divine time with this heavenly old boy, full of gossip, full of fun, but I put quite a lot of weight on. Then my stepmother who'd been a model at Hardy Amies got me a job as a house model, for five pounds a week. I stood for hours being pinned up and having measurements taken.'

Penny Graham, house model (far right) with Hardy Amies, 1959, at a dress rehearsal for a show, not quite sure where to position a flower

An alumna of the Catholic convent school Mayfield, Penny said to me, 'everyone our age would always have done a million little jobs. I'd left school with my head full of Georgette

Heyer, and I thought a duke was going to come along. We'd spent a lot of time looking up names in *Kelly's* [*Handbook to the Titled, Landed and Official Classes*] and practising writing our future surname. The future *hung* there: so exciting.'

But as the duke kept not quite materialising, the little jobs accrued. 'And as one didn't know where one was going, one didn't know whether one had arrived or not.' The only nagging question after you'd been in the same job for a few months was 'Should I move on now?'

'Had you had any intellectual encouragement or pressure from your parents to achieve anything in life?' I asked Penny, expecting and receiving the answer no.

'Intellectual! Pressure! There were just two layers of bookshelves in our entire house. If I did manage to get a modelling job or a journalism job, my father would say, "Oh, I hope that's not going to make you too big-headed."'

This was the whole tenor of many girls' upbringing and education – not to get too big-headed. 'Don't get in the way' was another piece of advice often given by parents – hence Penny's willingly scuttling downstairs to be out of sight at the antique shop when the 'famous people' came in. That advice was paired up with 'always make yourself useful'. It could be tricky trying to be both useful and not in the way. 'When, a few year later, I went to be interviewed by the editor of the *Daily Express*, I wrapped up his Christmas presents while he interviewed me – that was "being useful". He did give me the job, in the fashion department. But if only I'd believed in myself a bit more. I didn't have a core of inner self-belief.'

Penny's experience was the opposite of that of today's daughters who are praised to the skies for every tiny achievement from the potty onwards. 'All this – "oh darling, congratulations" – I had none of that.' When eventually she did become the fashion editor of the *Evening News*, and saw her own face advertised on the sides of buses, she told me, 'I could never really appreciate it was me. It said on the advertising bumph that I was read by 1,463,000 women. Golly!'

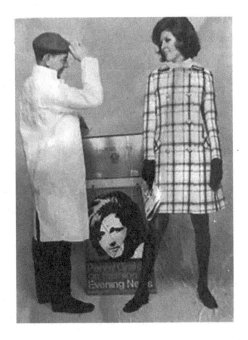

Publicity shots for Penny Graham as new fashion editor of the *Evening News*, 1968: 'I could never really appreciate it was me'

These young women were falling back on their inner 'sparkiness'. One of the key 'find yourself something to do' occupations was being a chalet girl: an irresistible idea, because it combined four glamorous concepts: abroad, snowy mountains, skiing and sociability. I spoke to some members of the 1970s and '80s chalet-girl brigade, and was impressed by the vigour with which they toiled for Supertravel or Murison Small. One of them, Kate Green (now deputy editor of *Country Life*), was a chalet girl at Courchevel for a group of Queen's Own Highlanders who, she told me, 'skied in their kilts. One of them decided to see if he could ski through the open French windows straight onto his bed.' He could.

To set the chalet-girling in its typical context, this was Kate's pre-chalet-girl trajectory: she was educated at St Audrie's School in Somerset, which she summed up in one word – 'Gothic'. Then she went for an audition at a drama school, discovered there were five hundred applicants for forty places, scaled down her ambitions, and did a secretarial course at the Alan Knight secretarial college in Guildford – 'quite progressive; we learned to use a stenograph instead of shorthand.' This was the fast-as-speech keyboard on which you could type a whole word at once by bashing down multiple letters in a 'chord'.

Then she put an advertisement in *Horse & Hound* offering her services as a 'Girl Friday'. 'Girl Friday', meaning 'young woman willing to do anything and everything, indoors and outdoors, as long as it's helpful to a handsome man' was an expression I heard often when people described to me their starting out. The Robinson Crusoe image appealed to them and to their mostly male employers. Kate was offered a job in a hunting hotel called The Crown in Exford, on Exmoor. This job turned out to be the English equivalent of chalet-girling, except that instead of getting all your work done as quickly as possible so you could go out and ski, you did it so you could go out and hunt. Kate found herself being receptionist, waitress, driver of a Land Rover with trailer, ironer of candlewax out of tablecloths with blotting paper, and bringer of tea trays to bedrooms, where occasionally she would open the door to find an amorous visiting Master of Fox Hounds on the bed waiting for her. At which point she would plonk the tea tray down and run.

Then she went to be a nanny and Girl Friday to an

Anglo-Irish family in Ireland who had no idea how to stop their baby crying, and Kate worked it out by flicking through her copy of Dr Spock till she found the bit on burping and winding; and then she went to be a secretary at a boys' prep school whose headmaster had a 'dim view of women and their abilities', and would say to his wife, 'Shirley, what are you doing? You know you're absolutely hopeless!' He was an eloquent dictator of letters, though, and Kate took dictation sitting on an armchair with both his Labradors resting their heads in her lap.

A month's Prue Leith cookery course in a house in Kensington came next (this was the mid-1980s) 'because I wanted to be a chalet girl', and in order to be one, she would need a repertoire of three-course supper menus for every evening of a week, plus a daily cake.

Once on the slopes, sleeping in a twin room in the chalet, near the washing machine room, the aim was to get the work done and be skiing yourself by noon. Dressed in their white Supertravel rugby shirts with a ski motif, the chalet girls waited for the water to take ages to boil at the high altitude. If they went over budget (the allocation was £4 per day per guest), their final week's salary was deducted accordingly. Changeover day was tough: eight hours in the coach accompanying the travel-sick guests back to the airport, and eight hours back again with the next batch. 'Girls, always go the extra mile' was the advice given pre-season at the Hans Place headquarters. Occasionally a chalet girl would take this too literally: fall in love with one of the guests, travel back to the airport and then to England with him on changeover day, and never return. This was seen as natural wastage.

There was a breathless sense of adventure in this job-to-job existence. Phoebe Fortescue's pre-chalet-girl trajectory in the late 1970s began, through university, with working in the basement of a diamond trading company near Hatton Garden, putting all the files going back to 1950 on microfiche. This was the kind of mind-numbing job girls were set to do: in basements, with microfiche, wading through files going back decades. Phoebe was paid £20 a day, which seemed a lot of money, so she kept at it. Her boss's PA (ah – this was the first time I heard the name 'PA' used instead of 'secretary'; it was a new trendy abbreviation, less demeaning-sounding) was madly in unrequited love with the boss, but the boss had a crush on Phoebe, making things awkward, and quite unpleasant when he came down to the strongroom to massage Phoebe's shoulders while she worked. (We last met Phoebe in *British Summer Time Begins*: she was the vicar's daughter whose highlight of the year was the annual trip to a restaurant, during the family's sojourn in Herne Bay.)

I discovered that the expression 'No, thank you, I'm quite happy standing', which we now associate with women over sixty politely declining the offer of a seat on a crowded tube train, was originally coined by young women in their late teens and early twenties politely declining the offer to sit on their boss's knee. Phoebe's boss at the diamond trading company was inspired by the innocence of this eighteen-year-old vicar's daughter in her Laura Ashley sailor dress, and summoned her to his office, 'where he delighted in showing me photographs of recent massacres in Angola, which was in its early years of civil war. He showed me piles of bodies of men with their willies cut off and put into their mouths – which he assured me was to stop their bodies exploding in the heat.'

This creepy working environment hardened Phoebe up for being an agency worker for the Solve Your Problem agency in Kensington. She found this job because she'd cooked a lunch for one Lady Munty, who'd said to her, 'You should work for Solve Your Problem. I'll ring them and tell them how marvellous you are and how you cooked me such a delicious lemon mousse.' It turned out that in order to get onto the Solve Your Problem agency's books, your reference had to be from a 'titled source'. So Lady Munty was ideal. The next thing Phoebe knew, she was doing random cooking and cleaning jobs all over London for people whose problems needed solving by the arrival of an instant nicely spoken girl willing to do anything. 'We've got a nice little ironing job for you,' the ladies who ran the agency told her one morning. 'We've got some clothes in from Paris.' Off Phoebe went to a flat near Sadler's Wells, 'and I opened the suitcase and it was full of sex gear: dog leads, satin dog collars, pink fluffy bras and fake leather whips'. In her Laura Ashley dress (again), with the chatelaine of the flat 'perching her bare buttocks on the ironing board and watching me,' Phoebe started ironing her way through the chatelaine's tools of trade, 'terrified that one of these items was going to melt into my iron.'

From there she was sent to cook for an Orthodox Jewish family in a house in a gated compound near Worthing. 'I was made to sleep on the floor of the larder on a mattress, and was given strict instructions about the Kosher two-kitchen arrangement – different pots and pans for meat days and dairy days. When I sliced a mango and a tomato when they should have been cubed, the whole lot was summarily binned, everything was criticised and I was humiliated in front of their family and guests. The final straw was when the family returned from their yacht for tea in the drawing room, and the master of the house screamed at me that I'd brought the wrong tea set. I apologised, saying I'd got it out of the correct Kosher cupboard, but he threw the tray onto the floor, smashing the cups and saucers, and made me clear up the debris.'

She left early the next morning, and reported the incident, and the mattress-in-larder existence, to the ladies at Solve Your

Problem, 'but they just tittered'. This was the world of 'find your-self something to do'. You never knew what was coming next.

To secure the deeply desired chalet-girl job with Supertravel, the only interview answer Phoebe needed up her sleeve was 'how would you garnish' various popular supper dishes, the correct replies being 'sprig of parsley', 'slice of tomato' and 'slice of cucumber.' She got the job and found herself in the mountains running a chalet for twelve, and sleeping on a mat-tress in a broom cupboard, which she considered fine, having experienced worse in Worthing. While out skiing after the morning ritual of changing twelve duvet covers and baking a cake, she met Nick Danziger who said, 'You're just the kind of person who should work for my friend who's starting a gallery in Cork Street.'

A typical evening in the chalet with guests, for hard-working chalet girl Phoebe Fortescue (far left)

So she did, and while there saved all her earnings to go to drama school. Then, after doing a Solve Your Problem job passing round canapés on the first night of a Jonathan Miller play at the Old Vic, she boldly sent him an invoice and a CV, with a covering note: 'If you're ever auditioning, would you consider me?' 'My agent got a call from them and I went and read for them, and was cast in their next play.'

Confidence very gradually grew for young women through these minion years when they threw themselves from job to job. By the age of twenty-five, the ones who'd left school at fifteen or sixteen already had nine or ten years of full-time work experience under their belts. There was a sense that 'a million little jobs' could and might eventually lead you to a big job – but only if you really and truly wanted one.

6

The Inspiration of Anna the Air Hostess

'Anna and Mary went to their little galley at the
tail end of the plane and started to sort out the
towels, soap and other toilet articles, replacing
those that had been used up'

from *Anna the Air Hostess* by
Cynthia Hunter, 1967

The schoolgirls who'd spent as much of their childhoods as
they could curled up with a good book had prepared themselves for adulthood by immersing themselves in enticing
grown-up worlds, such as the world of the working nurse
and the world of the working air hostess. Deep into the
1970s, girls at my school were still devouring and passing
round the *Sue Barton* series written in the 1930s and '40s,
starting with *Sue Barton, Student Nurse*, and proceeding
to *Sue Barton, Staff Nurse, Sue Barton, Neighbourhood
Nurse, Sue Barton, Visiting Nurse* and *Sue Barton,
Superintendent of Nurses*, at which point Sue Barton was
married with three children so had to give up being any kind

of nurse, only going back to work as a staff nurse when her husband was in a sanatorium with TB. The books, written in America by Helen Dore Boylston, who was best friends with Laura Ingalls Wilder, contained everything we craved from a girls'-school-story – uniforms, dorms, matrons – with the added bonus of ill patients and the prospect of a monthly wage.

One ninety-two-year-old patient whom eighteen-year-old Sue treats in *Sue Barton, Student Nurse* is an Army veteran who remembers being treated by Florence Nightingale in the Crimean War. The book was that old: published in 1936. But lots of girls at my school said they wanted to be nurses after reading it. 'The little crinoline cap was the climax and the reward for three months of desperate endeavour,' we read. How we longed for one! This was the next step up from our first powerful source of inspiration: the Ladybird Book *The Nurse*, from its 'People at Work' series, whose illustrations made Christmas Day in the children's ward, with one of the nurses thrumming out carols on the piano, look like the best party ever. It also showed us a deeply contented nurse sitting on her candlewick bedspread in her private bedroom on her afternoon off, knitting.

'A nurse must always rise to her feet when addressed by a doctor' was one of the instructions announced by the superintendent Miss Matthews to Sue Barton on her first morning in *Sue Barton, Student Nurse*. Miss Matthews explained, 'You must understand that you are rising, not to the man, but to his profession.' The role of female nurse as angelic helpmeet to male doctor, whose profession one should honour by rising to one's feet, was ingrained into an impressionable readership.

When it came to air-hostessing as a prospective career, the role model was Anna in *Anna the Air Hostess* – again, not an English work, but this time a Kenyan one, written in 1967 and first published in Nairobi. It, too, was in my school library, well thumbed. The author, Cynthia Hunter, conveyed the fulfilling life of the air hostess through the eyes of young Anna. We learned that, as well as walking up and down the aisle with the coffee pot, bringing succour and reassurance to every grateful passenger (a sort of Florence Nightingale of the skies), air hostesses actually scrambled and boiled the breakfast eggs while on the plane. It was an irresistible vision of keeping house at high altitude; and then you got a three-day stopover in Rome. Anna's excitement when she hears she's been selected for the Cairo trip is palpable. But two things go terribly wrong. First, on one of her flights, Anna is just serving out the coffee in the air when she notices oil pouring out of one of the engines. She mentions it to the pilot, and the plane has to do a forced landing in the Sahara Desert, everyone piling out down the safety slide. No one is killed, not even the baby on board, but the plane explodes. Anna receives a letter of congratulation from the authorities, praising her for her exemplary conduct.

A few days later, her heart is broken. Madly in love with Tom Clinton, her chief training officer, she returns to Nairobi Airport to find a terse letter from him explaining that he has left, to take up a job as a chief training steward in London.

The sympathetic senior air hostess in charge of the young air hostesses' welfare explains to a tearful Anna, who wonders if Tom will miss her, that men are different: 'I do know that men can put things to the back of their minds and concentrate entirely on what they are doing. Maybe in that way they are stronger than us.' We leave Anna in a state of wistful hopefulness that she'll be accepted for the next level of training: on the Super VC10s.

How nicely spoken these role models were! Both nursing and air-hostessing were clearly suitable jobs for young women of all social ranks, including pale English roses with posh voices. Passengers were used to hearing the question 'Coffee or tea, sir?' spoken in cut-glass accents by uniformed angels.

'And we had to know how to deliver a baby,' said Judy Price, who worked for British European Airways in the early 1950s. 'They showed us a film. I nearly fainted.'

Anna the Air Hostess, even with its catastrophes, did enough to inspire Elizabeth Ballantyne-Brown (born 1941). She found it in her local library when she was thirteen, devoured it, and wrote to BOAC on the strength of it as soon as she left school aged seventeen. Her father pooh-poohed the job that sounded so glamorous to her, calling it 'a flying waitress'. (Honestly! With one hand, fathers refused to countenance high academic achievement for their daughters; then those very same fathers belittled the jobs that were thus available to them.) But Elizabeth was determined. BOAC told her she was too young, and would 'need to do teaching or nursing training and come back to us when you're twenty-one' – hence her three years at the Edinburgh College of Domestic Science first, to pass the time until she was twenty-one.

Then she was off to the training school at London Airport (not called Heathrow till 1966) to learn everything from coffee-pouring on a backward-sloping raked aisle to life-saving and fire-fighting. 'Now, ladies,' said the female head of the course on the final day, 'there's something I have to tell you. You'll be going to beautiful places, spending time in hot, sunny countries with beautiful beaches. Later in the evening, when you're in your room, there may be a knock on your door. It might be your captain saying, "I've run out of toothpaste." Now, if that happens, do not open the door. Just squeeze the toothpaste through the keyhole.'

Of all the skills Elizabeth learned on that 1962 course, the one that has stayed most vividly with her is how to avoid being sexually assaulted by the captain. It proved useful. That knock on the door did happen during her year as an air hostess, and it was indeed the captain, and she didn't open the door.

Elizabeth Ballantyne-Brown air-hostessing, 1961

I didn't particularly go looking for people who had been air hostesses while researching this book. I just went looking for women in general, and was amazed by how many of them had spent time being air hostesses. It was one of those little jobs you could pick up before marriage and drop when you'd had enough of it. The enforced retirement age of thirty-five, or in some cases thirty-two, didn't matter a jot, as they would have left long before that anyway. The main annoyance was not that they couldn't be a bride, but that they couldn't be a bridesmaid, as it was impossible to commit to any dates, the rota being unpredictable and they might suddenly be called away to Geneva.

'Most of the pilots had been wartime pilots,' explained Judy Price. 'Those men were quite jokey. One of them flew very low indeed over the Scottish islands before landing in Glasgow, just for the fun of it. Another used to play a trick on passengers. He would put a mac on and sit in a passenger seat, looking exactly like a bored passenger. Then when the plane wouldn't leave, he started to fidget and look impatiently at his watch. Then he'd get up, walk into the cabin, start the engines and take off, to the horrified shock of the passengers.'

Air-hostessing had free foreign holidays built into it in a way that you don't feel it does now, looking at overworked cabin crew who get one night away in a Travelodge if they're lucky and who need to be plastered with make-up in order to hide the bags under their eyes. 'We were in Bermuda for a whole week between flights,' Elizabeth told me, 'with expenses to stay in nice hotels.' The job contained all the glamour of free travel abroad, in the days when most family holidays were spent at the English seaside, and when flying was still prohibitively expensive. Sukie Swan (born in 1948), who worked for BOAC in the early 1970s during the depths of the three-day week with its constant power cuts, had a marvellous time, frequently escaping for three weeks, spending three days each in New York, Los Angeles, Honolulu, Fiji and Sydney, a wad of cash given to her in an envelope on arrival in each place, as expenses. It made a pleasant change from huddling round the gas fire in dark Britain.

'To get in to BOAC,' she told me, 'you needed either nursing qualifications or languages.' 'Did you also need to be pretty?'

I asked her. 'You needed to be "in proportion" rather than pretty. We were all sent to the Elizabeth Arden beauty salon in Bond Street to do our make-up.' Sukie would marry aged twenty-six a man who lived opposite her parents. 'He saved me from the shelf, as he always says.'

One of my key 1950s and '60s floaters-about, Frances Pemberton, had a delightful spell as an air hostess in the mid-1950s, thanks to her boss Douglas Bader – who spent his time flying about in his own Dove plane visiting children all over the world who'd lost limbs, as he had in a plane crash in 1931 – saying to Frances, 'All my secretaries have gone on to be air hostesses. I'd go and do that too, if I were you.'

'I would never have had the initiative, but for his advice,' Frances said. 'He sent me off to Hunting-Clan Air Transport, based in a hangar at London Airport. We did trooping flights – taking National Service men out to Singapore and bringing them back. It took three weeks to go to Singapore and back, stopping off in Brindisi.'

From there she moved on to BOAC, 'getting the job because I knew about French cheese.' This job required more training in another hangar; and then she was off across the world on a Comet 4, 'a beautiful aeroplane, and half of it was first class.' Champagne-pouring was a major part of the job. 'Four days on Bondi Beach. Ten days in Bahrain with one of the girls who worked as an air hostess at Air Work – that was the airline where the debutantes worked. We went to parties with them in the desert.' But soon Frances grew 'tired of giving breakfast to tired, unshaven businessmen after a long night flight', and gave it up, to go and get married to a man she'd met at a party in Kent, 'but my heart wasn't in it [the marriage]'.

Frances Pemberton in her BOAC uniform

Air-hostessing didn't entirely live up to the expectations amassed from reading *Anna the Air Hostess*. 'I applied to Air France,' said Vicky Wilson (born 1950), 'hoping to be a ground hostess and doing things like welcoming Sacha Distel off the plane. But it wasn't quite as glamorous as that. The course before we started was rigorous, lots of it about ticketing, and we had to be dressed up to the nines, with heels at a precise height, and we had to know how to add the combined weights of people's suitcases to the tickets, and I couldn't add up. So planes were taking off overweight.' It was the typical self-deprecation of a woman laughing off her lack of a maths education. Even in the world of air-hostessing, where they thought they'd be safe from maths, earlier educational deficiencies could come back to haunt them.

Then Vicky left to became a teacher at Young England, the Montessori nursery school in St George's Square, Pimlico, of which she became the principal and owner by the age of twenty, thanks to financial help from her father, who agreed to buy the goodwill of the business for her when she was nineteen. (Montessori teaching was the one kind of teaching you could do without a maths O level, based as it was on learning through play.) She would later employ Lady Diana Spencer, who had floated up, entirely O level-less, through the nursery-school-teacher-and-nanny route to become the Princess of Wales.

7

Send Her Off to Yet Another Institution!

'Ann Stephens has begun her training at the
Middlesex Hospital, and has passed her first
examinations'

Stover School Magazine, 1959

Shoehorned into nursing, as it was one of the few careers
available to school leavers brought up to be useful and
helpful in the world, young women found themselves, once
again, ensconced in institutions where they were barked at
by older, unmarried women who were sticklers for tidiness.

Here's an example of the typical way a nursing career
got started.

With no hope of becoming a physiotherapist – St
Thomas's Hospital told her they'd keep the place open for
her 'for when she passed the science exams', but it was far
too late for that, after her virtually science-free schooling –
nineteen-year-old Diana Wright (born in 1936) was at a bit
of a loss as to what to do next. Her mother found her 'large
and unattractive' (subtext: not 'bedworthy' or easy to marry

off), and her father was cross that he'd had to pay for her education at all.

'I walked into my mother's club, the United Hunt Club in Upper Brook Street,' Diana told me, 'and found my father and mother sitting together on a sofa. They hadn't spoken since they got divorced at the end of the war. They told me, "You've been lazy and idle, and you're going to be a secretary." To which I replied, "No, I'm not." "Well, what are you going to be?" "A nurse," I said.'

And so it came about. Diana 'trotted off' (as she put it, suggesting eagerness but a lack of urgency – people were always 'trotting off' to interviews) to visit the Matron at the John Radcliffe Hospital in Oxford, who said to her, 'We're *much* the most popular nursing training place outside London,' and there was a place for her to start in the spring.

The next thing she knew, she was ticking off non-beautifying items on a clothes list again:

3 prs black lace-up shoes
6 prs black stockings
3 collar studs

... and so on. And then she was back in a boarding establishment, but this time sleeping in a Nissen hut with a whole lot of eighteen year olds. Bleary-eyed on her first morning, she was woken with a loud 'Get out of bed and say, "Good morning, Sister!"', and then it was eight weeks dressed in full uniform, learning the basics: bathing dummies, administering enemas to dummies, turning dummies, resuscitating dummies, giving practice injections to oranges, and endlessly making beds.

Many I spoke to were used to doing hospital corners, as the art had been drilled into them at their boarding schools. Tuck sheet into end of bed, lift flap on side, tuck hanging part in, lower flap, and then tuck that in. But in this new world of Nightingale Wards (long wards with thirty beds, fifteen down each side, exactly as in the Ladybird *Florence Nightingale*), even the beds themselves had to be brought into line, their wheels turned inwards towards each other symmetrically, like shy children's feet at a birthday party. The bed lamps had to be choreographed to swing in exactly the same direction, never mind whether or not they were pointing towards a book a patient might want to be reading.

At Bradford Royal, the wheels on the bed had to be lined up along a prescribed floorboard, and all the handles on the bottoms of the beds had to be pointing away from the door, as did all the pillowcase openings. At St Thomas's, 'if we let the corner of a patient's blanket so much as touch the floor we would get shouted at,' said Alison Willatts. 'The white counterpane had a Maltese cross on it, and if we didn't get it the right way up, there was hell to pay.' Jewish or Muslim patients could refuse a cross and have a plain counterpane instead, making their beds a bit less of a headache to assemble.

So many rules! 'You weren't allowed to fill a hot water bottle without a tray, a jug and a cloth,' said Diana Wright. 'And you were taught that whenever you went up to a patient to do anything, you had to, first, tell the patient what you were about to do, then close the window, and then draw the curtains.'

Closing the window seemed counter-intuitive, especially on a summer's day. But there was no questioning these institutions thick with traditions about how things must be done. Diana would soon learn that nurses weren't allowed to speak to doctors. 'If the telephone rang on a ward, and it was for Dr Harrison, I wasn't allowed to tell Dr Harrison directly. I had to say, "Sister, there's a call for Dr Harrison."'

She received her first pay cheque after a month. 'It was £8 2s 6d. I thought they must have made a mistake. I went to the finance office. "What d'you think you are?" said the woman behind the desk. "You're a first-year nurse. We keep you, wash your uniform and feed you."'

It seems extraordinary that she hadn't checked the monthly wage before starting, but there was real coyness in women when it came to mentioning money, seen as a rather vulgar subject, and they were expected gratefully to accept what they found in the envelope. Nursing was indeed the only paid training a young woman could do. But the food was 'lambs' hearts and lumpy custard in the nurses' dining room'; and if you were on night duty, it was 'hashed-up food from lunch, served up again at 2 a.m.' – 'I was just stunned by the horror,' said Diana.

The Ladybird book *The Nurse* hadn't mentioned any of this. The *Sue Barton* books had given an inkling of the tough life involved, but even they were sprinkled with more fairy dust than the reality had to offer.

Men were sent back to institutions, too, of course, after they left school, particularly when they did National Service, where they were sworn at, belittled and made to polish their shoes to a mirror-grade shine. Residential training, with its terrors, had the incomparable benefit of instilling in the trainee a whole habit of living. Helen Ball, senior police officer in the Metropolitan Police, gave me an enthusiastic description of life at her co-educational police college in Hendon in the 1980s, where in the evenings the trainees, accommodated on their single-sex floors of the residential tower block, practised arresting one another. What better way to learn and habituate yourself to your future procedures than in a cooped-up situation with other learners, where you could practise on each other? Trainee Catholic priests in Rome (I've seen it happen) practise doing confessions on each other, in role-play situations, one of them pretending to be pregnant out of wedlock.

But there was something particularly infantilising about the way that, in the period of this book, young women were corralled and bossed about by older women as soon as they emerged into adulthood and did any kind of training in a predominantly female occupation. We've seen it with the stern ladies who ran the secretarial colleges, but in the world of nursing training it was worse. Perhaps it was the uniforms, which gave nursing trainees a faceless identicalness that facilitated tyranny; perhaps it was the ghost of Florence Nightingale herself, revered for her withering strictness in the name of high standards; perhaps also it was the hideous sibilance of the word 'Nurse!' spoken in a rasping voice, but everyone I spoke to who trained to be a nurse from the 1950s to the 1970s shudders at the recollection of what happened when they did anything wrong. And there were hardly any male nurses in those days. 'Guy's Hospital was 99 per cent female nurses,' said Gill Robertson of her time there in the 1950s. 'The only male nurse was in "the special clinic", or "the clap clinic", hidden away.'

'Student Nurse Spooner!' Sister Lefever, the ward sister, barked at young Judy Spooner (born in 1954) in her first week at Jersey General. 'What on earth are you doing? I *hate* student nurses. The only people I hate more than them are PTSs [Preliminary Training School nurses].'

'That was us,' said Judy. She'd left Perry Cross Secondary Modern in Tamworth aged fifteen with no O levels, but had managed to do six O levels at Tamworth College of Further Education; she needed three to become a student nurse at Jersey General. 'At 11 every morning, after doing the bed baths, the junior student had to stand in front of Sister Lefever and recite the name, date, religion and diagnosis of every patient on the ward, and what had happened to them so far that day. If you got it wrong she'd yell at you and tell you to "get off the ward".'

Christina Ward, who trained at Leeds General Infirmary in

the mid-1970s, doing seven weeks in the pre-nursing school before being 'let loose in the ward', learned not to ask the sister questions. Her answer would be, 'That's for me to know and you to find out.' The general hospital rule was that, unless you were addressed first, a probationer nurse could only speak to a first-year nurse, a first-year to a second-year, a second-year to a third-year, a third-year to a staff nurse and a staff nurse to the sister. Tidiness of speech was as enforced as tidiness of bed coverings.

Dress codes were similarly terrifying. Of course you got sent back to change if you had a ladder in your tights, as did the trainee secretaries at the Ox & Cow. But even in a life-and-death crisis, you had to be wearing the right thing. 'A friend of mine,' said Patricia Heath, 'was on night duty desperately trying to resuscitate a man who'd had a cardiac arrest. Night Sister Brown came back from her tea break and was horrified. "Nurse!" she hissed. "You've got your cardigan on."'

Gill Robertson, her uniform attaining the standards of tidiness, neatness and cleanliness required, 1963

Swathes of girls who would nowadays become doctors became nurses, as we've seen with the grammar school that had a whole form called 'the Nursing Sixth'. For some, it was the fulfilment of a childhood dream: 'I wanted to be a nurse from when I was six and went to see a film about student nurses in a children's hospital,' said Pamela Jubb, born in 1948 and educated at Bradford Grammar. 'It didn't occur to me that I could be a doctor. The only person at my school who did become a doctor was the GP's daughter.'

For others, it was a compromise to which they were firmly guided by their parents. 'No one in my family had ever done A levels,' said Christine Padgett (the one who went to Buttershaw Comprehensive). 'My father was of the view that you had to go out and earn your living. My mum worked in a mill as a burler and mender, my dad was a police officer in the Bradford City force, and my brother joined the Army and then the police force.' Nursing seemed the ideal role for the daughter of this civic-duty-minded family, and Christine found herself on the Bolton Royd pre-nursing training course before becoming a pre-trainee at Bradford Royal Infirmary.

'My grandmother had brainwashed me into being a nurse,' said Liz Pierssene (born in 1936). Grandmotherly brainwashing was fairly common: a nurse's uniform for your seventh birthday, perhaps, followed by a drip-drip-drip of information about the joys of bandaging and the sweet satisfaction of making other people comfortable.

As with the abbreviations 'GCE' and 'CSE', which were redolent of high attainment and less high attainment in a girl's schooling, staining the lower-attainers for life, there were the two sets of contrasting nursing initials: 'SRN' and 'SEN', state-registered, and the lower rung of state-enrolled. State-enrolled required no O levels and just two years of training rather than three years, and was known as the more 'practical' wing of nursing, although the SRN type was pretty practical too. There were no state-registered nurses of colour at Leeds General Infirmary during Gail Nicolaidis's time there in 1964. 'If you were a person of colour you could do the "enrolled nursing", she told me. 'One of the girls I was at school with was Jamaican – we were exact equals in our qualifications, but Matron wouldn't have her. So she went to Bradford Royal instead. Bradford did accept nurses of colour.'

A nurse because her parents told her to be one, Allison Willatts had managed to cobble together a decent education, in spite of the fact that a teacher at Tudor Hall fell over and broke her leg at the tea after the Confirmation service, and 'it became clear she wasn't drinking tea at the time'. The achievement enabled her to train as a nurse at St Thomas's Hospital in London, after a year of being sent to live with an aunt and help with her six children, and another year of being an au pair in Flanders. 'You did what your parents told you to in those days,' Alison said. She would have preferred to fail those A levels, retake them at a sixth-form college and go to university to do social sciences, but she didn't quite succeed in failing them.

The nursing interview was always a frightening start.

'Whereabouts in the family do you come?' the Matron at Great Ormond Street asked Rosie Crichton, who, a glutton for punishment, had decided to train to be a nurse in the mid-1970s after her secretarial training at the Ox & Cow.

'I'm the third daughter down,' she replied.

'Ah – Daddy's little darling.'

She did not get the job from that sarcastic matron; but she did get into Westminster Hospital, which was 'quite a coup'. (Being accepted for training as a nurse at a London hospital had a similar cachet to being accepted as a secretary at the Foreign Office or House of Commons.)

As with mothers accompanying their fourteen-year-old daughters to factory interviews, parents often accompanied their (older but still teenaged) daughters to hospitals for nursing interviews and were interviewed themselves: sized up by the Matron who, by cross-examining the parent, gleaned a great deal about the daughter's upbringing, social status and possible inherited temperament. It certainly helped Alison Willatts's cause that her father was a surgeon in the Royal Navy and said his best nurses came from St Thomas's. Alison's mother gushingly relayed this information to the Matron, who lapped it up and took Alison on.

'Do you approve of your daughter leaving home?' the Matron at Jersey General asked Judy Spooner's mother, who was interviewed after Judy. 'Do you realise that the hospital will from now on be responsible for her moral welfare?'

'My mother had to give her written permission for me to work there,' said Judy. She did give it; and Judy started her training three months after her eighteenth birthday.

'I can see the Matron now,' said Gill Robertson, who, aged seventeen, travelled down from Nottinghamshire by train with her father to be interviewed at Guy's Hospital in 1953. 'She was called Jean Addison. She sat behind the desk in her navy dress, white collar and lovely cap: a pink and white English rose, hands beautifully manicured. She interviewed my father after me, and I was accepted.'

'Could you have been a doctor instead?' I asked her.

'About three girls in my year at the Lilley & Stone Foundation High School in Newark went on to do medicine,' she said, 'but 'I didn't aspire intellectually to that.' To get two A levels and thus be accepted into a London hospital was accolade enough.

'You're late, nurse!' were the first words barked to Gill by Sister Janet, the senior tutor, as she arrived, with her father, to start at the Preliminary Training School in a country mansion near Redhill called Holmesdale, on the dot of 2.30 p.m. The arrival window was between twelve and four. 'You'll be shown where to go, your father will be shown where you will be sleeping, and then he must go.'

It was just like the beginning of a black-and-white film set in a convent. Quaking, the new girls found their uniforms laid out on their beds. The first thing they had to do, with sweating hands, was learn how to assemble and put on their cap. 'A piece of linen with a starched cuff. Thread the cotton through a groove and pull it up to make exactly ten pleats. Pin the cap on with white hair grips.'

It was a bracing start, and Gill is still best friends with one of the four girls in her dorm, the fear having bonded them for life. The next lessons were bed-making, bed-bathing, and bandaging in herringbone formation with the overlapping segments exactly equal.

Holmesdale Preliminary Training School. Gill Robertson arrived in the middle of the 'arrival window', in September 1955, to be told, 'You're late, nurse!'

This was a world in which both cleanliness and tidiness were next to godliness. The first thing Alison Willatts had to do in her whole existence as a probationer nurse in 1967 was to wash the leaves of the rubber plant in the lobby of St Thomas's where the lifts were. 'We did an awful lot of cleaning,' she told me. 'Bed wheels, bed frames, pot plants ... we were all so terrified, we didn't make a fuss. It was nice to be given something specific to do that we wouldn't get wrong.' 'In the afternoons,' said Christina Ward, 'we cleaned all the lockers, while the patients dozed off to sleep with their pipes still going.' 'As a pre-trainee,' said Christine Padgett, 'I spent a lot of time polishing the stainless-steel bedpans.'

You can understand the obsession with cleanliness, although cleaning rubber-plant leaves, bed wheels and lockers seemed out of the expected remit of the caring nurse, and the tobacco smoke rather undermined the cleanliness drive; but why the obsession with tidiness? Why the absolute necessity not to be wearing a cardigan when you tried to resuscitate someone? Why the sarcasm when you broke a rule about personal appearance? 'I had a little curl coming out from under my cap,' recalled Christine, 'and Sister said, "Who do you think you are? Veronica Lake?"' The more I heard about the obsession with tidiness – for example, the way patients had to be propped upright in identical formation for Matron's ward round – the more I worried about tidiness's belittling centrality in so many of these institutions where young women were the underlings.

Poor ill patients: they probably just wanted to doze the morning away. But no. 'The Matron at the Bradford Royal, Miss Elizabeth Percy, was an absolute power,' recalled Patricia Heath, who was there in the late 1960s. 'She wore a green uniform dress with a blob of knitting on her head. She'd been trained in London during the war.' (Patricia added those details, London and war, as if to account for Miss Percy's extra level of iron-toughness.) 'She did a ward round every day. The patients were not allowed to be lying in their beds. They had to be sitting bolt upright in bed or in their chair. This was purely for tidiness purposes.' In order to remain upright in bed, a patient, whose urge was always to sink slowly downwards, needed to be almost trussed into the sheets, propped up so hard against the pillows and tucked in so rigidly that there was no possibility of slippage. Grimacing, pale, pinned into their upright positions, the patients were at least allowed to smoke – as were the nurses in their smoking lounge, but they had to take their apron off before they left the ward.

Patricia Heath (middle of second row) next to her friend Christine Padgett, 1974, just before they got their nursing exam results

Perhaps this regime of 'at least make it look as if you're not too ill' did have the desired effect of making patients feel less ill. I'm not sure, though, because former nurses have told me that patients used to spend much longer in hospital in those days than they do today. Nurses really got to know patients during their long stays. Every morning at 10 a.m. Patricia Heath took round the ward on a tray the mugs of coffee she'd made in the ward kitchen: 'coffee ground into a stockinette [which acted as a filter] and heaped into hot milk.' That was a good moment for a chat. 'We were with the patients, talking to them,' said Alison Willatts of Westminster Hospital. 'That's what's missing now. We knew who they were.'

There could be strange lapses in the cleanliness obsession. 'Speed up! You don't need hot water! Wash your hands in cold water! It'll work just the same!' said the Sister to Christina Ward, after she'd done a really pleasing bandage to an amputee, 'giving a good shape to the stump,' which she found a very satisfying task. 'And actually, cold water did work,' Christina admitted.

What was drilled into me while talking to these women was how they learned mainly on the job, rather than in the classroom as today's nurses do. Christina was left in charge for half an hour on her own, on her very first night in the ward at Leeds General Infirmary, and 'a patient was going berserk, shouting about there being birds on his bed, ducks and hens. It was the longest half-hour of my life. The Sister came back and said, "Oh, he's on DF118. They hallucinate on that." No book would have prepared me for that.'

Nor could a textbook really prepare you for seeing patients die. 'On my first ever day in the ward at Bradford Royal Infirmary,' said Christine Padgett, 'aged seventeen, I had to sit all day with a little girl who was dying. You didn't have anyone you could talk to about the trauma at the time. Two years ago I went to counselling as I was haunted by traumatic events like that, from my nursing days.' Rosie Crichton recalled a similarly haunting moment from the 1970s. 'I was on a cardiac-bypass ward and a chap of thirty-five was there – a very difficult man, always complaining. He died on my night shift. I was only twenty-one. A senior nurse from a different culture laid him out in a different way from the way I'd been trained to: she packed all his orifices with cotton wool. He looked so macabre and it really haunted me. I went home and burst into tears.'

Traumatic event number two was when Rosie was on night duty, doing overnight observations on a 'very large gentleman. Everything was done in the half-light. Towards dawn, he had a cardiac arrest. The other nurse and I tried to resuscitate him. We had one main night matron to contact when we couldn't cope. We kept trying to contact her, but she never came. We later realised that it was because the man was "of no fixed abode". She never came up. He died.'

So some patients were more equal than others in the NHS of those days.

Necks red from their collars starched as stiff as cardboard digging into them, feet aching from walking eight miles per day in their clumpy shoes (no plimsoll-style ones permitted, and they measured the distances with pedometers; but at least floors were mostly wooden in those days; concrete floors were worse for feet – as nurses noticed when the new tower-block wings started being built in the 1960s), boiling hot from the layers of obligatory clothing, fingers aching from removing and replacing every wired-in button each time their uniform went to the laundry, nurses got used to being walking bundles of discomfort.

Life was physically exhausting, as well as taxing on the knees. 'If we started our shift at 7.30 a.m.,' said Gail Nicolaidis, 'the first thing we did was get down on our knees round the dining table in the middle of the ward, and Sister would lead the prayers.' It wasn't the praying that gave them bad knees and bad backs for life, though; it was the turning. 'A lot of us former nurses have had knee and hip replacements,' said Christine Padgett. 'I don't think there's a single one of us that hasn't had a back injury,' said Alison Willatts. You can see why. There were no hoists or slide sheets to help them with the lifting and rolling over of patients. 'Two nurses stood opposite each other. One side pulled and the other pushed.' Every patient, whether skeletal or vast, had to be turned like this every two hours. 'If we mentioned to Sister that we had a back ache, she just told us we'd "lifted incorrectly".'

And what if you asked for a day off on a non-prescribed date? This was frowned upon, and was more visibly disapproved of if you were asking for a weekend off to get married. Alison Willatts's friend asked the ward sister if she could have a weekend off for her wedding, and was told she could have a half-day. 'So she left.'

'I was twenty-one when I got married in 1973,' said Christine Padgett, 'and the wedding was a week after my State [SRN] finals.' She was allowed to go to her own wedding, but asking for permission was not a pleasant experience. 'I asked Matron whether I could have a day off to get married. If you weren't qualified – and I hadn't got my results yet – she could say "no". Her first question to me was "Are you pregnant, nurse?"' Again, the rasping voice. The three 'super-strict' matrons at the hospital were unmarried, and saw no reason why their younglings should be allowed time off for an act of self-indulgence that would turn them from a Miss to a Mrs. There seemed to be a lingering air of bitterness among these older-generation unmarried ladies at the idea that the younger generation were having too much fun.

*

It was just as bad for young women training to be doctors. We last met Mary Piper in Chapter 2 – the girl who, determined to train to be a doctor, went back to school to improve on her A level B, D and E and eventually got in to the Royal Free Hospital. This was in 1966. Triumphantly, she had overcome the convention at Beckenham Grammar School in those days, that there were three suitable careers for the girls to go on to: nurse, teacher or secretary.

But, and you might have guessed it, even in the medical school, a rung above the nursing one, she found herself in an institution of abject fear run by formidable women. 'On my third day,' she told me, 'I did literally think, "What on earth am I doing here?" I mean, I'd been wanting to do this all my life, and it was insane.'

The Long Room in the Royal Free Medical School was 200 feet in length: a vast, echoing space smelling of formaldehyde. Lined up along both sides were cadavers on metal tables that the new students had to dissect. 'Four students to each body, two on each side. I was next to Sarah – perfect, confident, neat and tidy, and she had a boyfriend, while I just suffered from constant anxiety. We had to dissect the arm, and then draw it. Of course, my partner could do it all perfectly.'

'Do preserve the nerves and *don't* cut through them,' rasped the Professor of Anatomy, an austere woman, recalled Mary, 'with no sense of humour, just icy imperiousness.' The Royal Free used to be the London Medical School for Women and, even though it was now 50-50 men and women students, it retained the hard-edged-ness of the heroines who had fought to be doctors before the First World War.

Was it exciting, I asked Mary, when she started clinical work on the wards? 'Exciting? There was nothing exciting about it at all. It was terrifying. Every afternoon you'd be taught by the same person. It was just my luck to get the Dean.

She wore a tweed suit with a white blouse and a brooch. No make-up. I was taught by her all afternoon, every day for six weeks. One day she taught us how to use an ophthalmoscope. We were split up into pairs but there was an odd number and I hadn't paired up. "Girl!" she said. "You and I do it together." As I was looking into her eye with the ophthalmoscope – terrified – she said, "This is as close as you're ever going to get to a Dean."'

Mary worked her way up and eventually found an area of medicine that she loved and that suited her: being a geriatrician. 'But,' she said, 'I spent my whole career avoiding any formidable women who loomed into my reach. No man has ever scared me that much.'

PART III

THE TOE IN THE DOOR

8

How You Got Jobs (or Didn't)

'I'll take your brother if you take my sister'

Sarah Burns's brother to the managing director
of *Private Eye*, 1970

Sarah Burns's brother had fagged at Harrow for Andrew
Osmond, the original 'Lord Gnome', who in 1970 was the
managing director of *Private Eye*. One day in that year,
Sarah's brother offered to take Osmond's brother with him on
an archaeological dig in Crete if Osmond agreed to take Sarah
on as an assistant in the *Private Eye* offices. It was the way
such deals were done: young man helping his old fag-master's
brother in exchange for old fag-master helping his ex-fag's
sister in need of a job.

'It was pure nepotism,' admits Sarah, who had a great time
working at *Private Eye* with all the people who shaped the
magazine – 'Richard Ingrams, John Wells, Peter Cook, etc.'
She drove into Soho, parked her car outside the office in Greek
Street (unthinkable in today's world of gridlock, congestion
charge, parking fees and lack of spaces), worked from ten to

three thirty, and had every other Friday off. Three years later, she married into the Foreign Office, went to Romania, came back again three years after that, and went back to *Private Eye*, into the door of which she had already firmly got her toe.

The question was, and remains to this day, how did you get your toe into the door of the thing you really wanted to do? It puzzled and floored me when I set out with my English degree in 1984 and failed to get a job as a secretary at Faber & Faber, having answered an advertisement in the Creative and Media section of the *Guardian*. 'If it's any consolation,' Rosemary Goad's rejection letter said, 'you were second on the shortlist.' It wasn't much of a consolation for someone who dreamed of working in a publishing office (an imagined book-lined paradise where I would fall in love with an editor in a mothy V-neck), and was made more painful by imagining that letter being typed by the secretary who had got the job, or someone like her.

From what I could gather, chatting to people about how they did or didn't get their first jobs during the period of this book, there was a moment in about 1976 when the glut dried up. Everyone was now one of five thousand people applying for anything, and if you applied to hundreds of advertisements you'd be lucky to get a single interview. It was a sudden population explosion of aspiring young women who no longer saw marriage as their sole destiny – a great leap for society as a whole, but not much fun to be stuck in as tiny fish in this enormous shoal, especially after hearing how one's parents had walked into their jobs half-asleep and tossed them aside so disdainfully. 'I applied to 250 jobs after leaving UEA and coming home to Birmingham in 1976,' said Noelle Walsh, who would later become the editor of *Good Housekeeping*. 'I got one interview, and the guy said I could have the job if I slept with him. Instead of hitting him, or phoning his boss to complain, I just said, "Oh – oh no – I'm not doing that" – and left.'

The country was now bursting with female graduates desperate to get onto a rung of the ladder, lured by tales of how you could 'work your way up' from being a secretary or from working in a bookshop to commissioning and editing actual writing from Britain's great authors, but you must, simply must, get your toe in the door first.

Perhaps there were and have always been two parallel channels for trying to get jobs: the official one (scour advertisements, apply for everything, hear nothing, feel miserable, eventually get an interview, get called in for round two, get rejected), and the unofficial but far more effective channel: know someone who knows someone, and you're straight in – but NB, try never to say yes to getting-your-toe-in-the-door sex.

The exploiting of connections was brazen and unhidden. 'I worked for a Dorset MP who was a friend of my parents,' said Amanda Graham (born in 1959) – 'Jim Spicer – Sir James. Quite a lot of us girls from Dorset went to work for him in the House of Commons, and he was very patient and long-suffering.' (Actually, the expression Amanda used was 'Quite a lot of us useless girls went to work for him.' It was the typical self-deprecation of her generation educated far beneath their ability and drip-fed with a sense of their own lack of usefulness.) 'My mother said, "Jim, please could Amanda come and work for you?" I worked there for six months.'

'I got a job as a teacher at Downe House,' said Augusta Miller (born in 1936), 'because my references were Lord Norton and Sir Eric Seal.'

'My father said to the couturier Victor Stiebel, "I want a job for my daughter,"' said Jenny Boltwood (the one who would soon marry the much-older Swedish doctor her parents spotted on the beach in Majorca). 'My father had worked in the fashion world as the general manager of C&A Modes in Marble Arch, so he knew the people in the business.' Jenny worked at Stiebel as a junior vendeuse, sitting in one of the four corners of the salon with her senior vendeuse, Miss Joy.

And, in my ongoing enquiries to find out more about Jackie Laing, the woman in charge of the girls at Christie's, who'd promised me a turkey at Christmas, I found out that she was an old school friend of the managing director's wife. Of course she was.

I don't think it happens much nowadays, that when you happen to meet someone they happen to offer you a real, actual job, rather than its far weaker cousin, 'a week's work experience', but it did then. A tap on the shoulder in church; sitting next to someone on a bus; chatting to a dog walker in Hyde Park; I heard many stories of this kind of serendipitous meeting that led to full employment, from the 1950s to the 1970s, and was reminded of what it felt like to be thrown out of the meritocratic educational system into the chance-led adult world. 'Happenstance' was a word I heard spoken often, by older women who still used that old-fashioned word. 'All my jobs have come to me through happenstance,' said Ann Makower (born in 1934), who after Trinity College, Dublin, worked as a Cook's Girl in Italy in the 1950s, helping bewildered English tourists to have a slightly less bewildering time in the country of 'greasy' (as they called it) Italian food. Most things happened to her, she told me, by people saying, 'Oh, there's a job going where I work.' The girls who worked as secretaries at Spencer Stuart's very jolly management consultancy firm in Mayfair in the 1970s were given £100 if they introduced another friend of theirs who then got a job there. It was a word-of-mouth world.

The parish church seemed to play a large part in the nudging of young women towards the workplace. We've already seen Elspeth Allison who, having learned invalid cookery, was sent off to work as an au pair to the vicar's grandchildren, and Mary Piper who was given an introduction to a doctor at Guy's Hospital by her local vicar. Agneta Hinkley told me she went to work as a junior matron at Highfield School in 1946, her first job, thanks to the fact that the vicar's wife told her mother that her son had gone to school there. 'That job really put me on my feet,' said Agneta, after the 'quiet nervous breakdown' of her teens.

'I was in church with my parents,' said Gill Blenkinsop (born in 1944), 'and I was tapped on the shoulder by one of my parents' friends – he was the organist.'

Here we go again: a pivotal conversation about to take place in a church pew.

'The organist said, "You're a mathematician, aren't you? I work in ICI Dulux Paints and I can't add up. I need a mathematician for six months." He and I had a gin and tonic later that same day, and I had a job as a temporary clinical assistant – and I stayed at ICI for twenty-nine years. Personnel had no say in it at all.'

This was in 1968: the days when it was possible to bypass the scrutiny of 'Personnel', and go straight into a job thanks to a chance encounter in a church. Gill had read statistics at UCL. She described to me the university's 'vast computer, which took up two floors of a house in Bloomsbury. It was so huge that it had a name [Atlas], and was male [referred to as "he, him"].' To avoid having to go straight into becoming a systems analyst after university, which sounded a bit dismal, Gill accepted two jobs in that field but asked to defer. Off she went to do VSO (Voluntary Service Overseas) for a year, teaching English in Borneo, and then she drove back overland to England with six friends in two Land Rovers, taking six months over it – and ended up in church with her parents, which was how so many such adventures did end. It all came good. She'd gone right off the idea of being a systems analyst by then. The organist snapped her up to work in the Sales Department at ICI Dulux Paints in Slough.

Once you did get your toe in a door for six months, and proved yourself, you were usually kept on, if you asked to be. 'I wanted to stay on, so I went to the big boss and asked him whether I could be a sales rep. "Oh I'm terribly sorry, we don't have women in the sales force. But go to the marketing department – they do have women." So I did.'

The same happened to me at *Harpers & Queen* in 1985, where I got a six-month subediting job thanks to a kind friend, Isabella Palmer, suggesting I write to her friend Anthony Gardner who worked there as a subeditor, and thanks to one of the subs, Markie Robson-Scott, being away for six months' maternity leave. When the six life-changingly blissful months were almost up, my father said I *must* write a letter to the editor Willie Landels with the opening sentence, 'The time has come for us to talk about my future.' So I did, and the editor kept me on.

Life was still that good for some in 1985 – or that bad, for the ones who didn't know anyone who knew anyone. My toe was permitted to remain inside the door thanks to an editor's kindness and a firm's capacity in the mid-1980s boom to absorb one more employee.

The beneficiaries of nepotism were doubly lucky: not only were they handed a start in working life, but they found themselves in a world populated by their social and intellectual peers, where they instantly felt at home. That could feel extremely comfortable, even if some found the cosiness a bit stifling and felt a twinge of guilt about the word-of-mouth system that had so favoured them. For outsiders, it was a rankly unfair system that either excluded young women completely or made it much harder to get started.

The system was explained in all its cruelty to comprehensive-educated Helen Shay from Leeds, who went on to Manchester University in the mid-1970s to read English. 'At school we were sent to a careers officer. I told him I wanted to be a lawyer and he said, "Oh, for that, you'll need an uncle who's got a firm, who'll give you a job at the end of it." Well, I thought, OK, I can't be a lawyer in that case.' She went to a careers fair in the same year, 1973, and expressed her interest in being a lawyer to a solicitor at one of the stands, 'who gave me a bland, patronising smile, said nothing, and pointed vaguely to a leaflet, as if to say, "not with your accent". If I'd come from fee-paying Bradford Grammar, he would have been all over me.'

'Not with your accent.' A regional accent was a real hindrance. Employees at top firms wanted their executives to speak like people spoke on the BBC. Up till the middle period of this book, that meant no regional accents at all; then, very gradually, and broadly following BBC trends, a 'nicely tuned' Edinburgh accent was allowed, and then some of the more sparky northern accents; but things took a long time to change, and even now, having a Birmingham or a West Country accent can hinder you – as indeed (now) can having too plummy an accent.

Helen, who'd been dismissed in that way at the careers fair, told me that the pressure on bright girls like her was to become a teacher and go to one of the teacher training colleges that every town had. But many girls were heartily sick of school by then and had no intention of spending their working lives in one. Helen was determined to be a lawyer, and her mother went back to work to put her through law college: it was expensive, as there was no longer a grant for a law degree, and the Law Society had recently doubled the cost. So off Helen's mother went to 'an old mill on its last legs', a curtain factory where the workers were fighting for what little work there was, and her mother was 'up against competitive younger girls saving up for cars'. But she did earn the money through dogged piecework, and Helen thus could go to law college in Chester, and then she lodged in St John's Wood in London in the house of the grandmother of an aristocratic friend she'd made on the course. 'My friend could have her pick of the jobs. I had to apply for an awful lot before I got one.'

The door through which she eventually did get her toe in was that of a law firm in Huddersfield. 'I was their first-ever articled clerk, and I was the talk of the Huddersfield legal circle. The Sex Discrimination Act had just come in, in 1975, and they made me the offer as I think they were feeling a bit conspicuous about not yet having any female lawyers.'

The people who resented her presence were not the other lawyers or the clients but 'the secretaries from my back-ground'. They thought it hoity-toity of Helen to be going to meetings with partners while they were just sitting at their typewriters being secretaries. 'They would put telephone calls through to me, but they would just give me a line and I had to do all the plugs myself.'

Helen's urge to rise above what was expected of her had been passed down from her grandmother, Elsie Ward, born in 1899, who was put into domestic service aged fourteen, ran away, and went to work in a mill, mending the faults in men's suit cloth. 'I'm so proud of her,' said Helen. It was a slow process of self-betterment from generation to generation, leading to the liberating moment in 1982 when Helen, now a lawyer, got her own mortgage for a house of her own, the freedom for women to get mortgages in their own right having started only in the mid-1970s.

Helen Shay, on her graduation day in Manchester, 1978; and her grandmother Elsie Ward, who'd had no such opportunity, having had to go into domestic service aged fourteen

Likewise Mary Bennett, super-nanny, born in 1939, wanted to be a nanny and *not* a nurse. She had to fight for it. The careers officer in Torquay who came to her grammar school, just before Mary left aged sixteen, dismissed her career suggestion: 'Nobody has nannies these days.' 'So I didn't go home,' said Mary, 'I got straight onto a bus, went into town, bought *The Lady*, and saw so many advertisements for nannies, and that made my mind up.' It was a typical example of careers advice being plain wrong and out of touch. Meanwhile the careers officer had put her down as a nurse and had made an appointment for her to go along to the local children's ward. 'I went along – but I didn't want to look after poorly children, did I? Why would I?'

It simply wasn't her vocation to nurse ill children in hospitals, and she knew it. 'The district nurse in our village said to my mother that her brother was a housemaster at Marlborough and they were looking for a nursery-maid.' This was in 1955. Mary got her toe in the door of a lifetime of fulfilled nannyhood by going to work as under-nanny in that household of five children and a sixth one on the way. 'I wore my school dress,' she told me. 'I was paid £1 6s 9d a week, and my mother gave me a Post Office Savings book, as I didn't have a bank account.' From that job she graduated to being a proper nanny for various grand families, wearing a stripy dress with a white collar, from the uniform department at Harrods.

Labour exchanges were jobs cornucopias. The one on the Fulham Road in London was 'a big Victorian building that looked like a workhouse,' said Janet Garner (born in 1946; the one whose mother had said 'you're not clever enough' when Janet had mentioned anything she might want to do in adult life). She went there aged fifteen to be greeted by a woman flicking through 'long, narrow boxes full of files, and saying, "D'you fancy this, d'you fancy that – do you fancy Woolworths?"' A job was going in the head office of Woolworths on Kensington High Street, and Janet got it. Her daily task was to check whether employees who had been caught stealing were trying to work in another branch of the store under a different name, date of birth or National Insurance number. 'I spent hours and hours going through every name, checking their cards. Lots of times we did catch them.' The two women presiding over this little-known department of the Woolworths head office were Miss Judd and her underling, 'two single women in their forties, like dragons, immaculately dressed. They were so strict. We weren't allowed to talk while we worked. I got told off for having a hole in my cardigan.'

But she had a job, and was allowed to keep her weekly wage of £6 at the end of her first week, although 'after that, most of it went to Mum'. She carried on working there 'till I stupidly got married aged nineteen', having met a man in a coffee bar.

I was impressed by the young women who took one look at a job, or at a whole working world, and fled. Angela Tilby, Anglican priest and Canon Emeritus of Christ Church, Oxford, got a first in theology at Girton in 1972 and was told by the Ely Professor of Divinity, 'Although you got a first, Miss Tilby, it was not what I would call a distinguished first.' She passed the Civil Service exam and was invited for an interview at the Department of Agriculture and Fisheries. On the way up in the lift, the man standing next to her said to her, 'You're the first person I've seen smile in this place for twenty-five years.'

'I was offered the job,' Angela told me. 'But after that trip up in the lift, I knew I couldn't take it.'

Mary Villiers, fresh from Miss Judson's secretarial college, was invited to 10 Downing Street in 1954, thanks to Miss Judson's elevated connections, to do a quick typing and shorthand test before being offered a job there. 'I was shown round and saw all these young women cooped up like battery hens,' said Mary, 'tapping away. It was all so horrible that I failed the test deliberately. Miss Judson was absolutely incensed. "You've spoiled my reputation," she barked at me. Miss Judson's was a very snobbish outfit.'

What happened if you did dare to have a go at 'the milk round', as Sarah MacAulay, mentioned at the end of Chapter 2, did, thereby risking (a) not succeeding in getting a milk-round job even though you had tried and (b) doing badly in your university finals precisely because you'd spent too much time applying for jobs and going for interviews? It was indeed a risk to put yourself forward for the Real World in that way, from the weak position of female undergraduate-hood in the 1970s and '80s.

The forms you had to fill in for each of the merchant banks asked, 'Whom do you know at . . .' whichever bank you were applying to. 'The answer for me was "no one",' said Sarah. 'But reading history turned out to have been good for developing my skills at processing vast amounts of information, prioritising themes, formulating a strategy and trying to predict the future from the past.'

It was a gruelling process. There were three rounds of interviews for each of the fifteen banks she applied to: the first and second rounds in Cambridge, and the third in London, if you got that far. Nervously, Sarah travelled to London on the train to Samuel Montagu (this was in the spring of 1984). 'The first question the interviewer asked me was, "Did you read the *FT* this morning?" I admitted I hadn't actually read it. "I'm glad you said that," the interviewer said, "because they didn't publish it this morning."'

After the rounds of interviews, Sarah was offered three jobs out of the fifteen she applied for. That was a considerable achievement, considering that Kleinwort Benson (the bank at which she accepted the offer) had eight hundred applicants that year for ten posts.

It demonstrates the categorisation of young women by their education that Bee Bealey, a young woman of high intelligence, found herself – thanks to her low-aspiring schooling at her non-ambitious boarding school, followed by the semi-useless secretarial course at Mrs Thomsett's – pushing a tea trolley with an urn on it round Salomon's bank in about that same year. Tea lady and merchant banker: so near to each other in social class and in what their prospects might have been in infancy, yet now so far removed. 'The agency Kelly Girl found me that tea-lady job,' she told me. 'My boss was a lovely old Cockney lady with gout. She was always hovering with the trolley in a doorway, and taught me how to do it. On day one I wore my high-heeled Russell & Bromley shoes with gold chains, but no one wanted my tea. That's why my boss gave me a wrap-around pinny, just like she wore, and then they all flocked to me.' Clearly, bosses liked their tea-ladies to look like tea-ladies. Around that tea urn in the doorway, the employees from their various strata of social class and aspiration all congregated, having got their toes in at very different levels of pay.

Maggie Fergusson, as an Oxford undergraduate a few years later in 1986, knew she couldn't just hide away in the library and hope to 'get into publishing' after graduating, as she was going to need to make her own living and was switched on enough to realise that a job in publishing simply wouldn't pay the rent. Girls like her were the brave ones who dared to apply for 'milk round' jobs and dared to risk failing.

The one good thing about the milk round, she told me, was that applying was made straightforward: the merchant bankers came to Oxford to give their presentations. 'There was one from Goldman Sachs who looked like a god – a tall, blond, shining man.' As far removed as could be imagined from milkmen in their looks and gait, these job-delivery men 'gave out a strong message that the City was "booming" and that they would be able to take masses of new recruits.' I'm not sure that was truly the case, judging by Sarah MacAulay's stark Kleinwort Benson statistics, but it certainly inspired people like Maggie to have a go at applying.

The second time the bankers visited Oxford, this time to conduct the interviews, they set themselves up for a week, bizarrely, in twin-bedded rooms all over the Randolph Hotel. 'You and the interviewer sat opposite one another on the twin candlewick bedspreads,' said Maggie, 'your knees almost knocking against each other. If they'd had their heads half screwed on they would have realised I was not the right person to go into that world.' (Maggie was reading English and is now the literary editor of *The Tablet*. This is much more her natural environment.) 'There was no pressing or probing. They were all fascinated by my having been at Eton.' (She was one of a small number of girls who were educated there in the sixth form.)

When the day came for the interview with Mercury Asset Management, the investment arm of Warburgs in London, Maggie travelled up by train, having been told that the only job-specific question the chief man Stephen Zimmerman would ask was 'What dictates share prices?' To which the correct reply was 'Supply and demand.' She had it pat. 'But once again, they all asked me about Eton.' Were they captivated by the sense that she was, in a way, one of the boys? She got the job, with its salary of £12,000, which seemed like a fortune.

9

Life as a Secretary

'Elizabeth Thompson is very much enjoying
her interesting secretarial work at
Brompton Hospital'

'News of Old Girls', Lawnside school
magazine, 1974

In the great hierarchy of secretarial roles, starting from 'high powered' at the top and going downwards via 'long-standing', 'trusty', 'glorified', 'mousy' and 'new', the temporary secretary, or 'temp', found herself at the very bottom of the pile.

If, on leaving the secretarial course in those tricky years when getting jobs suddenly became hard, you hadn't managed to get your toe in the door anywhere, you were very likely to start out working as a temp. Temping was one of the loneliest jobs in the world. No one had any reason to be nice to you if you were the temp, or to make any effort to make friends, as you were only there for a week, or sometimes a day, or sometimes just a morning and you were sent somewhere else for the afternoon, drifting about from office to office in a cloud of your own impermanence.

In the early days of word processors and office computers, I was told, life for the temp was particularly tough. Every early word-processor system in every office was different. If you happened not to be 'proficient in WordStar' or whatever version was in use in that week's or day's office, you felt like 'the village idiot'. No one could be bothered to explain to you how their system worked, as you wouldn't be there for long, so you just prodded at various 'F' function keys, nervously and embarrassedly, terrified of deleting vital information. It was a horrible echo of being unpopular or 'sent to Coventry' at school. 'At the end of one of my one-day-long temping jobs,' recalled Caroline Donald, whose temping life in London began in 1984 after she'd left Cambridge with a history degree, 'the secretary who had brought me in was very annoyed that I hadn't paginated a document I'd been typing up, even though I hadn't been asked to and had no idea how to do it on that particular system. Nobody had checked in on me and I'd spent the day being totally ignored. They even passed the biscuits round the typing pool, missing me out, as if I were a ghost at the machine.'

For young women who had been brought up never to get in the way, it came naturally to make themselves invisible, sitting very still at their temporary workstation, drawing no attention to themselves, perhaps discreetly reading a book cradled on their lap until someone asked them to do something. It was normal practice for offices to get a temporary secretary in if anyone was away on holiday, even if there wasn't enough to do. 'At least make it *look* as if you're busy,' a passing man or higher-powered secretary would occasionally hiss. As a temp you felt a strange mixture of invisible and all-too-visible, waiting for the hours to pass.

Either you were given not nearly enough to do, or you were landed with a repetitively tedious task that no one else wanted to do, such as opening mountains of envelopes, or, as happened to Julia Wigan who typed letters for British Rail all day in an office behind Victoria Station, wearing headphones and typing from tapes for hours on end. 'You were allowed to put down every quarter of an hour as work. On the dot of five, I was out.' 'At half the temp jobs I had,' said Penny Sheehan, 'I typed about one letter a day. There wasn't nearly enough to do. I read the newspaper from cover to cover.'

'They treated you as if you were a piece of dust,' said various ex-temporary secretaries I spoke to. 'Impossibly toffee-nosed,' said Mary Villiers, recalling the 1950s architects she was sent to work for from Peter Jones's own agency for temps. One of the architects had such a plummy voice that he pronounced 'towel rail' as 'tollerah' and Mary couldn't make head or tail of his dictation. It does not reflect well on human nature that we're only reliably nice to people in lowlier stations than us when we know we're going to see them again, not bothering to invest our niceness in the passers-through. The only revenge a temp could get in this kind of situation was deliberately to put a grammatical mistake into the letter of a cold and haughty letter-dictator whom she would never have to re-meet.

You can see why, for the instinctively job-commitment-phobic 'floaters-about' of the early years of this book, the temping life was attractive. It could hardly be possible to wear a job more lightly. The temping agency, which you'd come across when passing its friendly notice on the door ('Come in for a cup of tea and a chat!'), sent you off to an address in the morning, and off you went with your *A to Z*, if it was in a city that had an *A to Z*, holding the map-book upside down to find your way there if it was southwards. Once inside the office, where you cared for nobody and nobody cared for you, you could plan your evening and indeed your whole future in the responsibility-free isolation of invisibility in a crowd. 'We did not take our temping jobs at all seriously,' Mary Villiers assured me. 'I recollect that time as one of terrific fun – going to dances after work, and so on. A lot of the fun was centred round the banking hall in Harrods, a good meeting place, where we sat around on the green sofas, gossiping with our friends.' Having been given a nice collection of fishing flies by one of her temporary bosses who was a keen angler, Mary was married by the age of twenty-three to Henry, whom she'd met at a party before a dance.

But, if the temping period was extended from months to years, and if, as happened more in the later years of this book, you really did want to 'get your toe into' the world of the office you were temping in, and advance in it, this enforced self-effacing existence could lead to a sense of failure and desolation, reinforcing the low self-esteem with which so many girls had been instilled. All too easily the temp assumed the role of phantom, never speaking, just silently making coffee for everyone else and vanishing into the city over lunchtime.

The late-1970s middle-class population explosion of aspirers made it hard even for highly educated graduates to get permanent jobs as secretaries in the 1980s, hence the often long-drawn-out temp existence. And it was the toe-in-the-door theory that made young women with university degrees go down this route. The idea was that if only you could get yourself physically inside the building you wanted to have a career in, this was a start. Once there, surely someone would spot you. You would make an incisive remark and they would realise you knew more about Sir Thomas More or Lloyd George than they did, and you'd soon be saying goodbye to the secretarial life.

When that didn't happen, you could soon be crying at your desk, powerless in your stuckness: tantalisingly close to where you wanted to be, but definitely not there. This happened to an Oxford graduate I spoke to, who, after a year of temping in the early 1980s, found herself holed up in a dead end as a secretary in a publishing house in the mid-1980s, working for the chairman's wife who, in her top role thanks to being the chairman's wife, had landed herself a job as a commissioning editor and 'did not show much talent at it'. 'Why did I even become a secretary?' she asks now. 'It was like putting Plan B before Plan A.'

But this was exactly what so many female graduates did: put Plan B before Plan A. And they found themselves stuck as secretaries in the back office of the art world where they never saw a work of art, or the publishing world where they never edited a sentence or met an author, or the music world where they never heard a live piece of music or met a musician. By the forward-looking 1980s, women were expecting to have at least a decade of working life before the possible interruptions of motherhood, so surely (you might have thought) they might have aimed high from the start. That chooser of 'Plan B' over 'Plan A' did actually apply for one milk-round job, at J. Walter Thompson (the firm into which my mother had breezed thirty years previously), but she got nowhere, as she hadn't done any research on the firm's profile. So she went to London, did the no-frills Pitman's course at Pitman's headquarters, and here she was, taking dictation from the chairman's wife, who was far too busy wildly sending off letters to celebrities asking them to write their memoirs for her, to bother to notice that she had a secretary with editorial talents. This situation was replicated all over Britain.

If, as occasionally happened, there was a single high-up person who did have a gift for nurturing the talents of younger women, upward movement for a secretary could take place. This was the tantalising thing that kept women having a go. In *British Summer Time Begins*, I mentioned the porousness that existed between the indoor and the outdoor worlds, in the days when front doors and back doors were left open all day and children rushed from house through garden and into meadow beyond. In the world of work, particularly in the more chaotic, eccentric, smaller and more personal offices without a stringent Personnel department keeping an eye on job descriptions, there could also be that porousness, and the luckier young women in this book were the beneficiaries of it. They did float up between translucent layers of job titles until, by some miracle, they found themselves producing television programmes, editing and commissioning books, or actually being lawyers.

For them, the secretarial existence that came first was invaluable training. 'You worked closely with the person at the highest level,' said Rosie de Courcy, who started as a secretary at Sphere Books in 1973 after leaving Cambridge with her English degree. 'You took dictation, so you heard from the horse's mouth how to express yourself. I was being dictated to by someone very, very clever: long editorial letters about shaping plots and characters. It was a privilege.' And she was spotted: 'My boss was fired and said, "I'm going to start a new firm. We want you to come, but not on any account as my secretary, as you're without doubt the worst secretary I've ever had." That's when it all began. I became a dogsbody editorial person, reading for dear life.'

Rosie de Courcy in 1973, just when she'd become a secretary at Sphere Books ... and in the late 1970s, when she was an editor

'Dogsbody editorial person' was in another league entirely from 'secretary'. The word 'editorial' had a thrilling glamour about it, even if it was paired up with 'dogsbody'. You were on the way up. And Rosie had managed it partly by being bad at being a secretary. It was self-defeating if you were too good at the lowly role. You'd get stuck in it.

The porousness could go in two directions, on the whims of the people in charge. 'I went up,' Rosie said, 'and a highly competent colleague went down to a more secretarial role and never came up again.' Poor woman! The truly thwarting-for-life injustices of the world of work put the more petty injustices of school life into perspective.

Rosie was clear that as a secretary, she preferred a male boss to a female one. 'A room falling silent when you came into it – a sense that they'd been talking about you behind your back – this is the way with female bosses.' With men, she said, there were two different kinds of bullying: the more blatant, swearing kind from the ones who'd risen through the sales side and worked their way up through the ranks, and the more subtle kind from 'very, very clever editorial men', who bullied by 'favouritising and blanking you'. The outward good manners of the 1950s and '60s had changed by the 1970s to a free-for-all when it came to speaking one's mind. 'There was a lot of shouting, swearing, crying, slamming doors and rushing off to the loo,' Rosie said. 'One woman, who played netball for Surrey, was built like a tank, and clearly didn't know her own strength, managed to knock out our female art director when things got out of hand after the art director hadn't liked the colour printing she'd used on a book cover. She was laid out flat.'

Men threw things. George Weidenfeld threw an inkwell at Mary Burd when she was his secretary in the 1960s. Anthony Eden, tyrannical about letters being flawless, threw an inkpot at Hermione Waterfield when she worked at the Foreign Office. 'I worked for him for a single day and never returned.'

The boss–secretary relationship was one that facilitated tyranny. True job satisfaction and domestic contentment for the most spoilt kind of man would consist of having both his 'nanny' (the older, long-standing secretary in a loose cardigan) and his 'mistress' (the young, sexy one in a tight cardigan whom he could have sexual fantasies about) always by his side in the daytime, and his wife cooking supper and bearing his children at home. So all around him were devoted female acolytes attending to his every need.

And, as Sharon Scard reminded me, secretaries were useful to their bosses not just to do the work but to help them (the bosses) on their way up the career ladder. 'My own boss liked me being a secretary and practically threw his files at me. He was a rugby player, only a couple of years older than me. Having a good secretary was really valuable to help *him* make his way up, because a good secretary has a lot of knowledge and manages the boss's workload.' This was 'secretary as rung of ladder for someone else' rather than 'secretary on rung of ladder for herself.' It was lucky that in the lawyer's office at Manor House in north London where Sharon worked, there happened to be a female partner called Maggie Wakelin-Saint, who herself had become a property lawyer without having been to university, and who spotted Sharon and trained her up: a secretary-to-lawyer porousness unthinkable today, which involved simply learning on the job.

The imperious shouting of female first names resounds through this 1945–1990 office world. 'Penneh!' (That was how the 'ex-Army posh boys' at the advertising agency where Penny Eyles worked in the early 1950s, after the weird time at Mr de la Warr's radionics lab, pronounced her first name when calling it.) 'Penneh! Would you book a table at Rules or Simpsons?' 'Penneh! Gray Dunn [the biscuit company] is coming in for a meeting. We'll need coffee for four, and biscuits: put out their products.' Having done that, Penny then had to go in and serve the coffee. (The ability to do a lightning change from secretary to waitress and back was a vital secretarial skill, often mentioned by my interviewees, some of whom had waitresses' aprons to put on for their bosses' lunches.) After those meetings, Penny had to take dictation of a report on it, and type it out, while her bosses went off for a long lunch, came back at three, and played chess till it was time for them to go home.

The worst thing was that, even as a non-temp, and having

worked for the same men for two years, she proved to be absolutely forgettable. 'I bumped into my former boss a few years later and he didn't have a clue who I was.'

Porousness worked its magic, again: Penny did a few more temporary secretarial jobs after that one and thought, 'there must be more to life than this.' Without that clanger of a realisation, there was no hope of going forward. Her parents' next-door neighbour, who had worked at Bush House during the war, had heard that the BBC was looking for people to work for its new channel, BBC2. Penny applied, and got a job as a producer's assistant. 'There were four of us: the director, his assistant, the other assistant, and little me who did all the secretarial work, typing memos and scripts and so on, but I was also sent out filming and to take notes and check on continuity.' Note, 'was sent': that was the casual imperiousness that allowed a chink of light into the secretarial existence, which itself might, if you were lucky, lead to a quick, quiet floating-upwards between the layers, and suddenly you were in the new land of the no-longer-just-a-secretary. 'Then I was sent up to the top floor of Television Centre to work for a very thin young man who looked about thirteen, with Sellotape round his glasses. He was a director called Ken Loach.' And Penny's career as a script supervisor took off, and she did it for forty years.

Occasionally I heard stories of secretaries who, quite by accident, found themselves briefly in positions of what turned out to be enormous power. Working as a secretary for EMI Records in the late 1970s, Sue Peart and the secretaries who worked with her, Bryony and Sandy, had a song played to them on the record player by their boss Clive Swan, head of the Licensed Repertoire Division. Then he said, 'Girls – would you buy this?' The song was 'Wuthering Heights' by Kate Bush. 'We just said, "Please play it again – and again,"' said

Sue. 'He could see we were instantly addicted. I flatter myself that the decision as to whether to take that song on was partly down to me, Bryony and Sandy.'

The fifteen-year-old commercial-class girls, meanwhile, were experiencing no existential angst about their secretarial or 'shorthand typist' roles. Well trained in secretarial skills from a very early age, they were thrilled to have a job and be instantly good at it. 'I proudly wore my high-heeled court shoes,' said Carole Ellis, who started in the office of Electric Washer Services in Leeds aged fifteen in 1958, 'and my soft-wool sweater was black by the end of the day from the carbon paper.' She clattered away on her Imperial Remington, never forgetting to indent after the 'Dear sir', as taught at school. Two years later, aged seventeen, she went to work for the publicity manager of Star Cinemas, whose offices were above the ice rink, and they all went bowling during the lunch hour. Fifteen-year-old Jean Dace, likewise, happily filled every day taking shorthand, copy typing and filing, first in the City and then at Cope's Pools.

So, there were the frivolous secretaries, for whom the whole thing was a short-lived bore to get through before marriage, and there were the later angst-ridden ones, for whom being a secretary was supposed to be the first rung of a ladder but sometimes they got stuck on it, and there were the vocational secretaries – the commercial-class girls – who were only too delighted to be part of a pool of like-minded typists earning a living straight out of school.

Joan Booth (born in Camberwell in 1932) was of the third sort. On leaving Sydenham Secondary Commercial School for Girls, aged fifteen, she went to the Labour Exchange for Central School Leavers with her mother. (So the Labour Exchange handily had different departments with different filing cabinets of available jobs, depending on which kind of school you'd just left.) In 1947 Joan got a temporary job at Thomas Cook's in the City and was taken on permanently after a month's trial, travelling from her parental home in Catford up to Central London every day through the bombed desolation. She worked in a little typing pool in the Shipping and Forwarding department, so the letters were all about transporting other people's luggage. The men called the 'girls' up to them to take dictation. It was easy to change jobs, Joan told me: shorthand typists were in huge demand, and she promptly left one job because 'they brought in wax recording cylinders, like rolling pins, which the men dictated into, and you put headphones on to listen to them, and there was one chap who coughed into his and all I could hear was his phlegmy coughing going straight into my ears – horrible.' Two jobs later, at a merchant company in Mincing Lane, she found herself working just for one man. 'So I'd stepped up from shorthand typist to secretary.' Progress was that smooth. Although she was wearing each job quite lightly, she was wearing the whole secretarial existence with pride.

Those fifteen-year-old school-leaver secretaries really could justifiably be called 'girls'. But for others it was a belittling noun. There was a secretarial agency slogan on the side of London buses in the 1950s: 'For Top Men, Top Girls.' The imbalance of the nouns was already starting to grate on London's working women, who mentally changed the wording to 'For Top Boys, Top Women'. As they knew, men were often far more boyish, with their lunchtime drinking and their playing office cricket with a ruler and a ball of scrunched-up paper, than the women they referred to as 'girls' were girlish. But for years, the slight harem overtones of the typing pool lingered, and if you were in one, you were still called one of the 'girls'.

Young women who associated being a secretary with the (to them) demeaning posture of taking dictation at knee level to a man, into a reporter's notebook with an elastic band to hold it open, and who did not want to be branded with the job title 'secretary', tended to use the expression 'I work for' instead. 'I work for George Weidenfeld,' Mary Burd learned to say at Weidenfeld's dinner parties in Eaton Square, to which she was sometimes invited after her busy day, which began with him dictating to her at lightning speed – seventeen letters in twenty minutes over breakfast. 'If I said "I'm George's secretary", the person I was sitting next to would turn away from me and talk to the person on the other side.'

I remember at Christie's in the early 1980s, when a male employee first encountered a female one, for example in the main hall or on the staff staircase, the question he euphemistically asked was 'Who do you work for?' It was expected that as a young woman you must be the secretary to someone, but 'work for' was the more tactful way of putting it.

'Work for' was also a nicely blurring way of expressing the fact that in many cases a secretarial job entailed making life easier for your boss in every aspect of his life: not just in typing his letters and organising his work meetings, but in more domestic tasks such as taking his shoes to the cobbler's and his shirts to the laundry, buying the birthday presents he was giving his children, filling his London refrigerator and discussing menus with his cook for his forthcoming weekend at his country residence. This holistic approach to 'working for' was widely adopted, and was actually often enjoyed by employees, who did not want to be chained to a desk all day typing his boring letters and were happy to be sent to Berry Bros. and Fortnum's to order ingredients for his home life.

Agnes Blane, multi-tasking secretary in the 1980s,
who helped her boss to run his two households

In her skirt made from a strip of flowery Liberty's material
that came with a ready-made elasticated waist and so 'made
you look like Two-Ton Tessie', her Hilditch & Key frilly shirt,
her wide white belt, her Benetton V-neck, her tartan tights,
her patent-leather pumps with detachable clips and bows,
her blue enamel 'planet' earrings, her velvet Alice band,
and her blue Loden coat, Agnes Blane, graduate of Durham
University, did exactly this kind of multifaceted 'secretarial'
job in the mid-1980s, working for a London art dealer. 'I was
really his Sloaney housekeeper/PA, and I managed his entire
life, including arranging the menus for his country weekend:
fish on Friday, game on Saturday and roast on Sunday.' Her
boss was a father, but single, so he needed his PA to be willing for her duties to spill over into the domestic realm. Penny
Sheehan, though, couldn't stand being 'PA' to 'a Greek man
who expected me to have dinner with him every night. It was
like being his lady-in-waiting.' 'I had to organise Edward
Heath's Sunday lunch parties and decide whom to invite,' said

Henrietta Mayhew, who worked as Heath's secretary in the late 1980s (he'd fallen asleep while interviewing her, and had woken up with a start, and asked her rather blurredly, 'What do you think of opera and ballet?'). 'I had a list of suitable ladies to invite: all widows of cabinet ministers. Then I had to tell his housekeeper who was coming.'

The secretaries who'd been educated at places like Miss Chynoweth's College in Eastbourne to 'know by heart the birthdays of all your boss's children' did very well in this kind of role. Agnes Blane had not been to such a place; she'd just done an audio-typing refresher course at Pitman's and could type at lightning speed (one hundred words per minute), but she was naturally helpful. 'I joined an agency and I was just the kind of person they knew they could place easily. I always got interviews.'

Firms tended to go one way or the other in their policy on which social class of secretary it would be their policy to recruit. A law firm of the more Old Etonian persuasion would go for the posher kind of secretary, as did 10 Downing Street and the Foreign Office; another firm would go for the more working-class kind, who'd been trained in commercial classes at school or at the less elite secretarial colleges. Applicants soon gleaned which firms they had any hope of getting into.

The lack of good English and maths teaching at school had repercussions in the secretarial life. Dot Hunter, working as a secretary at the BBC in the early 1980s, came back from lunch one day to find a man unloading heaps of cardboard boxes outside her office door. 'He showed me a packing list with my order for 666,666 bulldog clips, explaining that they only had twenty thousand in stock at the moment but the rest were on the way.' Actually, Dot said it wasn't innumeracy that had caused that mass over-ordering; it was

a typewriter key getting stuck down, causing the '6' to get
stuck up and keep repeating itself, and she hadn't noticed.
Alison Newton, working as a 'Girl Friday' at King Edward
VII's Hospital in London in the 1960s, was allowed to
hand round the digestive biscuits during Cabinet meetings
held in the hospital library when the prime minister Harold
Macmillan was in for a prostatectomy. 'Then,' she said,
'I had to type up the bulletin about him for the papers,
and I spelled it "prostectomy" by mistake, and that wrong
spelling was printed in the *Evening Standard*.' Nineteen-
year-old Rosie Crichton, who worked for the bursar of
Balliol College, Oxford, in the early 1970s, had been well
trained at the Ox & Cow in the drill for each morning: 'Go
into your boss's office and sharpen his pencils; never cross
your legs when taking dictation; never speak unless you're
spoken to – he's a busy man.' All very well, but she then had
to take dictation of the inventory of the college wine cellar:
a spelling nightmare for a young woman whose parents had
not prioritised their daughter's education and didn't really
want them to have to work: 'They felt that to find us a good
husband was a better way forward.'

The role of secretary as midwife to all official communi-
cation was eloquently conveyed to me by Caroline Chartres,
who in the 1970s worked first as a secretary to two lawyers
in London, one of whom was semi-retired and 'had too
much time on his hands. He dictated incredibly long letters
to me about solar panels. He liked someone to sit there and
take it all down.' You can see how doing that made this
man feel useful and relevant. To have someone sitting there
taking down his words was good 'optics', making him seem
useful. Then Caroline got a job as Diocesan Secretary to the
Archbishop at Lambeth Palace when Donald Coggan was still
the Archbishop of Canterbury and when 'hardly a loo seat in

a Kent vicarage could be signed off without the archiepiscopal signature. And the Archbishop was always off on one of his trips in the Anglican Communion.'

It certainly wasn't just men who kept women in secretarial roles – although, as I was often reminded, 'men would *never* type a letter'. In fact, as Shirley Trundle reminded me, recalling working as a young civil servant in the 1980s, anyone who was not a secretary was not even allowed to have a typewriter. 'It was a union thing. There was a strict demarcation of roles.' Woe betide you if you did a secretary's job for her. 'One colleague of mine secretly hid a typewriter in his cupboard, and if we desperately needed it we could borrow it when no one was looking.'

Women were just as much in charge of keeping women in their place as men were, as I discovered at Christie's with Jackie Laing, who kept the women on the straight and narrow. There were agencies, such as Miss Norma Skemp's agency in Queen Anne's Gate, which specialised as headhunters that placed 'top girls' in secretarial roles. I spoke to Liz Barrs, who after her time at the Whitehall Secretarial College under Miss Chynoweth, worked first for Miss Chynoweth herself as a secretary, and then for Norma Skemp as one of her interviewees, vetting possible secretaries to work at Church House, Clarence House and Goldman Sachs. This was the trajectory of women guiding other women into the ways of secretaryhood.

When, in the mid-1960s, Hermione Waterfield tried to leave the Foreign Office, where she'd been working as a secretary first in Brazil (where standards slipped and secretaries wore rollers in their hair in the afternoon if they were going out in the evening) and then in London, it was the 'Head of Women's Personnel, Miss D V Lee' (note, again, that dedicated head of personnel for women) who wanted to keep her in her place. 'You do know, don't you,' she said to Hermione, 'that once you're out you can never get back in? You'll never make anything of yourself.' The implication was that if you dared to quit such a prestigious secretarial position your prospects of climbing higher up the secretarial ladder would be scuppered.

10

Digs

'Bridget Brocklebank started her physiotherapy course in October 1971, and is living in the same hostel as Ann Bryant'

'News of Old Girls', Lawnside school
magazine, 1972

'I lived in a mansion flat in Kensington full of other girls.' 'I rented a room in a flat in Knightsbridge from a drunk landlord, who offered me a tumbler of sherry at 11 a.m., which I drank, and he said, "You'll do".' 'I lived in a hostel for young ladies in Queensgate.' 'I lived in a squat in North Audley Street.' 'I lodged in a ghastly flat in Kensington with a whole gang of us and a filthy kitchen.' 'A cockroach-ridden flat near Gloucester Road.' 'A mews house behind Harrods – a fluid arrangement, five of us in two bedrooms.'

The general theme, when I asked people where they'd lived when they started out making their way in the world of work and came to London to do so, was 'insalubrious lodgings in an upmarket district'.

What was going on here? The signals were confusing. Were they well off or not? Always the 'good' Central London addresses, and always the modifier: the drunk landlord, the filthy kitchen, the cockroaches, the dormitory arrangement. A lost, pre-fire-regulations, verminous London was portrayed to me in these glimpses: one in which old ladies made their living from cramming young lodgers into their spare bedrooms; one in which a young woman could (just) live in Central London on a secretarial wage, as long as she didn't mind queuing for the bathroom.

'Digs' was the word for these lodgings: temporary, rented, slightly shabby, and communal.

'At Miss Judson's secretarial college,' Amanda Theunissen told me, 'we'd been told it was unladylike to ask for more than five pounds a week.' Amanda started out as a temporary secretary on precisely that salary in 1962, lodged in a mews house in Kensington, and told me, 'the only way I could survive was to be taken out to dinner by a man three times a week. Some days I could live on Christmas cake from a fellow lodger's cookery class.'

That summed up the situation for young women starting out in the world of work: cohabitation with others in a similar situation, an early dependency on young men with 'proper' jobs to take them out and feed them (they could not have afforded to pay their share even if they'd wanted to); and the ongoing domestic science training happening all around them. Everyone I spoke to, apart from the few who went straight into banking, was paid what seems and seemed even then like a pittance when they started out; and the advice they'd been given from people like Miss Judson, plus an ingrained sense from their own upbringing that it was bad manners to mention money or to seem in any way financially greedy, kept women from asking for more or prying into how much the men of the same age earned. Augusta Miller, for example, starting out as a teacher at Downe House in 1956 aged twenty, was paid £80 a term – so inadequate that her father needed to lend her money to get by.

But the great thing was, they were getting away from home. There was a strong drive to move away from the stifling parental atmosphere and live independently, and this was possible to do when rents were affordable even at so-called 'smart' addresses. Annabel Charlesworth's first lodging place was with her grandmother in Cadogan Street, Central London, which turned out to be worse than staying at home: 'My grandmother lay in bed all day and picked up the receiver every time I got a telephone call, so she could listen in.' Above all, young women yearned to get away from this kind of eavesdropping, in the days when telephones were kept in halls and conversations were considered public property.

Young working-class women stayed at home for longer, living with their parents till marriage, brought up to believe it was their duty to contribute to the household income, and having to resort to telephone kiosks for conversations they didn't want their family to hear. Middle- and upper-class girls couldn't wait to get away, and did.

When it came to daily living conditions for young women in their digs, there was a strange veering between strict corralling and casual neglect.

Trainee nurses were corralled. It was all part of the 'send her off to yet another institution' mentality. Pay her £11 a month for a forty-eight-hour week (that was the trainee nurse's wage in the late 1960s), and keep her on the straight and in the narrow corridor. Tiny bedroom, candlewick bedspread, chair, washbasin, chest of drawers: that, plus communal dining-room meals, was all she was expected to require. The clanking sound I can't get out of my mind, from my many conversations with ex-nurses, is the one at the nurses' home attached to Guy's Hospital in the mid-1950s, recalled by Gill

Robertson: 'You pulled a heavy chain in the bathroom, not to flush a lavatory, but to unleash a stipulated shallow gush of water into the bath from the tap.' 'Sister's beady eye was always upon us,' Gill said, 'and she knew exactly what was going on.' It was strictly prohibited to pull that chain twice.

The nurses had to be in by ten every evening. If they were late, their name was put into a book and they were summoned to Matron's office the next day. Leeds General Infirmary allowed the nurses one 'late' night per week, the stipulated arrival time shifted to 11 p.m. Strictly no men were allowed in the bedrooms. On the one hand, the nurses were corralled and infantilised with these domestic restrictions; on the other hand, they were thrown straight into the deep end of adulthood when it came to dealing with medical horrors. 'On my first day in the operating theatre,' said Pamela Jubb, who started at the Nuffield Orthopaedic Centre in the mid-1960s, 'they amputated a leg and handed it to me. I had to take it to the sluice and get rid of all the forceps still attached to it. It was quite a shock. I'd only just left school.' Then she had to be tucked up in bed in the nurses' home by 10 p.m.

Pamela Jubb (second from left) and other nurses outside the nurses' home at the Nuffield Orthopaedic Centre, Oxford, 1965

The corralling was done to trainee teachers, too, for example at the College of Education in Birmingham, where Pat Benatmane trained in 1967: 'You had to be back by ten, but you could sign out for 11 p.m. at weekends.' In that year, she said, 'The government announced it wanted to double the number of teachers in Britain, so we were all crammed into an old Victorian building a long way from the campus. We had to walk a mile and a half to breakfast. So we hitch-hiked, but the authorities were horrified when they heard this, and said we needed to get written permission from our parents to be allowed to hitchhike to breakfast. I was the only one from our whole group who did get parental per-mission.' The girls were nineteen; the age of majority was still twenty-one, until 1969 when it would go down to eight-een. Judy Price, who trained as a teacher at Homerton in Cambridge in the mid-1950s, and all the other inmates, had to be 'in' every evening. 'It was like a school, to be honest. We got two passes per term for a 10 o'clock, and one per year for a May Ball.'

The rules had a bonding effect, those who were thrown together and institutionalised in this way still great friends half a century later, and still sharing stories about the day they were late back and got a drubbing.

Yet I was amazed at the glaring holes in some of the sys-tems. Anna Maxwell described life in her nurses' home at Westminster Hospital in the late 1970s. Her bedroom was standard nurses' home decor: 'Pale yellow paint, dark green candlewick bedspread, ghastly green carpet. There was no desk to study at, so we had to turn our top drawer upside down and use that to write on.' No one had considered the written-homework aspect of the trainee nurses' existence. But, worse, no one was properly guarding the front door. 'Members of the public could just walk in. I mean, there was a porter's lodge, but it faced away from the main entrance. I think the porter had a small mirror so he could check who was going in and out, but he didn't look in it much, and had no idea what was going on.' On top of this, the 'Vacant' and 'Engaged' signs on the bathrooms were movable from outside the doors. 'You could be sitting in the bath,' said Anna, 'and a total stranger would walk in.'

For the seventeen- and eighteen-year-old young women starting out training to be secretaries at the Ox & Cow in the early 1980s, the holes in the corralling system produced at first a kind of elation in the new recruits who'd just left school. Katie Thomas described the scene in the house she lodged in, in Canterbury Road, north Oxford: 'thirty girls in one house, and no one supervising us, just a "caretaker" if there was an issue'. Released from school and the world of rules and bedtimes, the girls went 'feral' in the cockroach-ridden house, Katie said, 'Smoking the moment we woke up in the mornings, using our tooth mugs as ashtrays, not cooking, because we all wanted to be thin, although there was a kitchen on each floor. The bath overflowed. Strands of hair blocked the plughole. There was no locked front door: we had to lock up our bikes, but not ourselves. We were a target for the Cirencester boys. I don't think the Oxford undergraduates were interested in us, as we were not "the smart set". We were just euphoric at being independent.'

Again, as with the under-guarded nurses' home at Westminster, there was the causal porousness between institutionalised girls and strangers who could just wander in. This situation might have been liberating to some, but it caused a nagging dread in others, making them nervous as they tried to get to sleep.

Katie entered into the spirit of the mad, rule-less existence. It was only a few weeks in to the secretarial course, when she became acquainted with the relentless humourlessness of the secretarial textbook and the hours and hours of shorthand practice, that she started thinking, 'Why did I make such bad choices?' and 'Actually, this isn't great.'

If there were supervisors of the digs, what were they like? The London ones were posher than seaside landladies, but apart from that they were similar: set in their ways, and not cosy. Mrs Bengough, in her mansion flat in Kensington, smoked all day and crammed her lodgers in: 'that was how she made her living,' Mary Burd told me. Commander Metheringham, a retired colonel who ran a hostel for young ladies in Queensgate in the late 1960s, charging five guineas a week, sounds cheerier than most: he gave all his lodgers a hearty breakfast: 'Cereal, eggs, bacon and toast,' said Sukie Swan, who was training to be a secretary at St James's College, and could then get by on lunch of bread and fruit 'borrowed' from the breakfast table, and supper for 3/6d at a café in South Kensington, or just cheese and biscuits in her shared bedroom. Miss Ling, who crammed nine female lodgers, all sharing one bathroom, into her house on Maids' Causeway in Cambridge in the mid-1970s, had 'bright orange hair, wore a flowery overall, and served us boiled beetroot with white sauce as a supper staple,' said Sue Peart, who lodged there while training to be a secretary at the Cambridge Tech. So, landlords and ladies came to different arrangements about which, if any, meals were included in the arrangements. The Maids' Causeway house had one communal room into which the lodgers were allowed to invite male undergraduates for tea: 'Chinless wonders, and we gave them tea and crumpets with golden syrup,' said Sue. It was all great fun, and the important thing was, she reminded me, 'we were getting a qualification that we *knew* would get us a job. It was the way in.'

Sue Peart (left) and her friend Gill, her roommate in their digs, both
of them doing secretarial training at Cambridge Tech, at the Pembroke
College Idlers' Club extravaganza, June 1976

Rosie Crichton was in a dormitory of eight in a house in
Norham Gardens, north Oxford, when training at the Ox &
Cow in the early 1970s – much more strictly corralled and
supervised than the girls in Canterbury Road would be in
the next decade. Again, the candlewick bedspread was her
salient memory. What was it about candlewick bedspreads?
The lodgers saw, touched and folded these items a great
deal in the more strictly run digs, making their beds every
day, which included putting this light, ridged, not-washed-
often-enough counterpane back on top of the eiderdown.
The Norham Gardens house had a stern landlady who

stipulated that her lodgers must be in by 10 p.m., and served them breakfast and supper in her dining room. 'The ones who hadn't boarded at school couldn't cope with the strict regime,' Rosie told me. 'No noise allowed, no record players, no boyfriends.' At the house, also in north Oxford, where Virginia Ironside lived and shared a room during her brief time there training to be a secretary in the early 1960s, the landlady kept a lit candle in the hall which the lodgers had to snuff out when they got back: 'In this way,' Virginia explained, 'she could measure what time the last one had arrived home.'

There was a strange expectation that young women somehow didn't mind where they slept. Having gathered information for *Terms & Conditions* about life in girls' boarding schools from the pupils' perspectives, I wanted to ask women who started out as young resident members of staff in such places what living conditions were like for them. Not much better, according to Agneta Hinkley, who started out as a junior matron at the boys' prep school Highfield in Hampshire in 1946. 'I lived in a dreadful little room,' she told me. 'A little slit in the wall at the top of the house, with bed, table, chair and Victorian washstand. A very old maid, called Mary, brought us our water every morning. We had to wait for the boys to finish in the bathrooms before it was our turn. There were eight baths per bathroom, and we had to have communal baths – me, the housekeeper and the music mistress.'

The boys washed their faces at washstands in the dormitories, and old Mary had to go round all twelve dormitories filling them with her watering can. 'She was eighty,' Agneta said, 'and had been doing this all her life.'

So, again we see the juxtaposition: the young woman on the cusp of adulthood, arriving in a new job, full of optimism, and the old woman who was a fixture and had been doing the same job in the same place for as long as anyone could remember. Queuing for a communal bathroom seemed fine for the young ones. They just hoped they would not still have to be queuing for the bathroom in middle or old age.

Wearing her stipulated junior matron's white overall and nurse's cap, Agneta was thrown straight into this insalubrious existence, enduring the same conditions as the boys, except that she didn't have to pee into a potty, as they did, rolling out of bed every morning to pee and say their prayers simultaneously. (Mary then had to empty the potties.) Agneta had to look after the three dorms, all named after naval captains, in which 'the babies' (youngest boys) slept. She spent the day, when the boys were at lessons, mending their clothes in a room called 'the Surgery'; 'there was a lot of mending to do,' she said, 'because the boys arrived in rags, as clothes were rationed and the mother was buying clothes for herself.'

The food was inadequate, and 'the majority of boys always had a spell in the san', but that changed in 1947 when a new housekeeper arrived who weighed twenty stone, and the food improved. It was a similar situation for Josephine Boyle, who worked at the boys' prep school in Sussex aged eighteen in 1952 when her parents hadn't allowed her to accept a journalism job. 'The boys were scrawny and malnourished,' she told me. 'It was a bit of a boy-farm, full of children from broken marriages who'd been dumped there. Quite a few of them stayed on for the holidays.' Josephine's room was a tiny box room with a lino floor.

'I got a job as a junior matron at a boys' prep school called Beachborough, near Stowe, when I was just seventeen,' said Richenda Miers (born in 1939). 'They took me on with no references, along with my friend Val Scott. We had bedrooms in the attic.' Again, the attic – and the rather unpleasant daily tasks. 'We had to stand outside the lavatories, when the boys queued up after breakfast, holding a list, and put a tick by their names if they'd "performed".'

A brief snobbism interlude here, recounted by Agneta Hinkley, telling me about her spell as junior matron living in the attic. 'The Mills family, who ran Highfield,' she told me, 'were really snobbish. I was always being put down as "not quite of the right class". My mother came to visit me one day, bringing my grandmother with her, who looked like Queen Mary. "We can't have them to tea, you know," Mrs Mills said to me, when I mentioned they were coming. When the car drew up on the gravel, Mr and Mrs Mills happened to be there, and knew they had to be introduced. Mr Mills said to my grandmother, "I'm sorry, I didn't quite get your name." She replied, "I'm Lady Mead-King." To which Mr Mills said, "Oh well – oh, my dear. Nora – won't these two ladies come in and have tea?"'

It was a bit of a Cinderella moment: young matron in attic suddenly called down into drawing room, invited to tea, along with her titled grandmother. 'You should have told me,' Mrs Mills hissed to Agneta under her breath.

When Augusta Miller started out as a music teacher at Downe House in 1956, she found that she, too, was living very much the same life as the girls. Everyone, staff and girls, had to dress up in their finery (long evening dresses) on Saturday evenings, but the staff swept straight up to high table, while the girls remained below the salt. After supper, the tables were pushed back for dancing, and the girls asked members of staff to partner them. 'You felt quite flattered to be asked,' said Augusta. Life was regimented: at the end of term, the teachers had to spend a whole day in the headmistress's stuffy drawing room, reading out the reports they'd written, 'And she would change them to her style of writing. She was an English scholar.' This ordeal took all day, and they were allowed to bring their embroidery – 'but not knitting: only "old maids" did knitting.'

But, when it came to living conditions, things got much more fun late at night. Six young teachers all lodged together in a house called St Peter's in the grounds, five minutes' walk away through dense woods. 'On summer nights, when the girls were all tucked up in bed, we dragged our mattresses out onto the lawn and slept under the stars.'

They were basking in the fact that, although living in an institution, they were no longer actually at school, so no one could stop them from doing this. When Augusta moved on to Sherborne School for Girls in 1961, the night-time japes continued: 'When the girls were in bed, we raced up and down the open-air swimming pool and then ate cold sausages swigged down with whisky at one of the housemistresses' houses.' Ah, so that was what was going on out of earshot of the girls after lights out.

Back in the urban world, the step up from the communal 'digs' existence was renting a bedsit. Hermione Waterfield described what hers was like in 1961, when both currency and addresses were still at Monopoly levels: salary £800 a year, rent £10 a week, for a bedsit on Marylebone High Street. 'Nine foot by twelve; two electric rings for cooking. I once had eleven people for a buffet supper. Roy Strong headed straight for the only chair, and everyone else sat on the bed or the windowsill.'

People were meeting new people in these cramped, affordable conditions, and this was what made things happen and life move on.

If you wanted to buy your own flat, until the mid-1970s

this was hard to do, because most building societies would not give mortgages to single women. When Sue Kipling made it her business to get out of the youth hostel in Stockton-on-Tees in which she'd been put up on her arrival at ICI in 1970, while the men were put up in hotels, even renting a flat on her own was frowned upon by the woman in charge of the youth hostel. 'She was gobsmacked: a young woman of twenty-one daring to set up house on her own! Women in the north-east did not do such a thing! When I came back to the hostel with new pillows I'd bought for my new rented flat, she was horrified.' Sue did manage to rent a flat – and she had to carry on renting for seven years, because it took her as long as that to get a mortgage. 'The Halifax wouldn't give one to a single woman, even though I was financially independent.' At last, aged twenty-eight in 1978, having changed building societies, she was able get a mortgage to buy her own house in Stockton. Virginia Ironside told me that when she wanted to buy her first flat in London as a successful young journalist and author in the early 1970s 'the Chelsea Building Society was the only company that allowed women to have mortgages'.

So this was 'Generation Rent', in its previous incarnation: young women floating about with not much cash in their pocket, relying on subsidised meals, finding it hard to buy property for themselves, kept vaguely aware that life might be more salubrious if they gave this existence up and became housewives instead. The push towards marriage was strong. But they were damned if they were going to give up this work lark without a fight.

Interlude

He Said to Her

Through the resounding injunctions, advice, criticism and vigorously declaimed rules of a hundred bossy ladies – words that still ring in the ears of the women to whom they were spoken – we've already heard a great many examples in this book of what 'she said to her'. I can add others, such as the editor who shut her eyes and said, 'Boring, boring, bored, bored!' when anyone suggested a new book idea to her, and the magazine editor who said, 'I Iate that! Hate that! Hate that!' when her underlings showed her the pages of a proposed layout. Rasping repetitions were a vicious verbal weapon.

I can also add the mothers and fellow women who were very much against women working. 'You shouldn't really have a job,' the mother of one woman I spoke to said to her in the early 1980s. 'You'd be taking the job from a man.' And a fellow mother at the school gate said to a female barrister in the 1970s, as they waited to collect their daughters from prep school, 'Oh, you poor thing! You work!'

But what did He say to Her? In the long game of consequences that was the unfolding life of a young woman making her way in the world of work in the second half of the twentieth century, here are some examples from the 'He said to

Her' section. All these were quoted to me by my interviewees, who heard them spoken.

'Silly cow!' *(Muttered by Sue Peart's first boss in the advertising department where she worked. He'd just put the receiver down after a conversation with his wife. He was having an affair.)*

'Problems with your floppies, Marianne?' *(Quoted by Barbara Rich, recalling her stockbroker boss in Holborn Viaduct leaning in close to the cleavage of curvaceous Marianne, one of the four secretaries, in the early days of floppy disks.)*

'Life's such a fight for you!' *(Said to Sue Kipling by one of her bosses at ICI's Billingham Plant where she worked as a chemist in 1980. With the esprit de l'escalier she wished she'd retorted, 'Well, you make it so.')*

'Because they are temperamentally and physiologically unsuited to it.' *(Surgeon's answer to Alison Keightley when she started at King's College Hospital as a young doctor in 1978, and asked him, 'Why do you think there are so few women in surgery?')*

'The young ladies just sit at the back of the class gossiping and doing their nails, and that would appeal to you.' *(Elizabeth Ballantyne-Brown's father to Elizabeth when she was seventeen in 1968. He'd just read an article in* The Times *about women going to study law at the Sorbonne.)*

'I want you to sleep with someone to get the story.' *(Fleet Street news editor to a young female reporter in 1960s.)*

'I'm not renewing your contract. There's nothing a woman can do that a man can't do better. If you're pretty, the audience will look at you rather than listen to you, and you're not pretty anyway. And my wife thinks you should be at home looking after your children.' *(Amanda Theunissen's boss at the BBC in 1970, where she'd been working in local news.)*

'We're having a large dinner party this evening. Would you like to come or would you be happier in the nursery watching TV?' *(Tactful question from the man of the house, firmly expecting the answer 'I'd be happier in the nursery, thank you', put to Mary Bennett when she was a live-in nanny in the 1970s. A nanny was not quite family and not quite a servant, so this was a tricky area.)*

'It helps me think when I'm writing.' *(Editor who liked to keep his hand on Caroline Stacey's breast while she was working for him as a researcher.)*

'I don't think women's voices really carry authority.' *(Said off-microphone by an Anglican priest who was responsible for producing the* Daily Service *on Radio 4, in 1973. Overheard by Angela Tilby when she was working at the BBC. 'He was echoing the view of another man at the BBC who said that "women should never be newsreaders because they would be too emotional and might cry when describing tragedies."')*

'You're doing a *very important* job.' *(With strong emphasis on the 'very important'. School inspector trying to be polite to Caroline Slowik, school cleaner, when he saw her carrying rubbish sacks in the 1980s. 'He was trying so hard to get it right,' she says.)*

'What are you doing here? We've got a no-woman rule in these chambers.' *(Said to Rose White when she arrived on her first day as a pupil in a barristers' chambers in 1969, before the Sex Discrimination Act of 1975. 'The usual excuse for this was that they didn't have any ladies' loos,' she said, 'but in this case they already had a female head clerk.')*

'But you'll say you won't be able to come in one morning, because you're doing a coffee morning.' *(Said to Sibella Laing by her interviewer when she went for an interview for a job at the British Council in Cairo in 1983, when she was a young diplomat's wife.)*

'Don't worry! I think of you as an honorary man!' *(Said by a partner to a young articled clerk at the solicitor's office in London where Margaret Whitehead worked in the 1970s. 'She took it as a compliment! I was appalled.')*

'Are you "Miss" or "Mrs" or do you insist on being called "Ms"?' *(The usual question that technical people asked when they rang you in the 1980s, as recalled by Caroline Stacey.)*

'Frightfully good pudding, dear!' *(Avuncular director for whom Christine Reddaway had cooked one of her director's all-male lunches in the late 1970s.)*

'Lady! I don't know how to cook. Find me a book!' *(Dirk Bogarde to Perina Braybrooke when she worked at John Sandoe's bookshop in the 1980s.)*

'It's not what you make, it's what you save.' *(Joy Burrows's husband to Joy, when she was not earning money, but saving money by running the marital household, doing the domestic work and growing the fruit and vegetables in their large garden, early 1960s.)*

'If you touch that again, I'll have them all out.' *(Barked to Celia Haddon by the compositor on the print floor when she touched the hot-metal page form, in Fleet Street, late 1960s. Women weren't allowed on the print floor. If a woman so much as touched a bit of lead, she could spark a mass strike.)*

'Oh, no, Elisabeth, you'd be far happier in the kitchen, getting married and having babies.' *(One of the directors of the fund management company in Edinburgh where Elisabeth Beccle had worked for three summers during university, when at the end of the third summer she asked for a permanent job, early 1980s.)*

'It's disgusting being taught by a pregnant woman.' *(Male undergraduate to the authorities at the Oxford college where Elizabeth Longrigg was a lecturer, mid-1960s.)*

'Have you got any hot pants? Have you got good legs? When can you start?' *(Peter Stringfellow to Denise Sherlock when she rang him in 1971 asking him for a job as a waitress at his Cinderellas Rockerfella's nightclub in Leeds. She got the job.)*

'All the breast.' *(Typical jokey message from man signing a secretary's leaving card in the magazine office where she worked, 1980s, recalled by Caroline Stacey.)*

PART IV

THE WORKING LIFE

II

'A Million and One Things to Do'

'To my office, where nothing to do'

Samuel Pepys

To what extent does 'waiting for a telephone call' count as 'being busy in the office'? To satisfy my curiosity, aroused when Rosemary Goad told me she had 'a million and one things to do' but couldn't name a single one of them, I asked people to reconstruct a typical afternoon in the office in the 1970s and '80s, and 'waiting for a phone call' was a frequent answer. This was a sort of limbo activity that justified one's continued employment. Someone's assistant had said their boss would 'ring you back in the afternoon'. So you couldn't go far, because the phone might ring. But nor were you actually doing anything. These were the fallow hours; the hours of chatting, making friends, and studying the daily habits of the twenty or so colleagues around you, with whom you spent a large fraction of your waking hours. You were on standby for work, as it were, rather than actually working.

One woman described her office day to me as 'just laughing all day long'.

There was more of this limbo-time in the office in those more amateurish, less efficiently costed days than there is today, when either you don't have a job at all, or if you do, every work-minute is squeezed out of you to ensure as lean an outfit as possible.

In my early 1980s office life I recall being given a whole afternoon to come up with a headline. (Admittedly it needed to be a punning headline.) Office life could not have been described as frenetic. Sometimes I had a whole afternoon to subedit the horoscope. If any of the twelve sections needed lengthening or shortening, you could tweak the prospects for your own star sign. At Christie's, I often waited till 11 a.m. before the first piece of paper arrived on my desk about a picture that needed to be transferred to South Kensington, along with the dreaded instruction: 'Ysenda: pls deal with.' Somehow, because I hadn't had to 'deal with' anything for over two hours, it was hard to rouse myself to fill in the form. An office-induced torpor descends in this kind of situation, a torpor echoed by my interviewees, who 'waited all day for a letter to type', 'had nothing to do except percolate the coffee', or 'sat all day with nothing to do while I was working at a state-owned company – I think it was the gas board.'

Even in the Tampax factory in Havant in Hampshire, where Eve Terry worked in the early 1970s, the conveyor belt would mysteriously slow down for fifteen minutes at a time, and hardly any tampons appeared. 'The flow changed from an avalanche to a trickle,' as Eve put it; a menstrual image in itself. This was when the tampon-box-juggling habit got going, and when Eve had time to fantasise about putting a 'help – rescue me!' note into one of the cardboard Tampax boxes it was her job to fill. Accidents did happen, she told me; she'd been informed (it might have been an exaggeration) that a previous employee's severed finger had been put into one of the paper wrappers with a tear-off strip, and boxed up.

Eve Terry didn't have any photographs of her taken at
the Tampax factory, but she drew this picture for me of herself
juggling Tampax boxes during quiet moments at the conveyor belt

'Nobody ever bothered me,' said Bee Bealey, describing her happy months being left alone as a receptionist at *Slimming World* magazine, whose editor was 'the thinnest person I'd ever seen'. 'It was solitary heaven. I read Proust.' Not just the beginning of Proust: the whole of Proust.

'Getting lipsticks out of our handbags and untwizzling them to compare the colours,' was how Caroline Stacey described Friday afternoons in winter at *Time Out* in the 1980s, when it was dark by 4.30. 'Then a cup of tea, a Bounty bar, a trip to the loo, another cup of tea, a bit of work.'

It was a whole way of life. But not having enough to do could be a long-drawn-out form of torture if you weren't allowed to sit down while doing the not-enough, and if you were constantly watched by your hawk-like boss. This was life in the stationery department in the gloomy windowless basement of Dickins & Jones in the early 1980s, as described by Agnes Blane. Armed with her archaeology degree from Durham University, she took the job at the fountain pen counter in the vain hope that she'd be able to 'work my way up in Dickins & Jones, as my father's best friend Alec had done at Harrods'.

'There was a woman in charge,' she told me: 'a woman who'd clawed her way up to being the manager of the stationery department. I aspired to that at first.' But life in the department was dismal. 'A woman called Karen was my supervisor, and she wouldn't allow me to sit down, ever, or even allow me to lean on the counter. I had to ask her permission to go to the loo: the allowance for that was seven minutes. I sat on the loo to have a rest and listened to my Walkman: Billy Joel and UB40.' That was seven minutes of respite before going back to the silent, carpeted, sales floor where not enough people were buying pens, and even if a few did buy them 'there was no commission in stationery – everyone wanted to work in the fashion department'. The carpet was alive with carpet bugs that bit her on the ankle. 'It was nine months of mind-numbing boredom,' said Agnes, 'and it wasn't just that I had to stand up all day. I had to stand up and *look interested*. Having done that job, I'm always polite to anyone who works behind a sales counter.' This harsh treatment was the last gasp of the Victorian and Edwardian world in which department store 'sales girls' were kept as boarders, squashed into dormitories in the attic or nearby hostels, and had to work from dawn till night-time.

So, un-talked-to temps, sales girls in the less-frequented departments, underlings in state-owned companies, subeditors and writers at the gentler end of journalism – all had not quite enough to do and were experiencing the truth of Parkinson's law. There was a bit of a 'grass is greener on the other side of the fence' syndrome, those with not enough to do envying the busier ones, and vice versa. The non-busy ones knew one thing for certain: time would pass more quickly if they were busy.

So, was this why Rosemary Goad was so coy when I asked her what the million and one things she had to do were? Were they too dull to name? A lot of putting pieces of paper into a tray and then not being able to find them? A lot of putting people through to other people on the telephone, thereby offloading the problem? Please tell me, I asked my interviewees, what you actually did and how busy you really were. I had noticed that whenever you watch a film or television series set in an office, the characters never seem to do any real work. They sip coffee at their desk and get distracted. It's a film convention, along with not eating the food in front of you at mealtimes; but does the not-doing-much-work-in-offices reflect reality, or at least the reality of the second half of the twentieth century?

As we've seen with the aged lawyer who liked to dictate long, slow, unnecessary letters to Caroline Chartres, bosses without enough to do sometimes justified their existence by being seen to give their secretaries something to do. That world of ease, of older men not in a hurry, and no one keeping a strict tab on things, was described to me by Annabel Charlesworth, who worked at the College of Arms for Colonel Walker, the Clarenceux King of Arms, in the early 1970s. 'He had exquisite manners, and would practically bow as I came through the door. He worked even less than I did, if that's possible. He only came up for two days a week. My office hours were ten till four, but on Fridays I was allowed to leave at 1 p.m.'

Not only was she wearing the job lightly; the job was wearing her lightly back. It was mutual, and no one was making much money or seemed to mind.

(That excessive bowing, done by the posher kind of men to female underlings, was mentioned to me a lot during my interviews. There was a great deal of ultra-gentlemanly 'After you'-ing, as bosses and secretaries went through doors or got into lifts together. It was a brief reversal of the hierarchy. Normality was resumed as soon as they got into the office. This kind of strained, almost embarrassed, politeness was especially marked in the older generation. 'I divided men into pre-war men and post-war men,' said Elizabeth Longrigg, who was a college lecturer at Oxford University in the 1960s. 'Pre-war men put on a special voice when speaking to a woman.')

In those days when you were allowed to bring your dog to work ('spaniels under the desks all over the place' as I heard the art world described), one thing that did go on was a lot of ringing up. The lost art of dialling telephone numbers was recalled to me variously: 'putting a pencil in the circles to do the dialling' (it stopped your index finger getting sore); 'cradling the telephone in the crook of my neck like a violin'; 'my long necklace getting caught up in the telephone wires', 'dialling a number, and you'd get straight through to the director of a large firm'. Telephoning did bypass the need to dictate or type a letter. Everyone was sneaking personal phone calls into the mix.

Far better, surely, to put your hand up to ask to go to the loo not out of the sheer physical strain and mental boredom of standing up all day with not enough to do, but out of the dire need for a few minutes' rest from the frenetic work. This tended to be the lot of the lower-down types in conglomerates who were kept harder at work, in groups or 'pools'. It happened to Frances Pemberton while working as a secretary at the Shell

Petroleum Company in the mid-1950s, working 'in the most awful typing pool – rows and rows of women, and we had to make nine carbon copies of everything, supervised by a strict upright woman in front'. It sounded worse than school. Nine carbon copies seemed an absurdly large number, requiring the fiddly layering of black, white, black, white, and making corrections nine times was no fun. The rule was 'hands up to be excused'. 'I went with Davina Gordon,' Frances said, 'and we spent a lot of time in the lav.' Offices later clamped down on this behaviour, and gave shorthand typists one single slot per mid-morning and mid-afternoon to go to the 'lav'. If they missed their slot, bad luck.

And far better than working in a lifeless fountain pen department was to work in a busy shop in the days of pneumatic tubes that sent money whizzing all over the ceilings and up and down through the floors. Some real action at last! Valerie Herron (born in 1938) worked in the cash office of Joplings department store in Sunderland straight after leaving school at fifteen, and described the jollity and the constant motion: the 'money put into rocket-things and sucked up – it went all round the shop right up to the cash office in the attic where we were. There were different chutes for the different departments, and the rockets contained the money plus two copies of the receipt. We had to take the bottom copy out and send the top one straight back with the change.' This all happened instantly, while the customer was standing at the counter chatting to the salesperson. No tills at Joplings: this was how customers paid – on the pneumatic superhighway. The hive of activity kept Valerie pleasingly busy up in the attic. She, and the girls like her who'd just left school and worked with her in the cash office, sat at 'great big high desks on high stools' and had to enter by hand into heavy ledgers every transaction they'd just done. They certainly felt needed.

'Lord, make me useful' is the prayer of all who enter the world of work. I could feel the satisfaction, still pleasing years later, of those who'd made twenty-four pairs of trousers per day, as fifteen-year-old Kathleen Hewitson did at Kauffmann's – impressive considering it took me a whole summer term in 1973 to make a single halter-neck dress (but that was without access to a sewing machine). Those factory girls really did have a million and one things to do, and did them all. 'We were used to working really hard,' said Judith Anderson, recalling her first job at Hepworth's tailoring factory on leaving school aged fifteen in 1962, where she and the girls opposite her on the line 'like the aisles at ASDA' made sixteen jackets an hour between them. If a mistake was made, such as a collar or lining being inside out, it was made sixty times, and the whole batch had to be unpicked by hand. 'You worried yourself sick,' Judith said, and thought, "We'll never get it done."' That was pressure.

Judith (third from left), aged twenty-three in 1970, at Hepworth's meeting, with other factory employees in their royal blue Hepworth's overalls

It was the same with making canvas water-containers for soldiers, as was done by seventeen-year-old Diana Brooks after her first two years of full-time work at the bikini factory near her home in Somerset, where she'd had to cut stiff metallic mesh all day with a hot knife. She got the hang of the bikini mesh, but when she moved to the water-containers factory, she made mistakes. 'The inspector came round, and I had to unpick all the top bits of mine, because they weren't good enough.' Both these jobs entailed standing up all day from 8 a.m. to 5 p.m. 'You just got on with it,' said Diana. 'You didn't have any other expectations. I lived at home and cycled three and a half miles to work and back in all weathers. My pay was three pounds a week. My brother and sister and I all gave half of our wages to our parents. They said, "If you don't like it, you can find somewhere else to live."' Diana soon did; she got married at eighteen to a man who worked on a farm.

The women I spoke to who went straight to work for banks on leaving school at fifteen or sixteen told me that they weren't allowed home in the evening till they'd done the 'balancing' at the end of the day. Any sloppiness during the day would catch up with them at that moment.

But in general, I got the strong impression that life was more laid back in offices and even factories through all the pre-computerised years to the end of the period of this book, allowing for strange bits of leeway, such as being allowed to make your own curtains on Saturdays, and no one noticing if you stole five reporter's notebooks plus a bunch of biros from the stationery cupboard. As long as the actual thing got done – the clothes made, the magazine published, the books balanced – there wasn't too much fuss about how it was achieved. In factories that ran on the piecework system, where you were paid in accordance with the amount of work you did, you could set your own pace. 'You'd think, "I need some money this week, so I'll go mad at work",' Judith Anderson said, recalling her piecework years at the Dewhirst tailoring factory in Sunderland.

The less disciplined, spreadsheet-free approach did mean, though, that young women sometimes started in new jobs and found everything in disarray: unsorted bits of paper all over the place, in-trays of unfinished business, furious people ringing up to complain, plus a filthy fridge. 'Going in and sorting things out for scatty men' was how one woman I spoke to, who started out as a secretary in a management consultancy firm in the early 1980s, described her job. As usual it was the woman's job to tidy it all up. Sue Peart recalled her arrival at *Cosmopolitan* magazine in the late 1970s, where it was more a case of sorting out the problems created by scatty women. 'My first day was pretty hellish. I was handed a pile of invoices that hadn't been processed. There was no system in place. It was chaos. I had to try to get to grips with it all, aligning every invoice with the article it applied to. And I had to clean the fridge, which was encrusted with mould: bags of dripping lettuce, cottage cheese that had gone green: it had all been in there for years.' Those were the seamy undersides of offices, where all too easily problems were no one's responsibility until they got really bad and started to smell. 'Are you going to come back tomorrow?' one of the (female) team asked her at the end of her first day. 'Yes, I am,' said Sue. 'Well, I'm only asking because the previous six haven't come back.'

Cosmopolitan did sound lively, though, under the editorship of Deirdre McSharry, who could be heard all day long in peals of laughter as she took calls from writers. 'She really brought out the best in us,' said Sue. 'She was a nurturing boss and she wanted us to get on in our careers. She allowed me to do a Certificate of Journalism on day release. She led us to believe it was our world and we could go out and grab it with both hands.'

So, along with making coffee for the whole office in the ancient percolator, and going to Berwick Street Market every Monday morning to buy a bunch of flowers to go on the windowsill in Deirdre's office, and going round the office with a tray at 5 p.m. every Friday giving everyone a thimbleful of white wine ('a nice Deirdre touch'), and as well as being mined for ideas by McSharry – who longed to know what her young employees were doing, wearing, and talking about, seeing these as a reflection of what her readers needed to read about – Sue was also enabled to make her way in the world of journalism, having started out as a secretary without a university degree. 'If we're going to do a piece on fellatio,' McSharry announced at one morning meeting, 'we'll first need to tell our readers how to spell it.' She was educating the nation, and helping her employees to forge their careers in the process.

Sue Peart in front of her desk at the *Cosmopolitan*
Twelfth Night Party, 1982

This was the kind of office hubbub that made the working day (a) enjoyable and (b) pass by quickly. In Fleet Street it had a more sexist edge to it: young reporters like Celia Haddon were sent out to do the 'pretty girl stories' for which they would be photographed, doing things like skiing down Britain's first artificial ski slope and making Britain's first car-to-car phone call across the Atlantic. 'A friend of mine,' said Celia, 'had to hatch an egg in her bra.' That was her 'pretty girl story', and it entailed walking around with an egg in her bra for a fortnight. It was all part of being the willing young female employee who would say yes to all tasks and assignments.

If you weren't firm about it, you'd be right back in the subservient role. Lots I spoke to said that even when they weren't secretaries any more, they were still asked to make coffee or to 'take a message from someone to someone else in another department', especially if their desk happened to be near the door. When in 1973 Hermione Waterfield became the first woman director at Christie's, on the same level as men who had secretaries, she was not allowed a secretary, as it was known that she had the secretarial skills herself. 'Well, they did give me an eighth of a secretary,' Hermione conceded, 'but she was always too busy working for the seven others.'

The female staff were at least allowed to wear trousers during the power cuts of that year, 'but as soon as the heating and lights came back on, we were told, "Back into skirts! Skirts and dresses only from now on."' So, freezing cold and with one-eighth of a secretary, Hermione shivered through the day and had to spend her weekends typing up the lists she'd made during the week.

The truth about unequal pay carrying on in the 1980s, long

after the Equal Pay Act of 1970 was supposed to put an end to such practices, was brought home to one woman from the art world whom I spoke to, who asked not to be named. 'I had two men in my department working for me,' she told me, 'young enough to be my sons. I'd taught them everything. A man from a building society rang me one day, asking me to confirm one of their salaries. I asked the boss of the department to tell me what the salary was – and found out it was 25 per cent more than I was paid. I was pretty cross. I did no more overtime from that moment on.'

This was the normality of male juniors being paid more than females senior to them, and it carried on under the radar, in a 'hush-hush' world where it was not thought quite polite to discuss what one was paid.

12

Smoke; Drink; Lunch

'Before a meeting begins, the secretary should
make sure that ashtrays are available and in
convenient positions'

from *Secretarial Duties* by John Harrison,
1967 edition

The levels of smoking and drinking were staggering.
Workplaces – and I'm including hospital wards here, as well as
offices (smoking in hospitals was not banned till 2003) – were
miasmas of fumes. 'People like you are switching to No.6,'
the 1970s Player's advertisement claimed enticingly, and by
'people like you' they intended to specify 'ordinary' people
both at home and at work, where the desk layout went 'in-
tray, out-tray, ashtray'.

Here's a snapshot of life in the fog.

In hospitals, where, as we've seen, patients were trussed
up at right angles into their sheets and blankets all morning
to look tidy for Matron, a common sight, as described to me
by Judy Spooner who trained as a nurse at Jersey General in

the mid-1970s, was 'a patient with an oxygen mask in one hand and a cigarette in the other'. They made the perfect complement to each other, in their way, one lengthening life, the other shortening it, and both making it more bearable while it lasted.

Every hospital patient was allocated an ashtray on his or her bedside table on arrival, and a spittoon to go with it. They dozed off with their cigarettes still alight or their pipes still smouldering, and the nurses had to swoop down to put them out – right out.

Surgeons smoked their way through surgery, GPs smoked their way through appointments, but hospital nurses had to go all the way to the smoking lounge, which could be as much as a fifteen-minute walk away, a quarter of a mile along endless corridors, and so thick with smoke when they arrived that they could hardly see the nurse puffing away in front of them.

Alcohol was served to patients as medicine. 'Guinness, light ale or sherry before lunch' was the norm at University College Hospital where Pamela Jubb worked as a nurse in the 1970s. 'The alcohol was supposed to boost the patients' appetite,' she explained. 'It was kept on the bottom of the medicine trolley.'

'Guinness being given to little old thin men who needed fattening up' was how pre-prandial life at Westminster Hospital in the 1970s was described to me. On Saturday nights at Leeds Royal Infirmary, the patients had a choice between sherry or a whole bottle of Tetley's beer. It certainly lightened the atmosphere.

There were rules; a sister at Jersey Royal was seen cutting up a patient's cigarettes in front of him when she'd caught him smoking at the wrong time of day (before breakfast). Sisters liked to be in control, but in general, smoke and alcohol in moderation were welcomed as part of the scenery, no one worrying that they might be in any way 'bad' for patients, everyone enjoying their more instantly discernible sedative effects. Patients up and about and on the mend were allowed out to the local pubs.

Away from hospitals, chain smoking was a way of getting through the working day. Sandie Higham, who worked at the fashion house Ellie & Goldstein in the 1980s, told me there was a 'no smoking in the design room' rule, 'because the design room was full of paper; but in the showroom, everyone was puffing like mad, the house models walking around through the fog of cigarette smoke.'

The piles of paper did not deter anyone in the world of journalism. 'Bins on fire at 7 a.m.' was how one newspaper office was summed up to me in six words. Smouldering bins, crumpled sheets of paper acting as kindling, kept life perpetually on edge. Smoking forty cigarettes a day was a way of getting through the stress of life as a tabloid journalist, as Celia Haddon told me, 'and I couldn't have stuck to the job without the alcohol.'

The drinking culture was an integral aspect of working life for a young tabloid journalist, and if you wanted to survive in it as a woman, you needed to take part. The only problem was, women weren't allowed into El Vino (known as the more 'intellectual' of the Fleet Street pubs) without a man to accompany them; nor were they allowed up to its bar to order drinks. (That restriction lasted till 1982, when the case of 'Gill and Coote v El Vino Co. Ltd' went to the Court of Appeal. Tessa Gill, a solicitor, and Anna Coote, a journalist, successfully challenged the ban on women being served at the bar of El Vino's; it was held to be a violation of the Sex Discrimination Act.)

So, in the 1960s and 1970s, a lot of the co-ed drinking took place at the White Swan in Fetter Lane, known as the Mucky Duck or 'the Mucky', a crowded pub that in those days smelled strongly of smoke, or the back bar of The Harrow, just off Fleet Street, where the smell of urine emanated from the gents. Part of Celia Haddon's initiation in 1965 was being taken to the Mucky and 'told how to drink', both at lunchtime and in the evening. As a woman, she was expected to buy her round when her turn came, just as the men did, but she must drink only half-pints, never pints. 'We were expected to behave like ladies, and it was unladylike to buy a whole pint for yourself.'

They went to the pub at lunchtime if they'd already finished their story; then back again in the evening, some of them 'drinking till the pubs closed' and then going on to the Wig and Pen drinking club till the small hours. 'One woman got so drunk,' Celia Haddon recalled, 'that she used to crawl down Fleet Street.'

Offices had drinks cupboards. Lynda Kitching, who worked as an office clerk at Barclays in Leeds in the late 1960s, told me that the bank manager's cupboard was groaning with alcohol, as customers would bring him a bottle of whisky or sherry as a gift. 'It was the way business was conducted,' she said: a drink to soften whatever blow might be being delivered, or whatever little difficulty needed to be discussed. The smell of sherry or whisky wafted through to the next-door office mid-morning, where Lynda was hand sorting cheques and typing out envelopes for bank statements. Unlike in the world of journalism, banking underlings were not invited to join in with the drinking culture.

Then it was time for lunch – if you were allowed lunch, that is. A startling incident illustrating the syndrome 'women instinctively regarded as second-class citizens' was described to me by Hermione Waterfield. It happened in the early 1970s

when she was working at Christie's, before she was a director. 'I was listing the contents of a stately home for insurance
or probate. There were four of us checking the paintings,
drawings and books around the house, and I was the only
woman. Tom Milnes Gaskell (from the silver department) was
summoned to lunch. I was listing the miniature portraits, and
we'd all been hard at it all morning. I could hear Tom calling
the coin specialist Richard Faulkner in the hall, discussing
breaking off for lunch: "Are you coming?" One of them said,
"What about Hermione?" Then I heard the factor of the
estate saying, "Does Hermione need lunch?"'

It was sort-of expected by the factor that she would 'work
through', subsisting on air and enthusiasm.

She jolly well did need lunch.

Usually, gratifyingly, the office or work lunch hour was
exactly that: a whole hour during which you did no work at
all, and either wandered about in the vicinity of the office
browsing in shops, or sat in a restaurant or café or on a bench
reading or chatting. For a lonely person, an hour could seem
long; too long. Barbara Pym described one of her solitary
female characters buying her *Evening Standard* at lunchtime
and reading it from cover to cover there and then, thus 'spoil-
ing her treat for later'.

Men tended to peel off from their female underlings at
the moment when the lunch hour struck. This was a blessing. The bankers who'd been at the drinks cupboard in the
morning 'went off to the pub for lunch and came back with
red faces, smelling of beer', recalled Lynda Kitching. 'That,
again, was how business was done – over lunch, or on the
golf course.' She, meanwhile, took a bus home for a cooked
lunch with her mother – there was just time within the hour
to make the return journey – and later she started bringing
in a box of homemade sandwiches to eat at the wooden table

in the small, smoky staffroom. She kept a tab on where the men went off to during the day. As well as seeing the older ones vanish off for lunch with each other and their clients, she noticed that some of her male colleagues the same age as her used to vanish off at teatime. 'They'd quietly go trotting off. "Where are you going?" I eventually asked one of them. "To college," he said. "We're doing banking exams."' Ah, she realised: the men (with O levels, just as she had from her grammar school) were being recruited for management, whereas the women were being recruited to remain in admin or on the counter, not needing to be trained for promotion, and would be lower paid.

The vanishing of the bosses gave the women who worked for them an oasis of peace and quiet. 'Having booked the table for two or four for the men at Rules or Simpson's,' said Penny Eyles, describing her time as a secretary to the 'ex-Army posh boys' at the advertising agency in the 1960s, 'I'd go and get a cheese and pickle sandwich for myself. Or I'd have my hair done at Hebe by the Aldwych: back-combed, dowsed in hairspray, and one emerged looking like one's mother, the whole creation shaking in the wind on Waterloo Bridge.'

So there was time for the whole washing, setting and being roasted under the dryer ceremony, as well as for the cheese and pickle sandwich that was eaten not at the desk but in a café where sandwiches were made especially for you before your very eyes, great dollops of pickle, or early forms of mayonnaise with skin on top, being spooned from tubs and slapped onto the white or brown sliced bread of your choice slathered with room-temperature butter.

The plainness of a custom-made sandwich served in this style is a lost delight, somehow impossible to recreate at home. It needed the brashness of an Italian behind the counter slashing it into approximate quarters with his long knife, in a hurry, to attain its not-quite-symmetrical but fresh perfection. Caroline Stacey remembered the notice behind the counter in the Italian café she used to go to in London: PLEASE DON'T ASK FOR CREDIT, AS A SMACK IN THE MOUTH OFTEN OFFENDS. No cheek, please; and anyway, customers were supposed to use their luncheon vouchers, worth 15p a day, eventually going up to 30p: a benign post-war initiative, designed to enable firms to subsidise employees' lunches without having to have their own canteen, but slowly declining in value as inflation rose.

On the menu at that café with the 'smack in the mouth' notice was a 'sow-sage sandwich', so pronounced, and the highly calorific item of fried breaded escalopes served in a bun. Lunch was proper fuel.

At small tables at the back of trattorias dotted about Central London, women meeting for lunch ate platefuls of spaghetti bolognese, or sometimes spaghetti *with* a breaded escalope, undergoing the waiter's phallic pepper-grinder ordeal and his sprinkling of vomit-smelling pre-grated Parmesan. There was a dearth of such jolly places in the non-central district of Leeds where Lynda Kitching worked in the 1970s: it was a café-less desert, she said: 'Just a few pubs and a post office.' To get a cup of coffee or a sandwich she would have needed to take a bus into the centre of Leeds.

There in the city centre, as Carole Ellis recalled, the Chinese restaurants that had opened in the mid-1950s were thriving. Sixteen-year-old Carole, working as a junior shorthand typist for Electric Washer Services in 1959, met her older sister Margaret, who was working as a shorthand typist for Somnus Bedding, once a week for lunch at their favourite Chinese restaurant, the Kee Hong on Boar Lane, which was packed, and they always chose their craved dish: chicken fried rice. She and Margaret, still both in their teens, noticed that the older married women (and they did seem much older, in their early twenties) went to Marks & Spencer and actually bought clothes. The most Carole and Margaret did was to browse in C&A.

Meanwhile, in London, Joan Booth (born 1932), who was working in the typing pool of the shipping and forwarding department of Thomas Cook, was going out to lunch every Friday at Swan & Edgar on Piccadilly Circus with her three best friends from the office, Janet, Jean and Brian, as a weekly payday treat. They always chose the curry.

Joan (far right) with her colleagues Brian, Janet and Jean, off to their weekly Friday lunch together at Swan & Edgar – 'our payday treat'

The first decade of this book was still the pre-dieting era, when rationing was either still going on or in recent memory, and everyone gratefully ate what was put in front of them. Later, that age of innocence would fade away and women would force themselves through the afternoon on a tub of cottage cheese, a few nuts from the local health-food shop, and a low-fat yoghurt; just one more aspect of the self-punishing regime they inflicted on themselves.

But in the 1950s it was meat, pastry, potatoes and boiled veg in the middle of the working day. Young women in factories ate a hot lunch at work and then went home for a cooked tea before going out for the evening. It was the way to survive, along with the sweets on Friday afternoons. They were all young and agile. Kathleen Hewitson ran home for a cooked lunch every day when she started at Kauffmann's aged fifteen: 'A mile, and I could do it in fifteen minutes.' But then she started having lunch at the office canteen, served by 'a lady who made lovely meals: meat pie and veg'. Audrey Loper, also in the early 1950s, ran home for lunch from Lister's, the vast silk and velvet factory in Bradford where she worked, but it was just for a plate of sandwiches because her divorced single mother was working too, in another mill: 'She was doing heavy work, carrying the tubs of wool around. She went shopping on the way home from work.'

Could the pressure to go home for lunch be another form of parental control, reaching its hand into a daughter's cusp of adulthood? This was certainly the case for Heather Hall (born in 1950), whom we last met with her CSEs 'not worth the paper they were written on' that she'd got at the secondary modern in Poole. She did get her Duke of Edinburgh Gold Award in 1964 – 'that was the one thing I excelled at' – and had no trouble whatsoever getting a job as a bank clerk at the Poole branch of Lloyds Bank, being offered a job there even before her maths O-level-less CSE results were in.

'My mother wanted me out at work so I could help with the household bills,' she told me. As for how much of her weekly wage she should hand over, 'My mother tried the "all of it". She was quite controlling. She said, "Give me all your money, and I'll buy you all your clothes." She'd go to fashion shops and say, "I've seen something that you'd like, Heather. I've put it aside. Let's go and have a look."'

Heather's reaction to this was 'certainly not'. She put her foot down and managed to keep half of her wages of £5 a week. Home life was not happy: 'My mother would push my father's buttons; he would lose his temper; she was subtle about it, pretending to be the victim. Actually it was he who was the victim.' Every single day, Heather had to go home from the bank, by bus, for a cooked lunch with the family. 'We were joined by my father, who got a lift home for lunch – he was a storeman at an engineering company. And my grandmother always came for lunch with us too.' There they all sat, in the stuffy kitchen, at a fully laid table with cloth napkins, tempers fraying. 'My mother always made us a three-course lunch: soup out of a packet, followed by braising steak or pork done in the oven, followed by pudding. And we'd have another cooked meal together in the evening.' It was an oppressive kind of domestic soft tyranny.

After lunch, Heather took the bus back to the bank and worked on until it was time to do the daily balancing of everything to the last penny. 'At the end of the day,' (I scribbled down these and many other bureaucratic processes in my notebook, struggling to keep up) 'two people would call back the balances so that the official bank ledger record matched the statement record that would go back to the customer.' Just as with Lynda Kitching at Barclays, 'Women weren't encouraged to sign up for the Institute of Bankers qualification.' Lurching from heavy lunch to heavy supper, Heather carried on living at home till she married at twenty-eight.

Heather Hall (far left) escaping from home supper
at a bank dinner-dance, 1974

The lunchtime dancing sessions at the Mecca Ballroom in
Leeds in the 1960s were a feature of the working day. Susan
Watson (the one who after her day's work in the tailoring
factory rushed out to the coffee bar) also rushed off at lunchtime to the Mecca Ballroom twice a week, running past the
slaughterhouse and grabbing a meat and potato pie from
the market on the way. 'The lunchtime sessions lasted from
11.30 to 2.30,' she told me, 'and all the local shop assistants
went, and the men from the barber's shop, and the girls from
the factory like me.' That, as well as the Conca d'Ora coffee
bar, was where they all met each other and where marriages
were made. Susan had broken the back of the day by doing
her morning's piecework in double-quick time, allowing for
a slackening off in the afternoon. On non-Mecca-Ballroom
days she had lunch in the office canteen at one of its two sit-
tings, ordering her meat and potato pie during the morning
tea break. Denise Sherlock (the one whose legs would a few

years later be found acceptable by Peter Stringfellow, who therefore employed her as a waitress) ran from Littlewoods, where she was working in the bra department, to the Mecca Ballroom for coffee and lunchtime dancing in the late 1960s. Jimmy Savile was the disc jockey.

Gill Blenkinsop, the one who landed the job in the sales department of ICI Dulux Paints in Slough through a chat with the organist at church, went off every day with her marketing and sales colleagues to the Greyhound pub in the back streets of Slough, 'run by two women who cooked a special every day', and they all played darts. 'I learned more about office etiquette and the way things really work in that pub than I ever did in the office.' This was 1969, and Gill was impressed by how little discrimination there was towards her, even though the firm was heavily male dominated. The darts games had a bonding effect. For this to happen a whole hour was needed, to walk there, have lunch, play darts and walk back: a break in the middle of the day that allowed for a change of scene and some exercise, in the days before 'capitalism stole the lunch hour', and the habit of the solitary working sandwich lunch took hold, dismally coined as 'al desko'.

The willingness of secretaries to help out as waitresses made lunchtimes run smoothly at lunch-party-giving offices. Each week at one of the management consultants in Central London whose ex-secretaries I spoke to, the firm held a lunch for clients. One of the receptionists, who happened to be a good cook, did the cooking, and the secretaries put on aprons and did the waitressing. They were paid in leftovers. At one point, three of the married partners were having affairs with three of the secretaries, so the changes of uniform at lunchtime just added to the sexy mix.

This doubling (or tripling) up of roles was at one remove from simply cooking directors' lunches as an official job, which lots of girls who'd learned to cook at finishing schools did end up doing, as there was high demand for this job. Caroline Goss, who'd been to Winkfield, signed up with an agency in Marylebone in 1978 that specialised in providing cooks for directors' lunches in the City. Entertaining was tax-deductible, and firms had accounts at Fortnum's and Harrods, so Caroline could arrive at 9.30 a.m. and order delicious, expensive ingredients that would be delivered an hour later. Dressed in their stripy shirts with white collars, the brokers and bankers would 'wander into the dining room at 12.30 and peruse the menu card – usually something like prawn cocktail, beef Wellington and apple crumble' – and would then sit down for a two-hour lunch while the women hovered, the waitresses having being sent by a different agency and the washers-up by yet another.

Having drunk quite a lot of vodka and tonic first, the men were red-faced before the lunch even started, and then they went on to white wine followed by a 'heavy red wine'.

'Were there any women at the lunches?' I asked her, to which she replied, 'No.'

Like the secretary-waitresses, Caroline was allowed to take the leftovers home, sharing them with the other staff; this worked best when they'd told her 'there might be twenty of us' but only ten turned up. There was then enough leftover food to live on for a day or so.

When men and women of a more senior variety started peeling off for lunch together, the women felt oddly compelled to keep up with the men's level of drinking. 'It was three-bottle lunches for two people,' said Rosie de Courcy, recalling her lunches with male authors when she started out as an editor in the mid-1970s, 'because I wanted to keep up with a hard-drinking man. If I wanted to keep up, I knew I had to learn to drink, swear and be unshockable.'

She tried not to bat an eyelid when one male author whom she was taking out to lunch at La Poule au Pot in Pimlico said to her across the table, 'I don't like the look of you. I want my editor to be big, burly, bearded and male.' She replied that she could always wear a beard, if that would make him feel better. Later she handed him back his manuscript marked with three hundred suggested corrections. 'I like this!' he said excitedly. 'Do you realise you've given me three hundred things to do?'

'A lot of them,' said Rosie, and by 'them' she meant male authors, 'wanted you to be a bossy schoolmistress.'

Lunch was just one of many work ordeals for Maggie Fergusson, who, within a day of arriving at Mercury Asset Management in 1986, having succeeded in the milk-round interviews at the hotel, knew she was in the wrong job. She wasn't interested enough in money. On the first morning, all the new graduate recruits were assembled and they had to go round the table saying what they'd done that summer. 'They'd been doing things like working on the Paris Bourse,' said Maggie, who had been doing no such thing. 'I knew it was a total and utter disaster. You had to be *really* interested in money. You were supposed to know the prices of all the shares on the FTSE 100.' Her job was to write reports on building-related matters such as whether Wimpey Homes were a good investment.

Far from being a restful hour to go and hide on a bench, the lunch hour was excruciating and demanding. 'Brokers would invite the chairman and financial director of a company to lunch, and we'd be invited, as people who might buy shares in the company,' Maggie explained. 'One day I had to go to lunch and meet the people from Todd plc, who made tunnel linings. They sat me bang next to the chairman. I couldn't think of a single thing to ask him. Because the firm was based in Lancashire, where my uncle was Lord Lieutenant, I thought I'd talk to him about that. He did *not* want to talk about my uncle.'

Her opening gambit having fallen flat, she then had to go through course after course of minuscule helpings, this being the heyday of nouvelle cuisine. 'Just a painting in sauce on the plate' was how she described a typical main course. By 3 p.m. on those lunch days, she was drained, faint with hunger, and feeling more than ever like a fish out of water, in this terrifying world where if you got into a lift with a senior banker, he would throw a quiz question at you about the price-earnings ratio of a particular share, and you were expected to know the answer. To dodge this, and to survive the long afternoon ahead, she went off to the ladies, locked herself in a cubicle, curled herself up on the floor and fell asleep.

13

Perks

'You won't have a large salary, but you will get tickets to Wimbledon, and you will meet the Queen'

Sir Oliver Millar, Keeper of the Queen's Pictures, interviewing Amanda Dickson for a job at Buckingham Palace as an assistant at the Royal Collection, 1988

So, you'd done the morning, had the cigarette, got through lunch, and now you needed to be propelled through the afternoon. What kept morale up was the thought that, at least, the place was giving you a few things for nothing.

Perks do go some way towards making up for a low salary. Small, freely given treats have a disproportionately cheering effect, giving employees the impression that the firm they work for has a fun-loving, kind and caring side in spite of its essential meanness. In the case of Amanda Dickson, quoted above, the firm was The Firm, and was offering her an annual salary in the region of £5,000, but she did indeed meet the

Queen, although the Wimbledon tickets never quite materialised and she didn't want to push her luck by mentioning or asking for them.

The withdrawal of perks, by the same token, has a disproportionately mood-lowering effect, hammering home to employees that the firm they work for is joyless and miserly to its core. The gradual withdrawal of perks has been the trend through the twenty-first century, due partly to the heavy taxing of perks, making the tax on items like company cars so onerous that it's cheaper to run your own, and partly to the general rationalisation and pruning of the workplace: fewer parties on boats, no free postage of Christmas cards, stationery cupboard kept locked, canteens hardly cheaper than real life, free medicals and gym membership given only because they'll make the employees stay alive and work for longer.

Rather in the same way that in our dying days we remember the family holidays (that's part of the point of family holidays, I'm told), in old age, recalling their first jobs, people seem to remember the perks. For the young women of this book, they tended not to be things as grand as company cars. You had to climb a long way before getting one of those. When Sandie Higham did get offered a company car in her late thirties, on becoming design director of the fashion house Ellie & Goldstein in the 1980s, she asked whether it could be a Mercedes two-seater, which was what her husband was given as an account executive of an advertising company. 'They said, "I don't think that's *quite* the impression we want to give," and I had to settle for a BMW.' Which doesn't sound too bad. The firm paid for all the petrol and it was basically hers to use as she pleased. She drove her mother straight down to Cap d'Antibes for a summer holiday.

This was a cut above the Christie's 'raw turkey at Christmas' in the spectrum of perks. But it is the small treats that people remember and treasure. Though Amanda Dickson didn't get the Wimbledon tickets, she told me that the Queen did give all the members of her household a sum of money at Christmas to choose a present for themselves at House of Fraser or the Army & Navy Stores. 'As a first-year employee, I had little to spend, but I chose a glass scent bottle. We were presented to Her Majesty in the Green Dining Room, where she gave us our gifts.' It was an example of the surprise-less present at which the Royal Family excels.

Denise Sherlock relished being allowed to buy marked-down stockings from the stockings counter when she worked at Bailey & Lockhart's department store in 1966. Kay Clayton, working as an assistant in the Partners' Dining Room at John Lewis, was thrilled by the 18 to 25 per cent discounts in the stores. Gill Robertson, working as a young nurse at Guy's Hospital in the mid-1950s, loved it that the London theatres and opera houses offered free tickets to the nurses: announcements of tickets on offer were pinned onto the noticeboard and the nurses took the 13 bus from London Bridge to the West End. Eve Terry was grateful that an allocation of free Tampax was given out to the female workers every month – not quite the required number of them, though, so in the tea breaks there was 'a bit of a black market in Tampax going on', as people frantically tried to acquire more at a knockdown price. Fleur Thomas, who worked as Betty Kenward's secretary at *Harpers & Queen* in the late 1980s, and spent many hours of her week keeping *Debrett's* up to date, trawling through the *Times* and *Telegraph* births and deaths announcements each day, and adding and crossing out names accordingly ('almost a full-time job in itself', as she recalled), loved it when she was suddenly informed that Mrs Kenward's driver, Peter, would be picking her up and taking her to the Royal Windsor Horse Show or the Badminton Horse Trials, for which Mrs Kenward had a spare ticket. 'And at Christmas she would sweetly surprise me by giving me luxury items that firms like Hermès and Louis Vuitton had given her during the year. She loved Floris Stephanotis and would give me Stephanotis soap and bath oil, her favourite Floris scent.' Life seemed kind, working for a woman who wanted to increase Fleur's happiness.

Fleur Thomas with her boss Betty Kenward, bestower of treats and surprise presents. Photograph by Barry Swaebe

The simple pleasure of tea from a trolley, or buns handed out in mid-morning, tweaked the working day into something approaching real enjoyment. Buckingham Palace elevenses, and tea at four, were served in porcelain cups, with biscuits, 'prepared by Sir Oliver Millar's PA,' said Amanda Dickson. 'No vending machines or ad hoc coffee breaks, and definitely no coffee mugs on desks.' The highlight of Carole Ellis's day, when she started working as a secretary to 'Mr Venmore' at the electrical shop in Leeds, was going to buy iced buns for the whole office at the Craven Dairies shop. Then she and another girl who was the same age (sixteen) went up to the top of the building, where there was a tiny kitchen next to a room where a man mended broken vacuum cleaners, put the kettle on, and tottered down two flights in their court heels carrying trays of tea and coffee. ('For a trolley, you needed a corridor' I was reminded by the ones who had to carry trays down flights of stairs.) A woman I spoke to who became a civil servant in the early 1970s straight after leaving Oxford – 'but we were definitely aiming for the more lowly jobs in the civil service,' she told me – recalled that the very first thing her secretary (yes, she had a secretary!) asked her was 'What time would you like your morning coffee, and what time would you like your afternoon tea?' The secretary – this being the civil service, she was of the 'posh' variety – made both hot drinks especially for her, and an older tea lady pushed a trolley round with a plate of cakes and biscuits. Lambeth Palace was also a trolley kind of place. 'The private secretary's secretary would ring round every morning at 10.45 and announce: "Coffee!"' said Caroline Chartres, 'And we'd all go up into the main office and help ourselves from the trolley: coffee in china cups. Then at 4 p.m. it was "Tea!" and up we'd go again.' These moments of punctuation imbued offices with a sense of gentility and gentleness; they had a similar effect to breaks in a cricket match.

Staff parties performed a useful function of releasing tensions, and not only sexual ones, sometimes just fear and dread. A terrifying matron would let her hair down for one glorious evening at the hospital 'knees-up'. 'Matron's Ball' at the Leeds General Infirmary, an annual Christmas event, enhanced the working life of Gail Nicolaidis, who started out there as a sister's aid straight after leaving school at sixteen in the mid-1960s, on a salary of £370 a year plus accommodation in the nurses' home. The ball took place in the town hall, everyone dressing up in their best. Gail wore a chiffon evening gown she'd made herself, having had sewing lessons in domestic science at school. Matron – scourge of the ward round – wearing a long glittery evening dress, and doing her best to smile and relax, suddenly seemed almost human. At one 1960s Matron's Ball Gail went to, the young medics got hold of Matron's lilac-coloured Morris Minor, which she kept parked outside the entrance, lifted it up, and plonked it on the floor of the hospital foyer – this was before revolving doors made such larks impossible.

Factory knees-ups, too, enhanced camaraderie. The children's Christmas party at the Tampax factory in Havant gave the children of the young mothers who worked there on the 'twilight shifts' something to console them for their mothers' evening absences from home – even if the mothers never quite owned up to what it was they were spending their evenings making. Of the tailoring factory Hepworth's in Sunderland where Judith Anderson worked in the 1960s and '70s, she said, 'They were good employers. They did everything for the staff: all kinds of social gatherings and Christmas parties. They had a knees-up for the whole factory in 1973 when Sunderland won the FA Cup.' 'At Christmas,' Judith said, 'they took the children of the staff to the pantomime and each child got a bag of sweets.' I asked her how these perks were paid for. Were they done purely out of generosity and paid for by the firm? She said that actually, she signed up to having a few shillings, and later 25p when decimal currency started, deducted from her weekly wage, to go towards the annual children's party. And when it came to drinks at the factory knees-ups at various disco venues across Sunderland, everyone was given a 'chit' to get one free drink, and after that they had to pay.

There was a general sense that as a factory employee you were never far from a party balloon. But there were fun-less perks too. At the larger factories, before launderettes started, employees were treated to the labour-saving perk of getting their washing done. Audrey Loper, the one who ran home for lunch from Lister's Mill in Bradford in the early 1950s, told me, 'Each department had a different day to get your family washing done. You brought it in, in a big bag, dropped it at the counter, and it would be done by the end of the day, in the factory's own big washing machines.' With a working daughter and working single mother living together, this was a godsend. It seemed like pure generosity on the part of the factory, but relieving women of this act of domestic drudgery released a whole cohort of them to work there.

Perks could divide as well as unify. In the world of the office, the knowledge that the senior men were quietly holding their meetings on the golf course was felt as decidedly unfair by their female colleagues who would have liked to be in on the discussions. 'A friend and I even started to learn to play golf so we could join them,' said Elisabeth Beccle, who worked as a fund manager in Edinburgh in the early 1980s, 'but we knew we'd never get as good as them.' The firm's

annual summer staff outing was a two-tier affair – a far cry
from everyone going off together in a communal charabanc.
'The senior fund managers went off to Muirfield for the day
to play golf and have lunch,' Elisabeth said, 'and the rest of
us – including all the female staff, regardless of their position
in the firm – went off in two coaches to Peebles Hydro for
a game of croquet, followed by lunch and a swim. It was
fifteen on the golf outing, and eighty-five of us at Peebles
Hydro.' The male senior managers, Elisabeth said, were
'old Edinburgh', in other words very much pre- any kind
of feminism awareness, and the golf club they went to was
Muirfield, where women weren't allowed to be members or
to go into the dining room. Elisabeth was a US equity fund
manager, and a number of the men at her level would have
been among the Muirfield golfing party from which she
was excluded.

'I wouldn't have called it a perk, exactly,' said Sue Kipling,
when I asked her about her rights as an employee at ICI's
Billingham Plant in the early 1970s to go to the various clubs
that belonged to ICI, all of them housed in beautiful old
houses with croquet lawns, called things like Norton Hall,
Wilton Castle and Winnington Hall. 'I would have called it
an entitlement.'

Yes, I do see there's a blurred patch where perk meets
entitlement. Joining ICI at her level in 1970, as the only
female researcher as opposed to lab assistant or secretary,
Sue expected her entitlements to include being allowed to
go to whichever club was the one nearest to her ICI plant –
Billingham's was Norton Hall. The men at her level all went
to them. 'But these places were still run like gentlemen's
clubs,' she told me, 'and it was made clear to me that women
were not welcome at them.'

When she went across the Pennines to visit ICI's

Winnington laboratory in Cheshire, she was put up for the night at their club, Winnington Hall, but was refused entry to the bar because it was men only. She hovered in the doorway until a man offered to get her a drink, which she then had to sip in the hall area. This situation echoed life inside the lab, where she had expected to be allowed to go along to the management meetings, as she was at a high enough level to do so, and blithely asked 'Can I come?' but then gleaned that she wasn't welcome, and heard on the grapevine that the meetings had had their names changed from 'management meetings' to 'chaps' meetings'.

It seemed to be easier to join in to office-club life if you were sporty. Duffield House, a Victorian pile in extensive grounds, was ICI Paints' country house in Stoke Poges, near the Slough plant where half of the company's paint was made. Gill Blenkinsop, working as a marketing coordinator, was given the role of chairman of the ICI Tennis Club. 'So many ICI families came to watch the cricket and tennis matches at weekends,' she told me. 'Socially, that was amazing.' The facilities were lavish. There were four hard tennis courts, six lawn tennis courts, a cricket pitch, a hockey pitch, a football pitch and a pavilion with a bar, as well as a dining room for those in high positions and bedrooms for business visitors from overseas. In proportion with the number of women working at ICI 'there was one ladies' tennis team and three men's teams', and there was also a bowls team for the retirees. 'We played the ICI Plastics division from Welwyn Garden City and the ICI Plant Protection from Sussex, as well as playing against other firms,' Gill said, reminding me that the big firms all had this kind of facility for healthy sporty activity – for example, Shell, BP and the Bank of England, and some department stores, too, such as Harrods.

A tennis afternoon at ICI's sports ground at Stoke Poges, 1982

Heather Hall, who worked as a bank clerk in Poole, jumped at the chance to join the Lloyds Bank sailing club, which enabled her to vanish off for whole weekends and get away from her oppressive parents. 'The bank provided a forty-three-foot-long yacht, moored at Gosport, that could take eight people. We'd hire it for £1.25 per day, and would sail up and down the Solent for the day, or we'd gather on a Friday evening, sail across the Channel through the night, arrive at Cherbourg at 6 a.m., have a whole day there and a good French meal on Saturday night, and arrive back on Sunday afternoon.' That was a whole weekend of family meals avoided. The yacht enhanced Lloyds' reputation as wealthy, healthy and fun-loving, as did the fact that the bank owned a tall ship and signed up to the Tall Ships Race, in which Heather took part: 'The bank flew us out to Kiel in Germany in 1972 and we picked up *Dark Horse*, a yacht with huge sails, at the marina and raced it back to Britain.' Lloyds was less competitive, sailing-wise, than the other banks, and never won a race in Heather's thirteen years there.

John Lewis had and still has its own hotels for its part-ners, the Odney Club near Cookham and Brownsea Castle near Poole; a perk Kay Clayton made and still makes the most of, not minding taking her mini-breaks in the company of colleagues. 'Just twenty pounds a night to stay there, and that included the food,' she was delighted to discover when she started in the 1980s; a perk to go alongside the annual bonus, and being allowed to go to the social club open every evening on the top floor of the flagship store in Oxford Street.

Long before expenses scandals, employees were positively encouraged to charge expenses to the firm. 'The first time I put in my expenses claim when I started as a Fleet Street journalist in the mid-1960s,' recalled Celia Haddon, 'I put in a claim for seven pounds and was told it wouldn't do. I simply had to put in a claim for at least twelve pounds.' Each week one of the male reporters would put in a claim for '£15: payment to contact', and the money would be split three ways, between the reporter and two members of staff on the news desk 'so that was an extra fiver for them each week'. Everyone would file endless claims for 'drinks to con-tact' and first-class train tickets.

Working as an announcer for Lord Harlech's new tele-vision channel HTV in 1968, Daphne Neville's only perk was a clothes allowance of £50 per year. This, on top of her annual salary of a mere £1,500, wasn't nearly enough for the glamorous roles she was expected to perform. In those early days of television, she and her fellow announcers suddenly became so famous that 'everywhere we went, e.g. M&S in Cardiff, there were queues of people wanting to touch us'. Daphne was invited to do endless public appearances, such as opening fetes and charity bazaars all over the west of England, for which (her contract stipulated) she was not allowed to be paid a single extra penny: 'we were supposed to be doing it for love'. So she turned up at these events, to be 'treated like the Queen, but wearing a top I'd bought for 2/6d.' It was simply expected that for a woman lucky enough to have landed such a celebrity job, the 'honour and glory of it' (as Daphne put it) would be remuneration enough.

Daphne Neville, television presenter for HTV, expected to 'dress like the Queen' to open bazaars and fetes, for no fee, on her tiny clothing allowance

When Betty Kenward came to the end of her life, she remembered Fleur Thomas in her will ('to my complete shock,' said Fleur), leaving her a few ornaments and items of furniture, which Fleur cherishes. So, the habit of giving small treats to people who worked for you sometimes led to greater acts of kindness, never forgotten. We remember life's perks on our deathbeds, and perhaps the givers of perks, on their deathbeds, die more contentedly for having bestowed them.

14

Machinery

'You have been promoted from the typing pool to become secretary to the Manager, who has never before had his own secretary. An additional small room has been acquired for you. Make a list of the furniture and equipment you will need'

test question from *Secretarial Duties* by
John Harrison, 8th edition, 1988

And still the working day ground on. There was no getting away from the hours and hours of having to give your waking life over to an institution that had nothing to do with you personally.

'It's a well-oiled machine,' I was told when I started at *Harpers & Queen* and was impressed by the seamless editing process from galley proofs to page proofs.

The 'well-oiled machine' was literal, too. Everyone I interviewed mentioned the noise of the appliances: the hydraulic lift powered by pistons in oil, with its 'clanking accordion doors', which took Penny Eyles, very slowly, up to her office in Little Essex Street when she worked as a secretary at Methuen publishers in the 1960s; the iron lungs in the polio ward at the Nuffield Orthopaedic Centre where Pamela Jubb worked as a nurse in the same decade ('all you could see were the children's heads sticking out'); the addictively ink-scented Banda machine operated by the 'delightful office typist' at the Inner London Education Authority where Philippa Millar worked in the 1970s; the 'great churning noises' emanating from the 'duplicating room' at Eton College where Angela Slater worked as the first female teacher, or 'beak', in the early 1980s. I kept being ambushed by clanking machinery and contraptions.

It was a loud, metallic, hydraulic, pneumatic world. Nurses were forever turning handles and pressing foot pumps to cause machines to elevate or descend. Telephonists were pulling and pushing plugs. The telephonist at Methuen was 'blind,' Penny Eyles told me, 'and dour, and sat in a metal cage in the middle of the building, in his tiny cupboard-office, listening in to all the telephone conversations' as he pulled the plugs in and out.

The pulling of handles also went on wherever any counting was going on. Barclays Bank, though it set up its first computers in 1969, still used National Cash Register adding machines when Lydia Kitching worked as a bank clerk there in the 1960s and '70s: 'The machine looked like a till, with a handle or "arm" at the side to pull down if you were adding a column of figures. It made a great clunking noise as you pulled.' And 'it could do take-away as well as addition,' she hastened to add, as if this justified the need for the metallic arm. Working as a young accountant in the early 1970s, Janet Walker went to audit a firm called Franklin Mint, which made limited-edition medals. It was still doing its adding-up with an abacus.

Everything rattled and shook. Factories were deafening, the noise of the machinery drowning out the Friday sing-songs. There was no question of chatting while you worked in the Tampax factory. Conversation had to be reserved for tea breaks. 'The buttonhole machine at William Read's,' Susan Watson told me, 'vibrated so much that it had to be clamped to the bench. It stitched one side of the buttonhole, and then a great big knife came down and slashed a hole in the middle of the stitching.' Above it all, going round and round, was the belt-driven machinery constantly juddering. 'You put twelve bobbins onto a machine,' was how Audrey Loper began her description of working 'on the winding' at Lister's Mill, 'and you tied the bobbins up to the cones ...' I scribbled it all down, trying to imagine it. This was factory life in all its high-decibel physicality.

You would expect such hubbub in places that physically made things, but the noise was also loud in offices, where mere letters were being typed and documents copied. 'In our first word-processing room in the early 1980s,' Sharon Scard recalled, 'the printer had to have a large plastic hood put over it to keep the noise down.'

The Roneo machine, an early form of copier that worked by forcing ink through waxed paper stencils, and could make about nine copies of anything before going faint, made a loud spinning noise as it rotated and spattered its operators with ink. Typewriters gradually grew quieter, from the din of mechanical Imperial Remingtons, via the clack-clack of golf-ball ones, to the quieter click-clack of electric typewriters, to the muffled tap-tap of electronic keyboards, which eventually brought to all offices a similar eerie hush to the one outside Lord Copper's office immortalised by Evelyn Waugh in his 1938 novel *Scoop*: 'The typewriters were of a special kind; their keys made no more sound than the drumming of a bishop's finger tips on an upholstered prie-dieu.' All keyboards were heading towards this eventual, solemn muffledness.

Taking me through the long process to reach this point, Vivien Ruddock reminded me that 'The great step forward was WYSIWYG.' That acronym, which happened to be pronounceable thanks to the position of its vowels, stood for 'What You See Is What You Get', and was a landmark in word processing. From that moment on, you could see on your screen the words in exactly the same position they would be in on the printed page. Of course, you could do that with an ordinary typewriter as well, where all you had was the piece of paper; but in that case, if you made a mistake, you had the soul-destroying job of erasing the mistake on the top copy and every carbon copy with your paintbrush of Tippex – or 'Tippet', as Betty Kenward at *Harpers & Queen* used to mispronounce the new-fangled white stuff, which dried up to a thick paste in its bottle if you didn't screw the lid on tightly enough.

As people described exactly what they had to do in the transitional days when mechanical objects gave way to computers, I took notes, and tried to make head or tail of what they were telling me about the gigantic contraptions they had to operate. Here's Kathy Hey, for example, describing what she had to do, aged twenty, when she was computer operator of the Central Processing Unit of Barclays Bank from 1969 to 1970. 'The unit was huge,' she said, 'eight feet tall, the size of the wall in my lounge. I was basically loading the computer. The programmers were the ones who went in and flicked the switches at the back. I was loading these enormous metal disks, two feet in diameter. There were four of them on a disk-unit that you took over and slotted in.' Information from all the bank branches was being fed into the main machine in this way. 'There was DOS and then there was TOS,' she explained. 'The disk-operated system and the tape-operated system. The tapes were more like huge cassettes.'

Lydia Kitching continued the theme. 'You had these hole-punched tapes, coiled up, and you had to feed them through the machine. You'd get nearly to the end, and it would go "ping", and that meant all your work was null and void, and you'd have to start all over again.'

It sounded unbelievably physically tiring and frustrating, and then there was D-Day: 'Decimal Day', 15 February 1971, when the whole banking system had to close down for two days while every single account was converted to pounds and 'new pence'. For this to happen, for some reason, the staff had to pretend to be customers paying in to the cashier with pretend coins.

'I was working at the Shepherd's Bush careers office of the Inner London Education Authority when they first had computers in 1979,' said Philippa Miller. She proceeded to describe the computer to me, and her description included the words 'mahogany', and 'green baize', and again, I scribbled it all down and tried to imagine the scene from the early life of computers. 'We were delivered a great big thing – well, a terminal – on four legs, a big, free-standing thing with a keyboard. To connect that to the mainframe computer at the headquarters in County Hall, you had to use a telephone. You'd dial the number and, as you dialled it, a piercing shriek was emitted by the handset. At that moment you had to put the handset into a special handset-shaped mahogany box with a green-baize lining, and shut the box hard with the handset inside it. This was the very first sort of modem: an acoustic modem. When it had done its booting up, the information came out onto a tractor-fed form.'

A tractor-fed form? It seemed to go wrong a lot. 'We weren't impressed. It was a very slow, frustrating process.'

The dawn of the computer age was a juddering, shrieking business.

A similar piercing shriek was emitted into your ear in the short-lived fax era of the final decade of this book, whenever you dialled a fax number. It was a shock if, intending to dial a telephone number, you dialled an almost identical fax number by mistake. Instead of the reassuring ringtone, you got a piercing shriek and no reply. So you slammed the phone down. It was thrilling to think that someone could type a twenty-page document in Australia and a copy of that very document could churn out into your office a few seconds later. But it was a miracle if something didn't go wrong. Either the document spewed out unstoppably, like an unspooling roll of lavatory paper, forgetting its key job of cutting off each page at the end, or it simply stopped: the machine jamming, a smudge of black ink on a crumpled accordion of shiny fax paper marking the moment it had juddered to a halt. It didn't help that fax machines tended to be kept in cupboards, so the operators were working in ill-lit, confined spaces.

Men built and mended the machinery, but it was women who were landed with it and expected to work it on a daily basis – somehow to un-jam the fax machine, for example, and replace the fax roll. 'The headmaster at the boys' prep school where I worked loved his Gestetner machine,' said Kate Green – the Gestetner being an even more primitive stencil-based copying machine than the Roneo. 'He was always trying to mend it himself. He had a very dim view of women and their abilities.' In the early days of computers, what usually happened was that the people at the coalface of office life – usually the junior women – just had a computer plonked on their desk one morning and were expected to use it from that moment on. And no one told them how to. Elspeth Allison, working as a secretary at a shoe wholesalers in Fleckney, Leicestershire, in the 1980s, was perfectly happy with her golf-ball typewriter: 'Smooth and posh. But my boss suddenly said, "You need a computer." And I thought, "Oh my Lord!" The office manager said, "Don't worry. It's easy." And there it was the next morning, on my desk. And it was impossible to work it. At the end of the day, half the letters weren't done. My boss was furious. "It's meant to make you faster!" he said. "Look at you!" I went home and cried and cried. I knew the boss wouldn't have a clue how to work it himself. There was literally one lad in the office who did know how to. I was just thrown in at the deep end.' This was typical.

Elspeth's boss dictated letters to her by shouting them from one end of the office to the other, so her nerves were pre-jangled, even before the computer arrived to make things worse.

The day came when everyone had to face the dreaded new item, the computer on their desk. It was being stuck at home on the morning after the hurricane of October 1987 that made Janet Walker, working as an accountant in television, decide that she simply must try to get to grips with the computer that had been given to her by the office – an unwanted present. She switched it on and spent the day grappling with its green words on a black background. She soon realised this life-improving device was a 'mixed blessing' because what happened was that everyone now expected her to do everything faster. 'A flashing green "greater than" symbol would appear,' recalled Barbara Rich, describing the experience of using her first computer – 'a "command prompt", and you'd have to type in a DOS prompt – a Disk Operated System prompt. You'd go into your program and you'd then have to navigate from menu to menu. You lived in absolute terror of pressing a wrong button and deleting the whole program.' It was all fraught with anxiety. The word 'menu' was supposed to make the options sound mouth-watering, but it didn't. As one ex-temp said to me, speaking from experience, 'If you pressed the wrong button, the whole computer system would go down.'

In the dying world of word processors, meanwhile – word processors being pre-computers that could do only words, not pictures, and were superseded even more quickly than the stagecoach was by the train – the working day for secretaries had swiftly degenerated to a grim existence of being in a pool of headphone-wearing women known as 'Word Processing', sitting in a room also known as 'Word Processing', typing letters they'd been sent on tapes by people they hadn't seen. ('Just give it to Word Processing and they'll do it.') 'You had to know all the different commands,' recalled Beryl Stoker, who did exactly this job at an accountancy firm in the 1980s. Nothing was intuitive with a word processor. You had to remember a hundred different 'semi-mnemonic key combinations' in order to do simple actions like use italics or bold, or move a paragraph down the page. 'Semi-mnemonic' was too generous. Those commands were not easy to remember. They just had a random letter of the alphabet attached to them. Temps who went from office to office needed to carry a notebook full of their own lists of different commands for all the different brands of word processor and 'software' they were supposedly 'proficient' in. But at least they still had a job. As soon as personal computers started arriving on every desk, the 'men who would never type a letter' suddenly did type their own letters, in their untrained, two-index-fingered way, and the demand for secretaries fell off a cliff.

Adrienne Waterfield, whose job it was to train two thousand members of staff over six years to use new office computers, said that the only way to do it was 'person to person'. It was no good sending people on courses laid on by specialised out-siders, who came to the office and tried to train the staff in a 'classroom' situation. 'Either they knew it already, in which case they took no notice of the lesson – some of them just sat at the back doing their Christmas cards – or they came out after a whole week of doing the course and still didn't know how to do it.' The difference in learning ability – and in the very desire to learn at all – in this area was huge. 'Some were quick to learn; with others I could spend days teaching them one to one, and they still couldn't get it into their thick heads.'

Thus the country juddered into the technological age.

PART V

LOVE INTEREST

15

Lust and Love in the Workplace

'It is difficult to generalise on questions of
relationship between employer and secretary,
but in all matters the secretary must
adapt herself to the methods preferred by
her employer'

from *Secretarial Duties* by John Harrison,
8th edition, 1988

The other main distraction to get everyone through the long
afternoon was speculating on who was in love with or having
an affair with whom. Proximity in the workplace was the
tinder before Tinder.

I need to make it clear, before we get into the lust and love
side of working life, that by no means all men were letches. It
would be malign and wrong to suggest that they were. Many
were good-mannered, enlightened, 100 per cent faithful to
their wives or partners, male or female, and totally 'safe in
taxis'; much nicer to work with and for, in fact, than some
of the women, who went around poisoning the working

environment with their subtle jealousies, favouritisms and moody silences.

'I loved the men! Such *gents*!' was how Virginia Ironside summed up her time as a young journalist in the early 1960s where she was employed as – that expression again – a 'Girl Friday' to two men, one of them Lionel Birch, who was 'the most-married man in the world – eight times', so he can't have been a total angel, but he was a delight to work with. Virginia loved going downstairs to the hot-metal room and chatting to the gents down there, too. But she did say that when it came to casual sex, the Cockney ones treated you 'like a princess', whereas for the public schoolboys it was 'just bonking'.

The test of a real 'gent' was not that he held the door open and said 'After you' in a zealously chivalrous manner, but that he was just normally polite, respectful and friendly, made you feel intelligent rather than stupid, valued your contributions and hard work, and treated you as worth listening to, not just speaking to. The non-'gent' was the obsequious holder-open-of-the-door who then couldn't remember your name when he shouted across the office at you. Most of us can shut our eyes and instantly recall the gents and the non-gents we have come across in our working lives. And most of us can recall women who fitted just as neatly into those two contrasting categories.

So, who pinched whose bottom? As I mentioned in the Introduction, it never happened to me. Not only did it never happen, but in the two 1980s offices where I worked, bottom-pinching didn't even seem a remotely likely activity. It simply wasn't in the vocabulary of the kind of courting and pining that were going on. By the 1980s, in civilised offices, fantasising had become internalised. All the sex was going on in the imagination. If two people were crazy about each other, they might just brush against each other briefly as they passed the photocopying machine, both equally desperate for a scarcely noticeable split-second of unleashed desire, before they put the lid firmly back on it and just glanced at each other from time to time for the rest of the day. If someone had an unrequited crush, they just sat at their desk looking sad.

When I came across bottom-pinching during my researches – men doing it to women, seniors to underlings, unasked, unwanted – it tended to be in the earlier decades of this book, in environments where the atmosphere was essentially male and intrinsically coarse-grained, and where women were treated more or less as living embodiments of the topless photo on the piece of cardboard behind the multipacks of Big D peanuts on a pub wall, which gradually revealed more naked breast at the moment of each ripping off of another packet. Woman as 'feast for the eyes' and 'butt of constant innuendo' was what had to be endured. 'I got pinched so badly on my bottom in the lift that I had a bruise for two weeks,' one woman who worked in Fleet Street in the 1960s told me; at that time, women weren't legally allowed to work after 10 p.m., and it was stipulated that a woman must wear a skirt, and the 'down-table subs' would call you over to the two tables where they worked, and you had to bend quite far over one of the tables to look at your story so the men on the other table could look up your skirt – this was just after miniskirts had come in. The atmosphere crackled with sex, and the lid was not kept on. Late at night, after all the women had gone home as per the 10 p.m. rule, one of the photographers put on porn movies in the newsroom. That same photographer took a ladder to his shoots so he could take a quick 'down shot' of a woman's breasts to keep for his personal pleasure.

This was straight in at the deep end for this young woman, who on her first morning, aged twenty-one, was shouted at so loudly and at such close quarters by her boss 'that I thought he'd broken my eardrum'. Her mistake was to have interviewed someone but forgotten to write down his telephone number. 'He shouted at everyone, but the sexual harassment was reserved for me. I got "bloody" and "fuck" the whole time during his bollockings – but I *had* been brought up on a farm.' So she was less shockable, when it came to both bad language and sex, than some who hadn't been brought up on farms.

The only way to keep her job was to buckle down in this atmosphere and get on with it. Men would come back from an overnight story, and as they wandered into the office, everyone shouted, 'Did you get your leg over?' This was daily office banter. 'Go there, cry, and tell them you'll be fired unless they talk to you' was the usual morning command. She learned to bribe policemen and doormen. She was seduced by the (married) literary editor, a rather pathetic figure who asked her to write her first ever review, and she was thrilled, being an English graduate. 'He took me out to dinner and got me into bed. And then said, "I want to run away with you to Ibiza."'

After that, when the fat, middle-aged chief sub started getting amorous, she found excuses. 'I'd say, "I've got a boyfriend" or "I can't sleep with anyone – I'm going to be celibate for three months" or "I've just had an abortion."' If you simply turned a male colleague down, she told me, he might stop doing you favours, or worse, penalise you or get you fired. 'There's no doubt in my mind that I would have been fired if I'd made a complaint about any of this.'

'I did go a bit mad when I was working on Fleet Street,' Virginia Ironside told me, speaking about her time there as a young pop-music columnist in early 1960s. 'I was an only child, my mother had left home when I was thirteen, and my father had recently married again – I felt extremely abandoned. As a result, I was desperate for affection – from anyone, really. This desperation coincided with the beginning of the Sixties, and the result was that I did sleep around. I just wanted people's arms around me, basically.

'But it was a very confusing time. No one knew where they stood, sexually. Society was turned on its head. The Pill had made no-risk sex available to everyone, and men were under the impression that once the fear of pregnancy was removed, women would be as keen on sex as they were. It didn't quite work like that.'

In the 'Mucky Duck' pub, she said, 'a journalist might knock ash from his cigarette down your cleavage, and if you bent over, he'd ping your suspenders. But it wasn't a hanging matter – it was basically playful and childish, rather than abusive. I think most men were terrified of women in those days, and this was a kind of teasing, a sign of affection. I didn't feel demeaned. I just felt, "Poor old bloke!" and said, "Ooh, naughty!" like someone in a *Carry On* film.'

Virginia had had no parental guidance on sex. Her mother had been an alcoholic – a very unhappy, though immensely successful, career woman – a fashion icon in the Sixties, as Professor of Fashion at the Royal College of Art. She'd had numerous affairs which basically ended her marriage.

'Like a lot of unhappy, confused girls at that time,' Virginia said, 'I went around with a diaphragm in my handbag. I'd go on an innocent date and bung it up myself on the off chance. Sex was a comfort to me, like a heroin fix. Having someone to hold me at night – which inevitably meant sex – made the next day much more bearable. Normally I'd wake every day in tears and feeling suicidal. After a night with a man, I felt calm and relaxed. I was just as responsible for all those one-night stands as the men were. I couldn't blame any of them. If I was often drunk, they were too. And they were often as young and confused as well. I don't agree when my contemporaries say, "Weren't we abused then!" It was a mutual thing. At least it was with me.'

Forward to the 1980s, by which time in 'my' offices such things were not remotely happening, and we have Melanie Cable-Alexander working as a young temp in the Private Clients department of a City merchant bank, where money-making on a massive scale seemed to be equated in the men's minds with their virility. Here, the sense of male sexual entitlement was still going strong. One of the bankers undid his flies one morning, slapped his penis onto the desk, and said, 'What d'you want to do with that?' Melanie, a convent girl, was rather flustered. She muttered softly, 'I'd like you to put it away,' and tried to go back to business as usual, typing letters to the great landowning families of Britain about how their portfolios were doing, making all the normal audio-typist spelling mistakes 'such as typing "a cute interest" when it should have been "acute interest".'

The bankers were taking drugs, Melanie told me. 'I thought they were just a bit hung-over in the mornings, but they were actually public-school kids taking cocaine to maintain their lifestyle – the easy money, the working all hours, the hard partying.' That plonking of the penis onto the desk was just the tip of their high-octane lifestyle.

Young women like Melanie, meanwhile, were simply doing their best to hold on to their jobs, emerging from childhoods of tamped-down self-esteem. One family member said to Melanie in her early teens she was willing to bet a million pounds that Melanie would never succeed in life. It would take a long time for her to build up her self-confidence.

Melanie Cable-Alexander, at the time when she was
working at the merchant bank, early 1980s

Having been at the Brooking School of Ballet and General
Education in Marylebone, run by the child-disliking Nesta
Brooking and Eleanor Hudson, where 'if your toes weren't
pointed enough you were caned on the legs and arms', Tessa
Skola told me, 'I was used to being abused.' When she was
thirteen in 1973, Miss Brooking told her, 'Your father's a
bastard and you're too close to your mother.' Tessa ran away
at fourteen, rang the Samaritans, and was allowed to leave
the hellhole at the end of that term, but the ground was
laid.

After a spell on stage at the Windmill Theatre aged seventeen, 'dancing in front of Japanese tourists and the odd dirty-mac man', Tessa worked as a cabaret dancer in clubs in Carnaby Street, and 'I'd get called names on stage: "You fucking slut" and so on.' This was the late 1970s. 'Other girls would go off to Claridge's with bankers after the show, and come back the next day with a black eye.' The stag-night men were the worst, Tessa told me. 'Their attitude to women was appalling. If they had a lap dancer squatting over them simulating sex, they'd be goading each other on. They weren't allowed to touch the girls: that was the rule. I looked through the curtains and saw the bottoms of the girls over the laps of the men – and the men's faces were utterly cold and emotionless. Either they were women-haters, or they came with all their neuroses and hate and took it out on them.'

This was the extreme example of the undermining of girls in childhood paving the way for their enduring of abuse in early adulthood.

Helen Shay, whom we last met when she eventually landed her job as a trainee lawyer at a solicitors' firm in Huddersfield, was sexually assaulted in the office car park in the early 1980s by one of the firm's clients. 'He seemed a nice guy – he worked nearby. He started dancing with me at an office social. Marvin Gaye's "Sexual Healing" was playing and he started rubbing up too much against me, so I pulled away and left early to avoid getting into anything, especially as he was a client and I also knew he was married. Then he followed me to the enclosed car park, and pinned himself against me outside my car. I told him to let me go but he persisted in trying to kiss and feel me. I was crying.' This went on for about five minutes until Helen managed to push him away and drive off.

'He came into the office the next day,' Helen said, 'and looked at me, and said, "Are you all right?" He was looking at me hard, to see if I was going to say anything to anyone. I said, "Yeah, I'm all right." It would never have occurred to me to report it. The recrimination would most likely have been for me, not for him.'

It was a culture of keeping quiet. Life at the ICI Billingham Plant in the 1970s for Sue Kipling as a young researcher was wall-to-wall sexual innuendo, but, as she said, 'I didn't complain about it. I knew that if I did, I wouldn't get anywhere.' She meant 'not get anywhere' in both senses: the complaint would not succeed in changing anything, and she would not get on in her career. 'The man who really resented me was training me, and I needed to learn from him.' So the two of them were stuck working together all day, and the way the man dealt with the situation was to load his instructions with innuendo, so that if ever he was explaining how a piston went in and out, he lifted his eyebrows up and down in nudge nudge, wink-wink way as he demonstrated how it went in and out and in and out. The way Sue dealt with this was to say, 'I need to write down exactly what you're saying.' She wrote his words down verbatim, with all the sexual connotations included, and read it all back to him afterwards. He did not like this. 'But if I'd complained, I would probably have been told, "You're not really suitable for this job in the lab. Let's remove you to a nice quiet office job."'

It was the scientific people in the lab who behaved the worst, Sue said, not the process workers on the plant, who were much more gent-like. In other words, it was the supposedly better-educated ones who were the worst. What's more, the scientific ones were mostly married, and their wives had no idea that their husbands kept pornographic magazines in the drawer of their lab desk. Whenever one of them went on a train to visit a lab at another plant, he came back with a new stash of top-shelf magazines he'd bought at the station, and the men then took turns with them, knowing which bottom drawer they were kept in. Sue met their wives at the occasional office 'do's, and she did wonder whether their husbands adopted an entirely different persona every evening, as soon as they walked in through the front door for their supper.

'Everything was designed to unnerve,' said Sue, 'including the fact that because there were so few women working at the plant, we had to use the revolting men's loos.' The only other woman working with her was such a fervent women's libber that she refused to wear a bra. 'The men could see all that she had, swinging about, and they enjoyed it,' Sue said. 'When she was out of earshot they'd discuss in front of me "how her tits moved" and so on.' This was the atmosphere in which Sue had no choice but to be steeped, if she wanted to pursue her career as a scientist.

Men tried it on; women fought them off. Mary Burd told me that George Weidenfeld 'tried it on in Prunier's restaurant' when one of his girlfriends had stood him up. She batted him away, and went back to her flat, where her flatmate, also a secretary, was having an affair with a boss, meeting him for trysts in Hyde Park. This was in the early 1960s, when Hyde Park was awash with bosses meeting up with their secretaries beside the Serpentine, and when one of the 'personal attributes' expected of a secretary in that decade's edition of the *Secretarial Duties* textbook was that she should 'be silent in matters such as her own personal troubles, office gossip and her employer's affairs and business'. But this kind of trying it on was still being done two decades later, even by men you might have expected to be more enlightened by then, and more at the end of the 'thinking about sex but not acting on it too impulsively' end of the spectrum. At a Christmas party in a restaurant, while Agnes Blane was working as a secretary for an architectural practice just off the King's Road in Chelsea in the early 1980s, one of the architects pinned her against the wall and 'rammed his tongue down my throat'. Again, nothing was said the next day.

Seniors were still doing it to juniors; this was the culture, in the dying days of the convention that the best compatibility and the most intoxicating sexual chemistry was between a high-powered man and a less high-powered woman who could be moulded to fit in with his ways. 'He had rogered her twice/And found it was nice/To be called "Mr Pritchard" in bed', as Richard Usborne's poem on the boss-secretary sexual fantasy went, quoted in Jeremy Lewis's *The Vintage Book of Office Life*. To be called Mr Pritchard in bed was the starting point of a man's fantasies.

Some did try to complain, but nothing was done. Daphne Neville, the one who was paid just £1,500 a year but treated like the Queen when opening fetes, eventually had to leave HTV, the final straw being that the management did nothing when she mentioned she had a stalker. 'Every day at 5 p.m.,' she told me, 'at the beginning of the children's slot, there was a programme called *It's Time For Me*. I was lowered down in a wicker basket, and told a story.' This, plus her daily continuity announcing and presenting, obviously drove one viewer into an obsessive state of desire, and he sent her a torrent of suggestive letters, and then came to her house to spy on her children. 'I put the letters on my boss's desk, to show him, but he did nothing about them,' she told me. 'I saw the pile of unopened envelopes on his desk.' She was expected to shut up and deal with it, and get on with the job.

Daphne Neville on HTV, 1969

Opinions varied among my interviewees as to whether sexual attention was offensive, or harmless, or even rather flattering. 'The idea that being wolf-whistled at was offensive! For goodness' sake, they were whistling because you were attractive!' said Angela Wheeler, who worked as a BOAC air hostess in the mid-1960s. She would not approve of today's threatened clampdowns on wolf-whistling. When she started as an air hostess, she quickly discovered that 'you only had to put on a uniform and you were a target. The presumption was that you were aching to get off at the next aeroplane stop and go to a hotel with them.' 'Them' being both male passengers and stewards, who were forever trying it on and lunging. 'We weren't humiliated by it,' Angela said. 'The amount of pinching of bottoms when we landed in Italy was quite amazing. We kept a count of the number of times our bottoms were pinched between the plane and the hotel room.' Jane Mackie said the same, about her time as an air hostess in the early 1950s. 'All the pilots wanted to do was to get into bed with you. You were beating them off all the time.'

It was both the women's looks and their uniforms that fed men's fantasies. And vice versa when it came to women fantasising about their male uniformed bosses, as Anna did in *Anna the Air Hostess*, although the women tended to be really and truly in love with the men they had crushes on. 'Three air hostesses on my course did marry first officers,' Angela Wheeler said, 'and once they met their Mr Right, they left.' For the men, it was a pressure-cooker situation when they had four ingredients working together: the prettiness of the young air hostesses, in those days when looks were one of the key factors in making them eligible for the job; the intrinsic irresistibility of the buttoned-up, tight-fitting, chic little uniforms, kindling a desperate urge to peel them off; the illicitness of doing such a thing; and the other chief nurturer of desire: constant proximity.

There was a feeling among the women of slight pity for the rather desperate, lunging men. 'I just thought, "Silly old bod," said Cicely McCulloch, when the retired Army major for whom she was working as a secretary at an animal charity in Bedford Square in 1966 stood behind her desk and tickled the back of her neck. Cicely just looked across the room at the other secretary and they both grimaced at each other. 'In the lift with a man who pinched our bottoms,' Angela Tilby said, 'we just thought, "Ridiculous!"'' Working as a young film-maker in 1977, Angela found herself sharing the working day with a 'real, old-fashioned sexist cameraman' whose van was full of nude posters and who leered at the girls in the film they were making about religious education.

When Margaret Wilson started out as a barrister's pupil in the mid-1960s, she got used to standing in the tea room and the robing rooms, overhearing the men discussing women's legs. It was all part of the legal landscape and soundscape of those days before the Sex Discrimination Act of 1975, which 'made a huge difference'. Before that, when Margaret was starting out, most chambers wouldn't take women, claiming that (a) that they didn't have the lavatories for it, (b) 'women would just go off and have babies', and (c) 'women were not suited to the Bar as their voices were too shrill'. Lots of solicitors' firms wrote back to female applicants saying, 'We don't take women.' Aspiring female solicitors kept a blacklist of the firms that did this. Margaret was determined to become a barrister, and to do so required her level of determination. To endure the banter was one of the many things required of her.

It was worse when one of the men really was serially having affairs with everyone in the department. One academic I chatted to, who started working in the sociology department of an English university in the 1980s, told me she was astonished to discover that one of her fellow academics, a man she had to work closely with, was serially sleeping with every single one of his PhD students and the majority of his junior staff. This was more than just 'trying it on'; it was a whole system of grooming and patronage, in which a highly intelligent man knew exactly how to plug in to what made each one of the women tick, and he set them against one another. If he didn't like a fellow female academic working at his level, he simply cut her off from teaching, wrecking her career. 'Luckily, the only woman the man didn't seem to fancy was me. But he was extra-nasty to women he didn't fancy.'

'Where am I going to sleep?' Rosie de Courcy asked the bestselling male author, in the summer of 1976, who had been so late delivering his manuscript that Rosie had to go all the way to his house – in fact, his 'ramshackle barn' – in Tuscany to collect it from him.

'There,' he replied, pointing to his four-poster double bed

up in the gallery. 'And he started telling me about the exciting sex we were going to have.' It didn't happen. Rosie climbed into her own sleeping bag on the sofa at bedtime, 'and I saw him in the middle of the night shining a torch into my face, but I was like a mummy in that sleeping bag.'

Alongside the men trying it on, there was a counter-attack from women in the form of 'if you've got it, flaunt it and have fun with it'. Working at the bookshop Truslove & Hanson in the mid-1960s, Lizie Byng climbed up a long ladder to fetch the leather photograph albums that were stored on a high shelf, wearing her black velvet hot pants and her pale-pink suede lace-up leather boots, 'and men would stand and watch me through the window'. Why not make the most of driving the whole passing population of Sloane Street crazy with desire? 'We got our bottoms pinched *the whole time*,' she told me, merrily, of her working life in London at that time. So it certainly wasn't just Italians who pinched bottoms, although Italians did so with the same uninhibitedness with which they pinched babies' chubby cheeks.

In retaliation, women knew how to exploit men. Working in television in 1981, Janet Walker told me, 'One of my colleagues, Emma, was big-breasted. If ever our department needed extra budget, they'd send Emma upstairs in her low-cut top. It was just a jolly good laugh and a way of getting what you wanted.' It worked a treat.

Just as proximity kindled lust, it could and did also kindle love: deep, long-lasting, Jane-Austen-quality love. If you were of the romantic type, proximity brought ample time to become deeply acquainted with all the adorable traits of the love-object, from the way they held a telephone receiver to the way they handed the surgical instruments to the surgeon, and thus to build up a rock-solid case for proposal and marriage. Just as going on holiday with someone is a true test of compatibility, so can working together be; both involving many, many hours, some stressful, some tedious.

'He could only see my eyes,' said Alison Willatts, recalling the weeks in the early 1970s when she, as a scrubbed-up nurse in an operating theatre at St Thomas's Hospital, was fallen in love with by her future husband, the anaesthetist at work in the same hushed room. 'We discovered we both liked music and going to the theatre,' she told me – the other kind of theatre – and they were off down the path of doctor-marries-nurse and lived happily ever after.

Doctor-marries-nurse was more usual than doctor-marries-doctor in those days. But, remember, those nurses, though perhaps not having university degrees as nurses have to have today, were cultured and self-educated, and a discerning man could spot that, even if all he had to go on was the eyes.

The sudden, startling declaration by the shy new chaplain to the Archbishop of Canterbury to a young secretary working at Lambeth Palace in the early 1980s was one of my two standout stories of love blossoming in the workplace. Drifting off to sleep at her school St Margaret's, Bushey, in dormitories named 'Winnington' and 'Ingram' after the sometime Bishop of London Arthur Winnington-Ingram, the young Caroline McLintock had no inkling she would one day marry the future Bishop of London.

Love blossomed over those cups of coffee and tea served from the trolley in Denby cups at 11 a.m. and 4 p.m. The two of them worked very closely together, but, in the incomparable way of British males at the opposite end of the spectrum from the bottom-pinching sort, the young Richard Chartres ('a young fogey', as Caroline said) didn't really know how to get the words out. His feelings were so internalised that she had no idea how far he'd got with them, or indeed that he had them at all.

He invited her to come and see Shakespeare's *Troilus and Cressida* with him in the West End. 'He'd booked tickets, as well as drinks in the interval,' Caroline told me, 'and we sipped our interval drinks, but he was strangely silent. I made polite conversation. Then we sat through the second half of the increasingly grim tragedy. When it was over we walked back from the Aldwych to Lambeth, and I tried to make conversation about London at night and the beauty of the river, but his silence became deeper and deeper. When we got to Lambeth Palace, where I'd left my car, he suddenly asked, "Would you like to come in for a glass of milk?" I said yes. He lived in the Footman's Tower, and we sat in his study. I drank the milk. He was still completely silent. I got up to leave, and was halfway across the room, when he said, "One of the things I meant to ask you was, would you consider marrying me?"'

Caroline was in a state of 'physical shock', she told me. It was her turn to be unable to speak. '"Don't answer me now," Richard said; then, quoting a colleague who had a remarkable gift for postponing any risk of a decision being made, "just let the idea float in the mind." I drove back to my flat, where my flatmates were all fast asleep. I knew I had to go back to work the next morning and face it.'

The next morning, she said, when she opened the great front door of Lambeth Palace to welcome a visitor to Archbishop Runcie, and 'the sunshine came pouring in from the courtyard, I had a sudden feeling of overwhelming conviction that I would marry him'.

The certainty swept away two of her rules for life: never marry a clergyman or a man with a beard. When the engagement was announced in the paper, the Archbishop's private secretary – who had worked with Richard for a long time and (not surprisingly) knew nothing of all this – fell down the stairs on her way to Caroline's office to check that the story wasn't a hoax. It was her turn to be speechless.

My second standout story of love blossoming in the workplace was Elspeth Allison describing how she and her future husband Alan fell in love in the van while working together at Initial Towel Supplies in Leicester in the early 1970s. Elspeth was a divorced mother of four by this time; the man she'd met while working for her parents' vicar's grandchild, and subsequently married, had left, and the maintenance money dried up when he lost his job, so Elspeth now needed to find a job that fitted in with the children's school hours. Being a driver for Initial Towel Supplies was that job.

'I did the city-centre route,' she told me, 'mainly offices and shops, delivering towels, tea towels, roller towels, and so on. We also did workwear: butchers' overalls and boiler suits. The best days were when our transport manager, Alan, came with us. I met him on the first day and found him quite dour. I mentioned this to the other women drivers in the canteen and they said, "Never say anything like that about Alan."'

She soon saw they were right. 'We just got on really well,' Elspeth said. 'Alan showed me how to fill up the van with diesel. Our romance started in the van. Sometimes I went to work in the evenings to do some mending for them – it earned me some extra money. Alan would always come in, so I wasn't on my own in the big warehouse.'

In coarser hands, such as we encountered in various workplaces earlier in this chapter, that scenario would have been a shoo-in for a lust-fest. But, here, real love developed. 'I used to get into a bit of a mess,' Elspeth said. 'One of the kids was in trouble at school, or the electricity at home got cut off because I hadn't paid the bill. Alan lent me the van to go to the Electricity Board and tell them they must give me some electricity. He helped all the time, and eventually he moved in with us, and he spent every penny on the house we still live in now.' Elspeth got pregnant, and carried on as a driver for Initial Towel Supplies until two days before their son was born. Then she gave up work for a few years, until going back to work as a secretary, in the very early days of word processors, at Goodwin Barsby heavy machinery.

Elspeth and Alan (centre) on their wedding day, 1982; they'd met working together at Initial Towel Supplies in Leicester

That was how true love in the workplace developed, in the more rarefied worlds where the life of the mind and the life of the imagination retained dominion over the life of the body, until someone, at last, summoned up the courage to say something.

16

Bumps in the Road

'Mrs Fletcher (Hilary Mackain) finds it "hopeless
to attempt free-lancing in the intervals between
the trek to and from school every day, and
twining herself round the kitchen sink"'

'News of Old Girls', Lawnside school
magazine, 1970

By 'bumps in the road' I mean pregnancy and the ensuing effect of motherhood on women being or not being given permission to continue down the road of making their way in the world of work in the second half of the twentieth century. By reproducing the next generation of the human race, many of them made themselves redundant in their current one.

Prior to the physical bump of a baby in the womb, there was the preceding psychological jolt of getting married, at which point some were expected to give up work there and then. 'It wasn't till 1964,' Lydia Kitching told me, 'that married women were allowed to work at Barclays Bank. Before that, they'd give a woman two hundred pounds in gratuity just before her marriage: "You've got to leave," they said, "but we'll give you two hundred pounds to help you on your way."'

Although the 'marriage bar' – the rule that women were obliged to give up their job on marriage in professions such as teaching and nursing – started being disbanded after the end of the Second World War, it lingered in the Foreign Office till 1973, and would only be knocked on the head once and for all with the Sex Discrimination Act two years later. 'I had to resign on marriage,' Elizabeth Nixon (born in 1945) told me. 'I was working as a secretary at the British Embassy in Beirut, where I met my husband. Every female in the Foreign Office had to resign on marriage. The reasoning was that a diplomatic career was mobile: diplomats needed to be absolutely free to move anywhere. If wives were working, that could be compromised.'

Even when this rule became obsolete, there was a lasting sense deep in the British psyche that marriage and work were somehow not compatible for a woman, and that a well-run household required one full-time stay-at-home spouse.

Many I spoke to gave up work on getting married, at both ends of the social spectrum. Lots did it willingly and happily. Marrie Walsh, who moved to England from Ireland in 1946 as part of a recruitment drive, when people went to Ireland from Birmingham after the war to collect as many factory workers and nurses as they could, told me, 'Married women didn't work in those days. Any man worth his salt would not let his wife work.' On arrival in England, aged seventeen, Marrie went straight to work at Wright's Ropes factory in Birmingham, lodging in a bombed house with holes in the roof. Marriage in 1952 to a master scaffolder was a rescue from that existence. Her husband bought a house in Liverpool, and Marrie's life from her wedding day on was pure domesticity: baking, cooking, sewing, knitting, cleaning, washing, and putting the washing through the Victorian mangle. She had no complaints about this. When her husband was injured in an accident at work, they had to take in lodgers to pay the mortgage and bills, and Marrie did the lodgers' washing as well as the family's. There would not have been a moment to spare to go out to do paid work, and anyway, she took pride in being a full-time wife and mother, and found it fulfilling.

At the other end of the spectrum, newly married wives were similarly subsumed into running households. Even if they did have domestic help, they were expected not to work. When Alison Carter married Peter Snow in 1964, she registered as a tutor with the agency Gabbitas and Thring, but Peter's mother said to her son, 'I really don't like this – Alison having to work. It looks as though you can't keep her.' Supporting a non-working wife was a social signaller to which husbands aspired.

Joy Burrows in 1963, on marrying her lawyer husband, whom she'd met at the local tennis club, settled straight down to make the curtains, decorate the house and manage the large garden in Prescot, Merseyside. 'I grew all the vegetables and fruit, and made jam and froze it. That was great. I never went back to work.' What's more, her husband came home to lunch every day, so she needed to get that ready.

She became part of the backbone of Britain's volunteers who propped up the country's good causes: married women who, thanks to such a kept existence, had time to work (unflaggingly and unpaid) for charities – in Joy's case, the Royal School for the Blind in Liverpool, for whom she worked as a volunteer for twenty-five years and was 'on the committee'.

When the physical baby bumps came along, to add to the marriage jolt, there was double reason to stop work. For Marrie Walsh, her domestic work merely increased when she became a mother, as, on top of doing all the domestic chores, bringing the children up and plaiting all her daughters' hair before school, she made every item of their clothing, from berets to cardigans to skirts with pleats.

'The fathers said, "I don't want my children to be latchkey kids,"' she told me. That was considered a dismal fate for a child: to come home to an empty house after school, one in which no one had been at home all day to keep it homely and prepare the tea or supper. Those I spoke to who did willingly give up work to become full-time mothers reminded me that motherhood is actually much harder work than paid work, and to do it properly you need to do it with a whole heart. 'Childcare is a love affair,' said Virginia Ironside, 'far more satisfying than a career.' Virginia, a single mother after divorcing a year after her son was born in 1973, specifically wanted to bring her son up herself and not hand him over to nannies and au pairs: 'I did *not* want him to have the same childhood as I had. I was always a latchkey kid. As soon as I could come home from school on my own, no one came to pick me up, and I had to make my own tea. So when my turn came to be a mother, I would do anything to make my son not know I worked. I let every spare room in the house, wrote or went to work only when my son was at school, and worked at Graham & Green on a Saturday when my ex-husband had him for the day.'

'My life really started when I married and had children,' said Gill Thomson (born in 1943), typical of the ones who happily cast their working life into the ditch on marriage. 'I'd done a secretarial course at the North of England Secretarial College and got a job as a secretary to the bursar at Leeds University. I hated it. The only nice thing was there were lots of students around, and I played for the university staff hockey team. I met my husband on the golf course, married him at twenty-two and gave up my job a few months after the wedding. I could be supported by my husband, who was a mechanical engineer.' It was a status symbol not to have to work, as well as a pleasure. Only when all the children went to full-time school did she get bored and went to work as a secretary for Barclays Bank. 'I've led a very boring life, really,' she told me.

Lots of the posh girls without a maths O level whom we met in the early chapters of this book walked happily from their 'million little jobs' to their one marriage, straight into a life of full-time wifehood, motherhood and domesticity, beginning with whole mornings spent writing thank you letters for the wedding presents. With domestic help, so they didn't have to do the washing-up, they became the rock on whom their husband relied to live his life, pursue his career and raise his family. Wifehood and motherhood were respected as vocations; there was no stigma about writing 'occupation: housewife' on a form. Domesticity as raison d'être was so entrenched that, when interviewing married actresses as a young journalist in the 1960s, Celia Haddon used to ask them questions like, 'How on earth do you manage to combine your career with being a mother?' And 'How do you find the time to cook your husband's supper?' When Daphne Neville, as a mother of three, landed her job as an announcer at HTV in 1968, the local newspaper headline was 'WIFE IN A WHIRL HARLECH'S NEW GIRL'. 'An attractive mother of three will spend four hours a day travelling to join the team of four announcers ...' it began. This was newsworthy enough to merit a half-page of coverage.

The food writer Josceline Dimbleby, who married David Dimbleby in 1967 aged twenty-three, remembers her eldest daughter saying to her, 'The thing is, Mum, you don't have "quality time" with us; you're just *there*.' The expression 'quality time' had recently been coined to describe the particular, glamorous kind of time a working mother supposedly had with her children if she worked and it was her day off. It might consist of a visit to the zoo, the seaside or a museum. More important than 'quality time', Josceline felt, and so did her daughter, was just being at home together on an ordinary weekday in the school holidays. 'As a child,' Josceline told me, 'I'd never had that day-to-day security. My mother married my stepfather when I was four. I always felt that for my children I just wanted to be there; that was why I'd decided not to become a professional singer after three years studying at the Guildhall School of Music. I wanted to be at home for my children, due to not having had time with my own mother. David *could* support me financially. Before my marriage I'd lived on ten pounds a week – an allowance from my father. The rent was six pounds a week, so I had four pounds for everything else. I was living with school friends in rented basements.' Marriage was her rescue from that. It was pure luck that a magazine happened to hear that she liked cooking, and she was asked to write a cookery piece for them. David then said to her, 'You ought to do a book,' and her first book, *A Taste of Dreams*, was commissioned by Hodder & Stoughton. David was so proud of his wife being a published author that he had her first three books bound in leather.

But having to admit your occupation was housewife could be dispiriting at dinner parties. It's not totally true that there was 'no stigma attached'. When Christabel Watson became a full-time wife and mother in her early twenties, after her brief racing-driver career in her turbo-charged Mini in the early 1960s, she did not enjoy the moment at dinner parties when the man next to her asked her 'What do you do?' and she replied, 'I do the garden.' 'The man always turned away and talked to the woman on the other side,' she told me. But the woman on the other side, in that upper-class social circle, would have been highly likely also to answer 'I do the garden.' 'School; children; garden; it was what you did,' Christabel said to me. Virginia Wright, wife of a diplomat, grew so tired of English men not talking to her at dinner parties that she just turned to them with the opening gambit, 'Now, what do you know about the sex life of the bumblebee?'

Christabel Watson (far right) as a debutante ... and then as a
successful racing driver for two years in the early 1960s, till she
became a stay-at-home wife and mother

For those who would have liked to carry on working through the early years of parenthood, the bumps in the road caused by marriage and pregnancy came as a sudden and nasty shock. Society continued to be clever at devising ways to dissuade mothers and even pregnant women from working. Right up to the 1990s, there was a persistent rumour that 'screens are bad for pregnant mothers' – it was believed they were dangerous to brain and body, like microwave ovens and 'carphones'.

Here are some baby-having moments from the world of work in the 1960s and early 1970s, as recalled to me by women who would have liked to carry on working.

'I think, Georgina, you'll have to leave here when you have your baby. This is International Planned Parenthood, and it wouldn't look right.' That was Georgina Harding's boss speaking to her in the late 1960s. Georgina (the one who'd been sent up north to look out for the Loch Ness Monster) was now in her late twenties and married, but it still wouldn't have 'looked right' for her carry on working at an organisation called International Planned Parenthood after having a baby.

'I became pregnant while working for George Weidenfeld in 1966,' said Mary Burd. 'There was no question that I would come back after having the baby. The notion that you'd come back was unthinkable. It didn't even occur to me.'

That expression 'it didn't even occur to me' was often said in my interviews. Certain things were so totally off the agenda that they didn't even swim into distant view as possibilities to be eliminated, and one of them was the idea of a young mother going back to work for George Weidenfeld. He might faint at the sight of a trace of regurgitated breast milk spotted on a secretary's shoulder.

'I had a baby, aged twenty-eight, in 1976, when I was a nurse,' said Pamela Jubb (who had also said to me, 'It didn't even occur to me that I could be a doctor.') 'When you had a baby, you had to leave your job. There was maternity pay for twelve weeks, and then you were out. It wasn't till after the Sex Discrimination Act of 1975 that they had to keep your job open for you. That simply wasn't available to nurses before then.' It was not totally accurate that 'you had to leave your job'. You were strongly encouraged to, though. Pamela did manage to carry on doing two night-time shifts per week when her babies were small; the job happened still to be there when she asked for it back; but 'we had no choice of hours: there was no flexibility just because you happened to have small children. I was awake for seventy-two hours at a stretch. I drove home after my shifts with the windows wide open and the radio on full blast. Then I fell fast asleep after lunch with my children, when we were watching television.' This was not sustainable.

Margaret Wilson, who had managed to become a successful barrister by the time her son was born in 1977, recalled of the Bar of those days, 'There was no such thing as maternity leave. It wasn't mentioned in the world I worked in. One just struggled on. I went back to work when my son was twelve weeks old. Nothing had changed by 1981, when my daughter Camilla was born.' The Employment Protection Act of 1975 had introduced the legal requirement for Maternity Leave and Maternity Pay, but it had not yet trickled down to the Law itself, when it came to barristers becoming mothers.

'There was a young unmarried lady who got pregnant at the tailoring factory where I worked,' said Susan Watson (this was in 1963). 'She carried on working till she was eight months pregnant, and then she was shipped off to a nursing home to have the baby, and she came back to work, and the baby was put up for adoption. We who worked with her were all her friends, and we stuck by her, all the way through it.' It was a typical, hushed-up workaday tragedy: mother submitting to enforced separation from her baby in perpetuity, and going straight back to work, as if childless, and as if nothing had happened.

Sweetly, and poignantly for anyone to whom such a thing happened, there was a system in place at some factories of helping future wives to build up a household linen inventory for their future marriage. 'At our factory, Kauffmann's,' said Kathleen Hewitson, 'it was called "The Cotton Club". We paid in a bit of money each week, and we picked a number – I was "week four". After four weeks, or whatever your number was, you'd get the money everyone had paid in, and you'd go out to buy towels and bedding for the "bottom drawer" – saving up for your marriage.' This system showed how certain the female workers were that they were heading for matrimony and needed to be ready when the moment came, in possession of the required double sheets and pillowcase sets.

'I'd graduated from university, and I'd done just one term of teaching,' said Philomena O'Hare, 'and then I got married and had a baby. [This was the early 1960s.] My husband was a town planner. No mothers worked outside the home in the suburb of Leeds where we lived. There we were, all these women, alone in our back gardens being miserable. Talking to children all day just drives you crackers.' Her achievement of getting a geography degree, thanks to the headmaster of her grammar school really pushing her academically and encouraging her to apply to university, felt as if it had been nullified, as she walked into motherhood and did not do any paid work for the next fifteen years.

Just as office bosses got to the tops of their professions on the backs of their highly competent secretaries, as recalled by Sharon Scard, husbands got to the top of their professions on the backs of their highly competent wives, who smoothed their paths by running the home, even as the 'bumps' of their pregnancies caused plunges downwards in their own career and job prospects. Judith Spooner (born in 1954), for example, met her husband in Germany when she was an Army nurse and he was a Captain in the Fusiliers. 'We met at a party in the Officers' Mess and got married a year later. You could stay on in the Army if you got married, but if you were pregnant, you couldn't.' Their twins were born in the military hospital in Aldershot, where Judy had formerly worked.

Another academic who asked to remain anonymous told me that, after marrying a fellow Cambridge student straight after finals in the late 1950s, she 'got a funny little teaching job at a school for the daughters of Army officers in Hitchin,' while her husband went to do postgraduate sociologist training at the London School of Economics. Their paths were already diverging, hers to the domestic realm, her husband's to academe. 'We had three children – and then I started working quite hard *for my husband*, helping him code and sort the research for his PhD. I explained it away and justified it as "well, it keeps my mind active and alert". But I was washing nappies, and he'd come downstairs and say, "What do you think of this?" showing me his work, and I would write a bit of the PhD for him. He was a productive academic, climbing the tree fast.' She found herself becoming more and more of a feminist as she watched this scenario unfold. 'It was not so much about being exploited as an academic worker. It was more that I was running the household entirely – he did almost nothing – and he was having the career.'

When, eventually, she got a three-year grant to do her own sociological research, her husband was at first 'condescendingly pleased about it,' she told me. The subject happened to be apposite: money and marriage. Having finished that piece of work, she got a job as a local health authority researcher. 'Don't talk to me about it,' her husband said to her. 'Boring, boring, boring! You're always talking about your work.'

So in that marriage, the absorption of one spouse into the other's working life went only one way.

'I got married in 1978,' said another woman I spoke to, who worked as a bank clerk on the South Coast, 'and my husband and I agreed that when I'd had a baby I would give up work.' 'My husband and I agreed . . .' Hmm. I got a sense that in those days, some women's marriage vows, if you read between the lines, actually went 'Love, honour and acquiesce'. 'My wife came round to my way of thinking!' was a much-used expression, spoken with a jocular twinkle by husbands, but the repercussions of 'coming round' could consign the acquiescer to being stuck on life's back-burner for years. 'I was a full-time mother for eight years,' this woman said. Much as she loved the company of her son, she badly wanted to do some part-time work. 'The bank asked me to go back, part-time, but my husband didn't want me to. I'd married a control freak, but he was so subtle about it that I didn't realise. When my son started going to nursery, I had free time, and my husband started to wonder what I was doing with my free time. He became jealous. When I suggested going back to work, he said, "Why would you need to? I pay all the bills for you." I protested, and I did go back, and I stuck at it for just a week, until I started being criticised for not running the house well enough.' The coercive control grew worse, until, in 1988, she mustered the courage to file for divorce. It was contested, and the divorce battle went on for four years, during which she was stuck living with the controlling husband, 'who did things like hide the car so I couldn't drive my son to school'.

And all this because 'we agreed ...'

'I married at twenty-three in 1982,' said Amanda Graham, 'had two daughters, and decided I was bored out of my brain. I was a housewife on a farm in the middle of nowhere in Somerset. That was when I realised I was completely ill-equipped for the real world. It does seem very sad that as children we weren't encouraged to do anything with our lives. (Amanda was one of the privately under-educated ones and had been to Fido May's secretarial college in Bridport, so at least she could do typing and shorthand.) 'In retrospect, I was very unproductive and wasted years – apart from having two gorgeous daughters,' she told me.

The art of fitting work round the edges of motherhood, and motherhood round the edges of work, and of devising a modus vivendi that made it possible to be a functioning employee or freelance worker as well as a functioning wife and mother, without being a functioning alcoholic or creating a dysfunctional family, was gradually being developed. For example, I kept my ears attuned for the first mention of the word 'crèche'. The date was 1970, and the place, surprisingly, Cobham Hall in Kent, a new boarding school for girls in an Elizabethan stately home. It had a futuristic founding headmistress, Miss Hancock, for whom installing a crèche in an outbuilding was an essential part of her vision. Nicky Laughland (born in 1942) got a job as a chemistry teacher there in 1970, when she had a young baby. 'The crèche was run by one of the parents,' she told me, 'and it was brilliant. Teachers could pop in and feed their baby at lunchtime, and there were cots upstairs. The boarders could help with the babies, taking them for pram walks after lunch. I worked at the school for thirty-two years, from the age of twenty-seven to sixty, as "Mrs Laughland", and I became the head of science and senior mistress.' The crèche made that continuity possible; but later, health and safety regulations would bring this in-house system run by enthusiastic amateurs to an end.

Grandparents and siblings helped with the modus vivendi, if they lived near enough and were willing to be on hand to take their grandchildren and nephews and nieces to and from school. 'I gave up work when I had a baby,' said Maureen Towndrow (born in 1953), who married aged eighteen and got a job as a 'progress chaser' for a building firm in Islington. 'I couldn't afford the childcare.' It was as simple as that. But as soon as both her sons were at school, she got a job in a school kitchen from nine till three; she and her sister took turns to do the school run. School dinner-lady-ing was the ideal job to fit in with motherhood, as it ended in mid-afternoon and you got school holidays.

'I worked in school kitchens in Yeovil,' said Diana Brooks (born in 1949), who had her first child aged twenty. 'I started with washing-up and scrubbing floors at the local junior school, and gradually worked my way up to assistant cook, before going to work at the local comprehensive. I walked a couple of miles to and from work, came home, prepared tea for the children, and then went back out to work at a private hospital for two hours.'

So that was not one but two jobs fitted in round the edges of motherhood; and her husband did not insist that she stay at home full-time. When I probed women more deeply about the blanket convention that 'any man worth his salt would not let his wife work', I discovered it was not as simple as that. It depended on the husbands and the presiding ethos of the area. While in some patches of Britain, as Philomena O'Hare described, whole streets of wives were stuck at home with the children all day in their separate houses, in others, wives did find ways of going out to work, encouraged by their husbands, who needed both the money and the non-demoralised wife. These wives and mothers found ways of fitting their jobs around the children, and places of work found ways to make it possible for them.

The main way of doing this was 'the twilight shift': going out to work from 5 or 6 p.m. to 10 p.m., as soon as the husband had got home from work. This was a lifesaver, both financially and in terms of morale. All the women I spoke to who did the twilight shift in various factories relished those four or five lucrative hours away from running the hotel of home. They seemed not to mind one bit missing evenings at home with their husbands. The twilight shift was what Eve Terry was doing in the Tampax factory in Havant in 1976. 'We were mostly young mums,' she told me. 'My husband was a teacher. He got home at 4.30 and I got the bus straight to the factory. Some of the other mums would have their own mums at home, bridging the gap till the husband came home.

We worked solidly from five to ten, with just one fifteen-minute tea break.'

In those fifteen-minute tea breaks, with all the hyper-efficiency and multitasking prowess of busy young mothers, the women would make straight for the ladies' cloakroom, where (if it was a Friday) some of them would put their rollers in if they were going out to the dance hall at 10 p.m. after work, and others would eat their sandwiches while scouring the catalogues for clothes and furniture, and others would devour their 'romance' comics, while all around them the more entrepreneurial ones were selling things to each other – jewellery, underwear and make-up – as a lucrative sideline. 'Those fifteen minutes were our only opportunity to talk to each other,' Eve said, and they made the most of it. 'I'd been on my own with a child all day, so it was nice to be with other adults, talking about babies and chatting about what we wanted to buy.'

'I went to do a twilight shift at George Bray's engineering from 5 p.m. to 9 p.m., when my son was five months old,' Denise Sherlock told me. This was in 1970. 'All I had to do was stamp the nuts that were going on gas boilers. It was very simple. I came out with five pounds a week.' When she got home just after nine, her husband took himself straight off to the pub for a pint for an hour, before last orders at 10 p.m. So that was two consecutive shifts of spouse-dodging per evening.

'Just absolute elation' was how Maria Wynne summed up to me her feelings on Friday evenings in the late 1970s, when she cycled home at 10 p.m. from her last twilight shift of the week, with her brown envelope containing £40 in cash for her week's work at Haffenden's hot water bottle and shuttlecock factory in Sandwich, Kent. 'That cycle ride home was the highlight of my week. The money I'd earned meant we could pay our bills for the week, and I could buy enough food for the family.'

The twilight shift, she told me, was 'a brilliant concept' dreamed up by factories – the half-length shift designed especially for young mothers.

'Didn't you dread having to go to work at the end of a long day with the children?' I asked her. 'Knowing you couldn't put your feet up but would have to stand up for four hours gluing ferrules into the insides of hot water bottles?'

'I didn't have to brace myself,' she said. 'I positively looked forward to it. I'd had a whole day at home with the children. I loved knowing I was going to be doing my bit to look after the family financially. It was a huge morale boost, an absolute godsend.'

She described the clanking machinery in the din so loud you couldn't have a conversation, and once again I scribbled down the process, trying to keep up: 'I lifted the rod up, to get one ferrule off it, and placed the ferrule in the rim of the hot water bottle, having first used a brush to line the inside with the hot, strong glue that brought my neck out in a rash. I had to keep my foot on the pedal to keep the rim open while I put the ferrule in. Then I quickly released the pedal and the top snapped shut, and my left hand was underneath the hot water bottle to catch it and put it onto the conveyor belt.' She did this three hundred times per shift, working with total concentration, strongly motivated by the piecework system: the more she did, the more she would be paid.

The punctuality requirements were merciless: 'if you were one minute late clocking in, you had fifteen minutes deducted from your pay, and you couldn't leave a moment before 10 p.m., or your pay would also be docked by fifteen minutes.' Just as at the Tampax factory, there was one fifteen-minute break, when Maria stood at the side of the room having her snack and a drink from her Thermos.

So, four nights per week, the home-evening was eliminated:

no supper à deux after the children's bedtime, no flopping down to listen to the radio or watch television, no early night with a good book; instead, a bracing, short, sharp weekday-evening shift, and an exhilarating, empowering feeling of independence.

17

Being an Extension of One's Husband

'(Margaret Cosgrove) is now living in Belgium where
her husband has an interesting and important post'

'News of Old Girls', Lawnside school
magazine, 1972

'And then Patrick was Ambassador to Saudi . . .'

It's a whole way of talking: the wife, quietly proud of her
high-achieving husband, who followed him to wherever his
career took him, and, by doing so, became an extension of
him. Diplomats' wives, Army wives, clergy wives, headmasters' wives, all of these were not only married to the job, but
by being so, actually did an essential part of the job, usually
unpaid. They all speak like this. It's part of the background
hum of ageing British wifehood and widowhood.

'One was supporting him.'

'My father took me for a walk when I was engaged, and said
to me, "You do realise, don't you, that you're not marrying
Douglas. You're marrying the regiment." He was absolutely
right. I followed the drum everywhere Douglas went.'

'It was so hot and sweaty in Singapore! James went through three khaki shirts a day.'

'Looking after the lower ranks? Yes, one did. One was doing the rounds, and keeping an eye on the other ranks' wives to make sure they were all right.'

'My career was an Army wife, alas! No; it was lovely.'

'I'd been an Army child. So it was completely normal for me as the wife of a diplomat to pack up a house and move every few years.'

'I didn't get any pay, but I did get free Romanian lessons.'

'Stuart would come home from the embassy in the evening and we'd learn four pages of Arabic together by rote.'

'It's the story of my marriage: wherever one's husband's career took him, one went.'

Those are the voices of what used to be termed 'the trailing wife', eventually amended to 'the trailing spouse' when the possibility dawned that the trailing person might not necessarily be a woman. I was struck by the cheerful, non-self-pitying attitudes. That use of the word 'one' rather than 'I' to describe themselves was not merely the ingrainedly unemotional vocabulary of the upper-class drawl; it deflected the attention away from the speaker into the realm of what was the norm and what was expected. These women were driven by a strong sense of duty, as well as of loyalty to their husbands.

The two categories of trailing wife were those who went abroad (military and diplomatic wives) and the ones who trailed from tied house to tied house in Britain (clergy and housemasters' or headmasters' wives). All of them coped with being carried along in the slipstream and being expected to take part, in a sort of unspoken 'two-for-the-price-of-one' deal. The level of their being subsumed into their husband's role is exemplified by the commonly spoken 1970s term 'Mrs Headmaster', lazily used by fathers who could hardly be bothered to remember the name of the headmaster, let alone that of his wife. The wife's identity was wrapped up in her husband's job title to that extreme extent.

'Did you resent it?' I asked Diana Russell, who, after telling me about her life as an Army wife, proceeded to recount a terrifying incident. Staying at The Grand Hotel in Brighton with her husband James Russell during their tenth consecutive Conservative Party conference together, in October 1984, when he was chairman and treasurer of the constituency (Basingstoke), she was blown out of bed, and so was he, at 3 a.m. when the IRA bomb exploded. They would have been killed if they'd happened to be sleeping on another floor, which they nearly were. Instead, they were alive, in a state of shock, in their nightclothes, and they were kitted out the next morning at Marks & Spencer.

'Resent it? No one has *ever* asked me that question,' she replied. Then, after a thoughtful silence: 'Well, I suppose it wasn't easy. You were brought up to follow in their footsteps and support them.'

Just to recap a typical 'little jobs before marriage' trajectory: in the late 1950s, Diana's job before marriage had been working in the Grafton Coffee House off Berkeley Square, an upmarket establishment run by a Miss Corbett, who, as so often with the members of the upper classes, was no stickler for hygiene. If there were any items of food that looked slightly 'off', Miss Corbett would just say, 'Don't worry – just wash it in vinegar.' And if something fell on the floor, she'd say, 'Just pick it up! And wipe it!' Diana lived in typical 'digs': a mews house in Rutland Gate, which she shared with two friends: rent £4 a week. When she met her future husband, James Russell, at an officers' dance 'when the Camerons [Cameron Highlanders] were stationed at Dover', he took down her telephone number on the back of a cigarette packet. (The romantic thrill of having a regiment stationed nearby had not changed since the days of Jane Austen. Or perhaps it was the very fact of having read Jane Austen's novels that made young women equate 'Camerons stationed at Dover' with the prospect of high romance.) Diana swerved at the last minute from her intended secretarial course route, married James aged twenty, and off they sailed to Singapore.

For these women, the 'bumps in the road' of marriage were so severe that they were bumped clean out of their own possible jobs-and-careers paths and landed deeply in the groove of their husband's. On doing so, they were not only cast into the role of facilitating and easing his job by doing vital bits of it, but were also often soon having his babies, in whichever diplomatic or Army outpost they happened to find themselves in.

They had four immediate hurdles to contend with.

First, the journey. 'We went out with the regiment,' Diana Russell told me, meaning 'out to Singapore'. This was in 1960. She described the two separate worlds on board ship: the world of the officers and their wives, and the less salubrious world of the soldiers, known as 'the jocks'. 'The jocks slept down low in bunks, which were more like shelves, stacked up, three in a pile, with sexy pictures on both sides of the beds. Lots of them weren't married, but the few jocks' wives who did come slept on a different deck from ours.'

Instantly the wives were institutionalised in this two-tier existence, and then the climate changed from freezing to boiling as they contemplated their new life far from home and had to clamber through the jocks' quarters to find their trunks full of summer clothing.

Then, the arrival at the house which wasn't their own home. 'Ours was a huge old colonial house,' Diana Russell said, 'set in a lovely park, with bougainvillea, birds and butterflies. But it had been used as a prison for eighty prisoners of war in the Second World War. I've seen ghosts, I feel ghosts, and I did *not* like that house at all – particularly our bedroom, which still had a huge rust mark on the floor where the prisoners had had their cauldron to boil up water. Not a breath of air, and the doors banged. My successor in that room couldn't sleep in there, either. A ghost said to her, "You've got to help me leave." It was a trapped spirit who'd got left behind.'

'We never had a home as such,' said Richenda Miers, who married her Cameron Highlander Douglas Miers in 1959. 'I had a roaming life all over the world and we lived in over twenty houses. Most of them were like council houses, but our house in Singapore was beautiful. It had been one of the staff houses for Changi Jail. The furniture belonged to the Army. It was identical wherever you went, and they provided the china. We didn't bother to put up shelves.'

So, the nesting urge of a young wife was not pandered to. Having given up those premarital jobs that they'd worn lightly, Army and diplomatic wives now found themselves having to wear their domestic lives lightly, flitting from abode to abode, never getting too attached. Their marriages did give them a certain status that they would perhaps not have been able to achieve on their own merit, in those days of female under-education, and many of them emphasised to me what a privilege it was to live in another country and have a chance to explore, learn and make friends with people from other cultures; but the sacrifice they made for this was great. For diplomats' wives, the act of home furnishing sounded a little bit less impersonal: they were encouraged to bring their own interior belongings across oceans, so their ready-furnished houses felt a bit more like home; but moving 'got harder and harder', as Virginia Wright (wife of Patrick, eventual Ambassador in Saudi and later head of the diplomatic service) said to me – 'unpacking the same awful old things': their belongings that had followed them round the world. 'Bring your own saddles and tapestries,' they were advised, before moving to Cairo. 'Tapestries!' said Virginia. 'But the walls were huge and our small pictures looked like pinpricks on them.'

Richenda Miers and her husband Douglas, 1980s.
'You're marrying the regiment.'

Third, the giving birth as a trailing spouse abroad. It didn't sound much fun. Sarah Burns, the one who'd landed the job at *Private Eye* thanks to the Old Harrovians' job deal for siblings, made a determined effort not to have her baby in a Romanian hospital when she was newly married to her diplomat husband in 1977, because she knew that patients in Romanian hospitals under Ceausescu had to share a hospital bed, sleeping head to toe. She managed to get back to London just in time to give birth, and while there watched the Bucharest earthquake on television.

Jane Nicholson (born in 1941), the wife of a diplomat in Romania in the 1960s, did give birth in a Bucharest hospital, and she knew there were microphones planted round the walls of her hospital room, so local spies could tune in to her in labour, listening out for any politically subversive sentiments she might utter in that uninhibited situation. Sue Teale (born in 1941), an Army officer's wife who went to live in Munster in Germany aged twenty-two, when her husband was stationed there with the 15th/19th The King's Royal Hussars, had to give birth in the military hospital there: 'very primitive; no antenatal classes at all, hardly any check-ups, creeper growing into the wards through the windows. I had a German midwife who didn't speak a word of English, and husbands weren't allowed to be with their wives for the birth.'

'If you'd been to boarding school,' she added, 'that did toughen you up a bit.'

It certainly did. 'The carapace', as some described it to me, was useful. It was what supposedly 'privileged' British girls developed through their spartan and sometimes traumatic childhoods. Virginia Wright said to me, 'I came to England from India in 1946. My father, who'd been in the Indian Army, had died of polio. My mother married again, and we stayed with my new stepfather's relations. It gave me quite a carapace. I had to have one. And I would need it for life as a diplomatic wife.'

For the final hurdle, there were the locals among whom you found yourself living. Here's a glimpse of Communist Bucharest in the late 1960s, as recalled by Jane Nicholson: 'The small kitchen in our big old house (provided by the embassy) was crawling with cockroaches up and down the walls. They sent me a cleaner who helped me unpack, when I was very pregnant. I lost all my jewellery and my shoes. So I found my own cleaner. She cut out cardboard teeth and stuck them into her mouth to count as teeth, and they got soggy during the day. I managed to get a Romanian nanny, but I was pretty sure she was spying on me. There were seventy-four microphones hidden around the house. My husband and I went for walks if we wanted to discuss anything. Every time we left the house we were followed. One day we had a picnic in the hills with another diplomatic family. I knew our listeners were hiding in the bushes. I took them the leftovers from our lunch.'

The conflicting feelings were of loathing for the spying and pity for the hungry locals in the impoverished, tooth-decaying country. The man who came to help them for diplomatic receptions used to pour any leftover chocolate mousse straight down his throat.

For a contrasting glimpse of 'the locals among whom you found yourself living', here's a snapshot of wealthy Washington, DC, at the dawn of 1963 from Virginia Wright's experience, when her husband was private secretary to the Ambassador there. 'On the night of 22 November 1963, the day President Kennedy was assassinated, we'd been due to go to a Republican friend's drinks party, but it had to be cancelled. It was reinstated forty days later. There we all were, sipping our drinks in the drawing room, when the host said, "Now, everybody, let's drink to the bastard's death." Well, my husband and I walked out.'

Virginia Wright and her husband Patrick arriving at a
diplomatic cocktail party in Cairo, 1968

The qualities drilled into these women while they'd been
growing up came to the fore in this alien, institutionalised
existence far from home: duty, a lack of self-pity, the habit of
'looking after those less fortunate than ourselves', and a willingness to put their own ambitions, such as they were, aside.
They also drew strongly on the school-prefect qualities they'd
acquired in their teens, either through being prefects themselves, or by gleaning the required attributes from the prefect
they'd looked up to or had a crush on. Just as they might
once have comforted a homesick New Girl in her dormitory,
they now kept a kindly eye on the wives from the lower ranks
of the Army or the lower grades of the diplomatic service,
calling in on them to check that they were all right. 'I found
one young soldier's wife, from the Gorbals,' recalled Diana
Russell, 'scrubbing her kitchen floor, even though the Army
had provided her with a cleaner. The Chinese cleaner was

sitting on the table, watching her, while she was scrubbing away.' The multiple rungs of the international class system were encapsulated in that scene: officer's wife, jock's wife, Chinese migrant cleaner, each of them trying to negotiate what was expected of them in the isolated bubble of an Army camp in Singapore in the 1960s.

'We officers' wives were really unqualified social workers,' said Sue Teale, again, speaking in a head-girly tone. 'It was awful for the soldiers' wives stuck out in the middle of nowhere. They hadn't been to boarding school, so they were really homesick; mostly Geordie girls. I went to see one poor lass, in about 1963, who desperately wanted to go home. I had to explain to her that if she went home, she wouldn't be able to come out again. She decided not to go.'

'You were damned if you did, and damned if you didn't,' said Penny Holt (born in 1938) of the (to her) rather thankless task of 'being responsible for all the company's families, making sure everyone was fine' in her role as wife to her husband Paddy, who was an officer in the Queen's Own Highlanders. 'I used to go and call on the wives. I sometimes took my little daughter along with me – that worked well. It broke the ice. If they had immaculate houses, they were delighted to see you. If they didn't, they were not.'

The head-girly convention extended to senior officers' wives looking after newly married ones. When Lynette Burns's husband was sent from the Army camp where they lived in Germany to a tour in Northern Ireland in 1974, Lynette was not allowed to go with him, and had to stay in Germany with their young child. 'One newly married lieutenant's wife,' she told me, 'who lived off-camp on a German estate twenty miles from any other officers' wives, came to share my flat with me when our husbands were both in Northern Ireland. She'd been frightened, living alone. Every time the senior officer came to visit her, she'd nearly passed out with fear, petrified that he was bringing news that her husband had been killed. He'd said to her, "Don't worry; I would have had a padre or a nurse with me if the news had been bad."' This constant half-expectation of dreadful news was what the wives had to live with.

'The wives were expected to do a lot of the welfare work that later became professionalised,' explained Veronica Goodenough, speaking of the diplomatic service, but it was the same in the Army. 'The wife of the head of chancery [the political section of an embassy] was expected to look after all the other wives and their families. But we often felt ill-equipped to do that – we'd had no training, and most of us didn't feel in the least bit qualified.' The problems they encountered could be really bad: profound homesickness, thoughts of suicide, wives on the verge of divorce because their husbands were having affairs, wives on the verge of nervous breakdowns. There's now an official job title for the professionals who take on what used to be the wives' role: 'community liaison officer'.

Lynette kept her own worrying at bay, while her husband was on tour in Northern Ireland, by keeping busy running social activities for the wives: endless bingo evenings, whist drives and coffee mornings, plus running the badminton club and serving lunch to 275 regimental wives and their children every Sunday. (The expression 'coffee morning', which expanded what used to be known as 'elevenses' into something you spent your whole morning doing, somehow summed up the way time hung heavily.) Then she started a hairdressing salon on the camp (which had once been an SS headquarters), kitted out with hairdryers, and it was a great success, just like an English hairdresser's: a haven of 'cold wave perms', and a home from home.

Expected to entertain, run clubs, keep everyone else's peckers up as well as their own, and be a rock of domestic reliability for their career-ladder-climbing husbands, were the wives remunerated financially or allowed to get local jobs and earn salaries of their own? Until much later in the period of this book, they were not. Lynette told me that the clients in her hair salon on the Army camp in Germany did pay her, but that 'it was very difficult, at that time, to work in the German economy, because you weren't allowed to take a position away from a German person'. Veronica Goodenough, whose husband's first diplomatic post was as a junior diplomat in the embassy in Athens in 1967, did manage to work as a 'fill-in temp' secretary to her husband, followed by another temporary job as a social secretary at the residence. But she was paid a tiny amount for these jobs, and counted herself lucky. At the time, a diplomat's wife was obliged to obtain the Ambassador's specific permission to take a job in the embassy or elsewhere. Sibella Laing, for example (born in 1949), a Cambridge graduate, had to give up her job working for the British Council when she married into the Foreign Office in 1972. Living in Jeddah as a diplomat's wife, she longed to work. She needed to ask for special permission from the British Ambassador, who allowed her to join the British Council as a locally engaged employee. 'The baby came with me in a carrycot to the office,' she told me. Later on, a general rule was introduced that all diplomatic service spouses could apply to work as 'locally engaged' in the embassy (or related organisations such as the British Council), employed and paid like any other qualified local staff, and not by the FCO in London.

Generally, though, men were used to the idea that the wife would run the household and be at home to bring up the children, and that if he wanted to give a cocktail party or dinner party to entertain the local dignitaries, she would sort it, as willing oiler-of-the-wheels of their existence. This changed in 1973, when diplomatic service women officers no longer had to resign on marriage. It was at about this time that the expression 'diplomatic spouse' took over from 'diplomatic wife'. It was unthinkable that a male 'spouse' would be treated as a two-for-one spare part in the way wives had been; unthinkable also that he would not be allowed to work. Thus in the 1980s the convention shifted, and the Foreign Office started encouraging the 'spouse' to work while the other one was in post, in order to help pay off their mortgage back home and earn their own pension.

'I'll sort this out. Get the wife on the phone.'

That was an imaginary (but all-too-real) typical father late at night, as recalled by headmaster's wife Elizabeth Kefford (born in 1940), who while working as a secretary to the headmaster of a boys' prep school in Winchester in the early 1960s, had met her future husband Michael, who was a classics master there. This was another charming 'love in the workplace' story, or 'Love in a School Climate'. 'I was at my typewriter in the office one morning,' Elizabeth said, 'and Michael started talking to me through the window. Then I went back for supper in the dining hall after the boys had gone to bed, and that's where I got to know Michael better . . . and we went to the pub, and for swims and walks.'

Before she knew it, she was married to him, aged twenty-four, and they went to live in a cottage in the grounds of a prep school in Hampshire run by Michael's father, 'who was a *dear*; devoted to his job, good with the boys, and I helped: I did some secretarial stuff for my father-in-law.' Then Michael became a housemaster at a school in Croydon, and one night a week Elizabeth 'did' the boys' evening refreshment of cocoa and biscuits. She loved being part of it all and became used to helping out; and then Michael became headmaster of a prep school in Bristol and then of the Pilgrims' School in Winchester. 'Some of the boys are still in touch,' she told me. 'One of them read from *The Pilgrim's Progress* at Michael's funeral.'

'When a headmaster's job was advertised in those days,' she told me, 'it specifically said, "Wife is expected to take part." The husband didn't get the job unless the wife was willing and able to take part. That went back to the Victorian convention of a man and his wife running a school together, the wife helping on the domestic front and being a house-mother type. Most schools wanted a married couple.'

The role of headmaster's wife was pretty much a full-time job. As well as bringing up their own son and daughter, 'I had to organise the troupe of domestic cleaners, supervise the matrons, check the menus, ring the parents if a boy was unwell and do a lot of hostess work on match days. On Sunday morning, my job was cleaning the boys' lavatories, as well as having lunch for the visiting preacher under control. Find me a headmaster's wife who has not cleaned the boys' lavatories!'

And at 11 p.m. the telephone might ring – that was because, far away, a mother was in distress about some injustice her son had mentioned, and her husband had had a couple of drinks, and said, 'I'll sort this out. Get the wife on the phone.' Elizabeth was expected to field the torrent that came out of the receiver at her. She got used to it. Later, when Michael became headmaster of the Pilgrims' School, one of her jobs was to fill twenty Christmas stockings for the choristers.

Any remuneration for all this? I asked her. 'When I started, many schools were not offering to pay the wife anything. The understanding was that any remuneration was "contained in your husband's salary". That was not very good for self-esteem! I was paid, in 1974, about one thousand pounds a year, and the Pilgrims' School was a bit more generous. Michael did say to me, "Don't worry. I won't go anywhere where they don't pay the wife."'

That split-second mention of self-esteem reminded me just what a boost it is to self-esteem to be paid money specifically to oneself; this was captured in the exhilaration Maria Wynne (quoted in the previous chapter) felt as she cycled home with her pay packet at the end of a week of twilight shifts. 'Contained in your husband's salary' is no substitute for that.

Clergy wives found themselves similarly subsumed, and they were not remunerated at all, just given a tied house to live in. 'His work involved both of us,' Caroline Chartres said, simply and happily, of starting out as wife to the vicar of St Stephen's, Rochester Row. 'And we both believed in hospitality. I had privileged access to a social cross-section you would not have unless you were a criminal lawyer. My lack of a game plan for my own career fitted in well. If I'd been a highly motivated career person, it would have been much harder.' But she did fit in a three-year teacher training course round the edges of this existence. 'And we started having babies. It was *not* isolating. I had a place at the heart of a community.'

'The moment I got married I gave up my teaching job,' said Vivien Wilson, who married a curate from the evangelical end of the Church of England spectrum when she was twenty-three, in 1956. 'I became a curate's wife. I ran the ladies' groups and the toddler groups and the Young People's Fellowship, all in our vicarage in Sheffield: seventy people, every Friday night. Michael was paid. I've never been paid as a vicar's wife. We lived at a time when you learned to live with that. It's fine, because you love the Lord, and love serving

Him and you're married to someone who has the same vision as you have. I just loved to support my husband, feeding him and watering him. He was the preacher, I was the supporter. He radiated his love for God and he radiated his love for me. Every night he said, "I love you, Viv", and I said, "I love you, Michael."'

Epilogue

Revenge

'When I became the first woman director of Christie's in 1973,' Hermione Waterfield told me, 'I tried ringing Miss D V Lee to tell her, but she'd just died.'

Miss D V Lee, whom we came across briefly in Chapter 9, 'Life as a Secretary', was the head of women's personnel at the Foreign Office who'd told Hermione that if she had the temerity to leave her secretarial job, she would 'never get back in' and would 'never make anything of herself'.

So it was a real pity that she'd died, because one of the sweetest aspects of career success later in life, for anyone who has been predicted to have a life of nonachievement by their teachers, parents or bosses, is to be able ring them up and mention it.

And all too often, in the case of the women in this book, it was too late. The person had died. It had taken that long: sometimes a whole long marriage, and years of bringing up children, and sometimes a divorce, before it was possible to get a dose of late education or training and thus a fulfilling job for the second half of life. By that time, the old baggy-cardigan-wearing teacher who'd told them they were 'not university material', or the blinkered father who had not seen any need to educate his daughters, or the arrogant boss who'd called them 'Thingummy' across the office, or the senior partner who'd put his hand on their knee while dictating the first letter of the day, were either in their coffins or untraceable in retirement.

Hermione Waterfield, on her first day as the first woman director of Christie's, 1973

But still, the overwhelming feeling was 'two fingers up to them', even if the desired recipient was no longer alive to be at the receiving end of this sign. Most of my interviewees – certainly the ones born in the 1930s and '40s – were polite types who would not usually use the term 'two fingers up', even less do the 'V for victory' sign the 'wrong way round'; but so strong was their sense that their life prospects had been smothered by the adults supposed to be guiding them through their teens, or employing them as they set out into adulthood, that they spoke the words and did the gesture, into thin air. 'It was all about sticking two fingers up to my father,' said Cicely McCulloch (on the telephone, so I couldn't see whether she was doing it) of her later career. It was her father's pronouncement – 'There's no point in your having a career, because you're perfectly bedworthy and will get married' – that opened this book, and is perhaps the key quotation on the 'how things were' side.

'I was forty-two when my father died,' Cicely said, 'and I started my career as a relationship counsellor when I was forty-four.' This was late revenge, but better late than never.

Cicely McCulloch, relationship counsellor, who only dared to escape the confines of her parents' theory that 'daughters didn't need a career' in her mid-forties, after her father had died

The urge to prove one's discouragers, ignorers and demeaners wrong is a powerful force, and can remain undiminished decades later. 'Fifty per cent of my teachers were discouraging rather than encouraging', said Jo Fairley, now one of the UK's leading entrepreneurs. The chief culprit at Bromley High School for Girls was Mrs Wootton, who made the notorious 'If you manage to be so much as a Girl Friday, I'll eat my hat' comment. 'That spurred me into proving her wrong,' Jo told me. 'Every time I start a new project, there's still a little bit of "showing Mrs Wootton".' That 'burning desire to grasp the world and be *in* the world' that she described to me had been ignited precisely by the negative forces designed to snuff out any self-belief in the girls. It morphed into a burning desire, which still burns to this day, to prove the naysayer wrong. Discouragement can have the opposite of the desired effect.

For Jo it was a spur. But, as she said, for some of the other girls at Bromley High, that discouragement damped down their self-esteem to such an extent that they never recovered. It depended on temperament. You needed a bit of fiery vengefulness to fight your way beyond the low horizons predicted for you.

One thing to be said for the era of this book was that a young woman on leaving school or university did not walk straight into a void of unemployedness. There was a path instantly open to her. 'At the present time, the demand for the well-trained secretary is greater than the number requiring posts.' So went the first sentence of the principal's introduction to the prospectus of the Queen's Secretarial College of 1973. In other words, do this course costing your parents £270 for the year, and you'll never be short of a job. With a sharp burst of training, you could go straight into the world of paid work. 'In every profession, business or philanthropic organisation,' said the prospectus, 'as well as the arts, the well-run office must play its part.'

It must. But once there, in her smart skirt and blouse, how on earth did the young woman progress along that path to a more eminent form of existence? As we've seen, luck played a large part in what happened next. You could

work for a kind or a nasty boss, who did or didn't spot your
potential and do something about it, and you could marry
a nice or nasty husband, who did or didn't give you the
spiritual freedom to carve out your own career round the
edges of wifehood and motherhood, or even right down the
middle of them.

The young mothers and other volunteers who ran the
Oxfam shop in Headingley, 1969 ... and their proud
announcement on the shop window

Remember those young mothers stuck alone in their houses
and back gardens in the suburbs of Leeds in the early 1960s,
being 'driven crackers' by the tedium and repetitiveness of
looking after their children on their own all day? That existence was described to me by Philomena O'Hare, a geography
graduate, expected by her husband to stay at home and not
work. Her first quiet act of rebellion was to get a system of
babysitting going among the twelve mothers in the street.
'We paid each other with Ludo counters. Red was for an
hour, black for half an hour.' So they could all now slip out
during the daytime, or in the evening if they were lucky. Then
Philomena set up the first Oxfam shop in Headingley, which

expanded into four Oxfam shops, one of them housed in an old Barclays Bank that offered them its premises. These were run by those local mothers, all unpaid but delighted to get out of the house and be busy, and they brought their children to work with them. 'Someone brought in an old potty,' Philomena told me, 'and my friend Veronica went out to the back lane and filled it with bluebells and put it in the window, and customers poured in.' That flower-filled potty in the shop window somehow proclaimed the liberation of these mothers from their domestic isolation.

It was fifteen years of bringing up children later before Philomena felt free to do a secretarial course at the Yorkshire Ladies' Secretarial College, and even then, in the late 1970s, when she answered her first job advertisement, it turned out to be working for a manager who set up lunchtime events in a local pub for semi-naked dancing girls whom he called 'Bouncing Betty and Big Bertha'. 'But I'm a feminist!' Philomena protested, and walked out.

The exhilaration of a late, career-enabling education was recalled to me with the same sense of blissful release with which others had described the liberation of the factory twilight shift. 'I started an Open University course when I was thirty-four,' said Amanda Graham – the one who'd been holed up on a farm with two young children, and had thought, 'This is it,' with a mounting sense of dismay. 'My sense of self-esteem was at rock bottom when I left my first husband.' She sailed into a much happier second marriage, had two more children, and got straight down to studying for a history degree. 'I wrote my first essay in hospital when I'd just given birth to my fourth child. Working towards a degree was a fantastic antidote to child-rearing and domesticity.'

With admirable empathy, the Open University did not insist

on a maths O level to do this, so it was genuinely 'open' to swathes of women stymied by the lack of one at the end of their school education. But they did have to do a 'foundation year' to bolster the vestiges of their general knowledge. This entailed English language, English literature, history, philosophy and music. 'It was wonderful – so stimulating,' said Amanda, 'but I remember being utterly amazed by what I didn't know. I discovered how exciting learning was.' That she discovered this so late was 'tragic', she said, but she was too busy being excited to brood on it. 'I got up at 5 a.m. to study, before the children were awake, and it gave me a buzz for the rest of the day.' The course went on for six years, and Amanda graduated aged forty, with a first in history, and became a teacher.

'It was the "University of the Second Chance",' Helen York said, speaking of the Open University, which similarly saved her; she'd done very well at her grammar school, achieving four A levels, but had joined the Women's Royal Naval Service instead of going to university, because that was the path her mother insisted on for her. 'My family wouldn't give me any money to go to university,' she told me, 'and in order to do a secretarial course, I would have had to carry on living at home, as I had no money, and I did not want to be at home with my stepfather for one more moment.' So the WRNS had been the only option, and she'd got married aged twenty to a naval pilot. She started the Open University course aged thirty-three, when she was pregnant, and was delighted that 'they didn't judge you on your previous achievements'. The six-year degree could be fitted around motherhood. 'But I'd sit down to watch a video lecture on the Italian Renaissance and find that someone had taped over it.' That was a hazard of an academic working from home, 1980s-style. But it was not as bad as what a friend of hers on the same course had to endure: 'She had a drunken, violent husband, and she had to wait till he was in a drunken stupor before she started studying in the evenings.'

Being amazed to find out what one didn't know was brought home to me by Christabel Watson, who did a degree in history of art at Warwick University in her fifties, in the early 1970s. 'I had to ask my husband, "What is an essay?"' Having left school at sixteen, she had never written or even come across this brand of short-form non-fiction prose.

'I redeemed my misspent youth!' said Elizabeth Kefford, the headmaster's wife, with the typical self-teasing tone of her generation. By 'misspent youth' she did not mean 'going to hen nights in Magaluf', as it might mean now; she meant 'doing fairly disastrously' in her A levels, and not going to university but straight to a secretarial course in Edinburgh. She was one of my oldest late-graduates, achieving her BSc from the Open University when she was sixty-four, after her husband had retired. 'I had no idea whether I was thick or lazy, but I got a 2:1 honours. I proved I could do it.' In her case, this was not done in order to start a late-life career. It was work for work's sake, and was intrinsically worth it, both for itself and as late proof that she was neither 'thick' nor 'lazy'.

'Children arrived. I became very domestic.' This syndrome, which happened to so many wives and mothers, was described by among others Sukie Swan, whom we met in the 'digs' chapter (landlord: Commander Metheringham) and the air-hostessing chapter, and whose husband 'saved her from the shelf' when she was twenty-six. She had wanted to study law at university, but realised she couldn't, as she had never done Latin at school, and Latin was a requirement for law in the 1960s – the lack of school Latin teaching was another lopping-off of possibilities for the leaving school-girl. Aged forty-three, still trading on the A levels she had managed to get all those years ago, she managed to get in to Southampton University to read law (Latin was no longer a requirement by then). And she taught happily at that university for ten years.

Jenny Boltwood, aged forty-two, graduating with a B.Ed (Hons), when she became a teacher. 'I wanted to show them' – meaning show her late husband and her late father what she could achieve

'I definitely thought, "Boo sucks!"' was Jenny Boltwood's polite way of expressing her feelings, on getting a teaching degree in her late thirties. Jenny was the one whose parents had married her off to the Swedish doctor they'd met on the beach in Majorca when she was eighteen and he thirty-nine. After his early death, she married again, to a man who already had three children, and they had a son, 'and when I was thirty-four I thought I ought to educate myself.' In order to do this, she had to go right back to where she'd left off, leaving Northwood College for Young Ladies aged fifteen with zero qualifications, because her father had just retired and claimed he couldn't afford to pay for her education any more. 'So in my thirties, I had to do English, maths, human biology and history O levels, and an English A level.' Only then was she armed with the qualifications needed for a teaching degree, which she did. 'Part of the reason I did it all,' she told me, 'was to show them.'

'Show whom?' I asked.

'Well, my parents, and also my first husband, who'd been so shocked that I didn't have any qualifications. He'd died long ago, and my father had sadly died too, but my mother did come to the degree ceremony.'

Some were getting revenge by proxy, on behalf of their mothers and grandmothers, such as lawyer Helen Shay whose grandmother Elsie had gone into domestic service aged fourteen in 1913, and had then run away to work in a mill, but had had no opportunity to achieve further career advancement. Her destiny was to live through two world wars and bring up six children.

'My mother,' said Janet Walker, now the Bursar of Eton, who trained as an accountant at Price Waterhouse in the 1970s, 'told me she remembered crying in the school library when she realised she would have to leave school early. She was at a grammar school in Bristol, and she did well in her O levels, and she'd just started in the sixth form. But her mother had died, and there was no money, and she was needed as an earner, so she had to leave. She worked at the Prudential till she got married aged nineteen. I remind myself often of this, and of how lucky I've been.'

The abrupt cut-off of a girl's education was brutal. In many families it was totally necessary: the daughter, as soon as the law permitted her to leave school, was propelled into work to help pay the household bills. There was no time to think or plan ahead. If the money wasn't earned that very week, the electricity would be cut off. This was especially true in households with feckless fathers, addicted to drinking or gambling, of whom there was a large number.

So the daughters just got on with it, day in, day out. In a way, the lack of choice in the matter spared them all kinds of soul-searching. There was no 'What on earth should I do next?', just an instant 'I am doing this job right now and will carry on doing it till I get married.'

And then the marriages, too often entered into as an easy escape route from drudgery, were sometimes a disaster. Secondary modern girl Janet Garner, who in 1965 'stupidly' got married to the man she'd met in a coffee bar while working at Woolworths headquarters, divorced him in 1972 and never got the £6 a week maintenance money she was owed. 'So I just got extra jobs.' Then she had a second disastrous marriage, and then she worked as a school cook in Crawley, and then (in her mid-thirties) at Sainsbury's. And then: the light-bulb moment. 'There must be something better than this,' she thought. 'I asked for office work,' she told me, 'but I was told, "No – you have no qualifications."'

'There must be something better than this' was the realisation you needed to be struck by, in order to grab hold of the world's rails and climb out of your low-paid predicament. Janet discovered TOPS: the Training Opportunities Scheme, an inspired idea (piloted in the Harold Wilson government in 1975) to give late education to the educationally deprived. 'I got forty pounds a week to go to Crawley College,' Janet explained. 'We did bookkeeping, typing, audio-typing and business studies: just an eighteen-week course, with exams at the end. I loved it. I passed with a distinction. I'd never passed anything in my life, apart from a driving test. It gave me a bit of confidence.'

Off she went, within minutes, to work as a temp at British Caledonian Airways at Gatwick, and they offered her a permanent job, and then British Caledonian was taken over by British Airways, and BA sent her on its computer course, and she started doing check-in desk shifts at the airport in 1987, aged just over forty, wearing her red, white and blue uniform. Emotions ran high in the check-in zone, she told me: 'Lots dropped dead while queuing at the check-in,' she said. 'It was the stress.'

Then – the icing on the cake – she was able to get a mortgage to buy her council house for £19,400 in the mid-1980s. So she benefited first from a Harold Wilson scheme and then from a Margaret Thatcher one. Quite a few women I interviewed had bought their council house under that scheme and were grateful for it, whatever their 'politics' might now be. 'You shouldn't do that, Janet,' her mother advised her, terrified that her daughter was taking on more than she could cope with financially. But this was a new Janet. Her timidity had gone, and her new confident self dared to give the house-buying a go. She did pay off the mortgage, and now lives in her own house in the West Country.

Sal Rivière was one of the army of women I spoke to who'd undergone the 'leave school at sixteen and learn to type' trajectory, as imposed on them by their school, their mother, their father, and society as a whole. She spoke for many when she said to me, 'I made damn sure my own daughter went to university.'

That sent a bit of a shiver down my spine, because it explained in a nutshell today's phenomenon of the pushy mother. Not that Sal was particularly pushy; she was just ambitious for her daughter, as were so many of her generation, and you can see why. It was to keep open the avenues of possibility that had been closed to them. Ah, so is that why today's daughters are made to take their Key Stage 2 maths workbook in their rucksack on the plane to the family holiday? To make damn sure they get into university, as their forebears couldn't? I think it is. The revenge for which so many of the women in this book still thirst is being taken, willingly or unwillingly, by their daughters, granddaughters and great-granddaughters.

ACKNOWLEDGEMENTS

I'm immensely grateful to everyone I interviewed for this book, as well as to the people who kindly and thoughtfully suggested people I should interview. Even if in the end I didn't individually quote everyone I chatted to, what each person said went deeply into the mix of my thoughts, and became a vital part of the atmosphere and backdrop of the book.

Huge thanks to Jane Aitken, Elspeth Allison, Judith Anderson, Helen Ball, Elizabeth Ballantyne-Brown, Lesley Bamford, Margaret Bamford, Liz Barrs, Bee Bealey, Elisabeth Beccle, Pat Benatmane, Ann Bennett, Elizabeth Bennett, Mary Bennett, Catherine Benson, Agnes Blanc, Gill Blenkinsop, Jenny Boltwood, Joan Booth, Beatrice Bowen, Jan Bower, Josephine Boyle, Lucinda Boyle, Perina Braybrooke, Tessa Brewer, Diana Brooks, Mary Burd, Sarah Burns, Joy Burrows, Louisa Butcher, Lizie Byng, Melanie Cable-Alexander, Sue Cameron, Raine Capara, Glena Chadwick, Annabel Charlesworth, Caroline Chartres, Kay Clayton, Joy Constantinides, Rosie de Courcy, Rosie Crichton, Ann Crookenden, Jane Cussons, Jean Dace, Jean Davis, Valerie Dawes, Josceline Dimbleby, Caroline Donald, Violet Downton, Carole Ellis, Alexandra Etherington, Penny Eyles, Lynette Ellis, Lucy Evans, Jo Fairley, Maggie Fergusson, Phoebe Fortescue, Janet Garner, Edith Gilfillan, Veronica Goodenough, Caroline Goss, Amanda Graham, Penny Graham, Kate Green, Celia Haddon, Heather Hall,

Penrose Halson, Gillie Hanbury, Georgina Harding, Sally Haynes, Patricia Heath, Glenda Herron, Valerie Herron, Kathy Hey, Denise Heywood, Kathleen Hewitson, Sandie Higham, Angela Hill, Agneta Hinkley, Penny Holt, Corty Howard, Jan Hunt, Dot Hunter, Virginia Ironside, Liz Jones, Pamela Jubb, Elizabeth Kefford, Alison Keightley, Sue Kipling, Jackie Kingsley, Lydia Kitching, Sibella Laing, Rhoda Lapish, Nicky Laughland, Henrietta Lindsell, Elizabeth Longrigg, Audrey Loper, Sarah MacAulay, Jane Mackie, Anne Makower, Claudia Maxtone Graham, Anna Maxwell, Henrietta Mayhew, Cicely McCulloch, Jennifer McGrandle, Nonnie Meynell, Richenda Miers, Augusta Miller, Phillipa Miller, the late Sally Moore, Amicia de Moubray, Fiona Naylor, Daphne Neville, Alison Newton, Jane Nicholson, Gail Nicolaidis, Janet Norfolk, Bumble Ogilvy-Wedderburn, Anne Oldroyd, Philomena O'Hare, Ali O'Neale, Elizabeth Nixon, Christine Padgett, Caroline Paterson, Sue Peart, Frances Pemberton, Liz Pierssene, Mary Piper, Helen Powell, Judy Price, Sue Rawlinson, Christine Reddaway, Barbara Rich, Sal Rivière, Gill Robertson, Elizabeth Rolston, Alice Rourke, Sophia Ruck, Vivien Ruddock, Diana Russell, Sharon Scard, Helen Shay, Penny Sheehan, Denise Sherlock, Tessa Skola, Angela Slater, Caroline Slowik, Judy Spooner, Caroline Stacey, Beryl Stoker, Sukie Swan, Sue Teale, Eve Terry, Amanda Theunissen, Fleur Thomas, Katie Thomas, Gill Thomson, Angela Tilby, Maureen Towndrow, Camilla Trimble, Shirley Trundle, Mary Villiers, Janet Walker, Marrie Walsh, Noelle Walsh, Christina Ward, Rebecca Warren, Adrienne Waterfield, Hermione Waterfield, Caroline Watson, Christabel Watson, Susan Watson, Alex Wheadon, Angela Wheeler, Margaret Whitehead, Rose White, Julia Wigan, Alison Willatts, Maureen Wright, Margaret Wilson, Vicky Wilson, Vivien Wilson, Diana Wright, Virginia Wright,

Maria Wynne, Gwen Yarker, Helen York, and others who asked not to be named, but thank you all.

And to those who have helped me with suggestions, introductions, thoughts and encouragement: my immense thanks to Peter Arbuthnot, Diana Baumann, Sue Cameron, Carole Dace, Gerard Evans, Serena Evans, Neil Heron, Julia Korner, David Kynaston, Mary Miers, Georgina Montagu, Harriet Mould, Wendy Phillips, Markie Robson-Scott, my sister Livia Sevier, Gabrielle Speaight, Nina Stibbe, Cicely Taylor, Uta Thompson, Julie Welch and Andrew Wilson. Veronica Goodenough, Penrose Halson, Cicely McCulloch, Cicely Taylor and my mother Claudia Maxtone Graham very kindly read and edited early copies of the manuscript.

Thank you to my wonderful agent Sophie Scard at United Agents; to my brilliant editor Richard Beswick at Little, Brown, and thank you to my copy-editor Lynn Brown, to project editor Jon Appleton, production controller Marie Hrynczak and designer Bekki Guyatt at Little, Brown – and to publicist Lucy Martin and marketeer Lilly Cox for your wonderful work and help.

Thank you to Karol, Mila and all the staff at my haven of a writing café, Le Pain Quotidien on Parsons Green.

Thank you to my sons Toby, Charles and Francis, and to my husband Michael Maxtone-Smith, media lawyer by trade, reader, editor and pianist by nature, always the first to read anything I write.